CW00767680

Authorware®

AN INTRODUCTION TO MULTIMEDIA

Second Edition

SIMON HOOPER
University of Minnesota

PH
PTR
PRENTICE HALL
Upper Saddle River, New Jersey 07458

Library of Congress Cataloging-in-Publication Data

Hooper, Simon.
  Authorware: an introduction to multimedia 2/E / Simon Hooper.
      p.   cm.
    Includes bibliographical references and index.
    ISBN 0-13-096130-2 (pbk.)
    1. Multimedia.   2. Macromedia Authorware   I. Title.
  QA76.575.H68   1998
  006.7'869—dc21   98–26044
                                                       CIP

Publisher: **ALAN APT**
Editor-in-chief: **MARCIA HORTON**
Managing editor: **EILEEN CLARK**
Vice-president of production and manufacturing: **DAVID W. RICCARDI**
Production editor: **KATHARITA LAMOZA**
Art director: **MICHELE GIUSTI**
Cover designer: **JAYNE CONTE**
Manufacturing buyer: **DONNA SULLIVAN**
Compositor: **PREPARÉ/EMILCOMP**

© 1999, 1997 by Prentice-Hall, Inc.
Simon & Schuster / A Viacom Company
Upper Saddle River, New Jersey 07458

Printed in the United States of America

10 9 8 7 6 5 4

ISBN 0-13-096130-2

Prentice-Hall International (UK) Limited, London
Prentice-Hall of Australia Pty. Limited, Sydney
Prentice-Hall Canada, Inc., Toronto
Prentice-Hall Hispanoamericana, S.A., Mexico
Prentice-Hall of India Private Limited, New Delhi
Prentice-Hall of Japan, Inc., Tokyo
Simon & Schuster Asia Pte. Ltd., Singapore
Editora Prentice-Hall do Brasil, Ltda., Rio de Janeiro
Prentice-Hall, Upper Saddle River, NJ

Dedication
To Lucy, TL, Sara, Gabi, and Jack

Contents

Preface

WHAT'S AVAILABLE IN THIS TEXT?

Learning to use Authorware can be a demanding task, even for experienced computer users. Although the application is tremendously enjoyable to use, it is also sophisticated and takes many months, or even years, to master. Unfortunately, learning Authorware from a manual can be particularly puzzling. Manuals often include detailed information that sometimes cloud critical concepts resulting in confusion and frustration.

My goal has been to develop a different kind of "book" that will get closer to the experience of learning from a personal tutor. The book uses a multidimensional approach to learning by using various resources to teach, illustrate, and supplement the learning experience. Three resources make-up the entire text: the book, a CD-ROM, and a supporting Web site.

THE BOOK

The first resource is the book. The text differs from a manual in important ways. First, it focuses on Authorware's critical features and ignores detail that can be learned more easily when important fundamental knowledge has been learned. Every chapter includes a brief list of objectives that are intended to steer the reader away from distracting information and to focus on critical ideas.

Second, the text builds on the belief that you will learn to develop multimedia most effectively by developing a project as you learn. The text includes a series of projects that provide first-hand experience with the content addressed in the chapter. Each project builds on the work completed in the previous project, leading to the completion of an interactive multimedia kiosk. The topic addressed in the project is one that will interest many people: the process of buying your first house. The graphics, sounds, and text files needed to complete the projects are included on the accompanying CD-ROM disc. After completing a project, I hope that you will be in a much better position to understand the rest of the chapter. Many chapters also include additional follow-along activities that outline important ideas and help you to learn-by-doing in a guided setting.

Third, most chapters include exercises that are intended to leave you with a rich and work-ing knowledge of the design process. In many cases, the concepts go beyond simply learning Authorware and address issues essential in the design and development processes. For exam-ple, topics such as screen design, bit-depth, and cross-platform file development will provide important background information that transcends the development platform.

THE CD-ROM

The second resource is a CD-ROM that runs both on Macintosh and PCs. When you run the CD on a Macintosh you will only see the Mac files. When you run the CD on a PC you will only see the PC files. The CD contains a working version of Authorware 4, videos, support files, and project files.

Authorware 4

The CD contains both Macintosh and PC versions of Authorware that you can transfer to your computer. The software is know as the Working Model. The Working Model is a limited ver-sion of Authorware that allows you to save small files containing up to 50 icons. You can also use the Working Model to open each of the Authorware support files on the CD. (See the sec-tion on page xvii entitled Support Files.)

You can use the Working Model to build the projects that accompany the text. However, you will not be able to save your files if you exceed the icon limit. To save larger files you will need a commercial version of Authorware.

To install the working model on your computer:

Macintosh Users

Double-click on the file titled *Authorware 4 Working Model* on the first level of the CD. The application is designed to install the Working Model on your computer. Follow the instructions to complete the installation process.

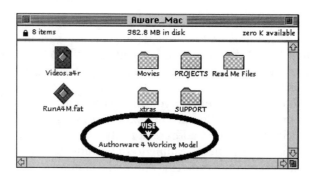

PC Users

Double-click on the file titled *Awworkng* on the first level of the CD. The application is designed to install the Working Model on your computer. Follow the instructions to complete the installation process.

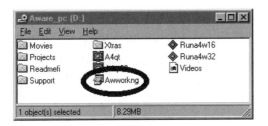

VIDEOS

The videos explain ideas presented in each chapter and illustrate important design concepts. Ideas that are difficult to understand by reading alone are demonstrated in these videos that play on your computer monitor. The videos are developed in QuickTime and will run on Macintosh and PC computers.

To Run the CD-ROM Videos

The CD-ROM contains digital videos that have been created in QuickTime® format. To run these files you must have a copy of QuickTime for the Macintosh or the PC installed on your computer. QuickTime is preloaded onto many computers, however, if it is not already installed on your computer you can download it over the Internet at the following address:

```
http://quicktime.apple.com/sw/sw3.html
```

QuickTime movies will usually run faster on Macintosh computers than on PCs. If you are waiting long periods for the videos to run on a PC, free-up all available RAM by turning off all unnecessary TSRs and programs, including network drivers and connections.

Macintosh Users

Open (double click on) the file titled *Videos.a4r* to start the application.

Videos.a4r

Windows 3.1 Users

Run the application titled RUNA4W16.EXE

Runa4w16.e...

At the dialog box, open the CD-ROM drive (in the following illustration, it's the "e:" drive), select the file titled *videos.a4r*, and click on OK.

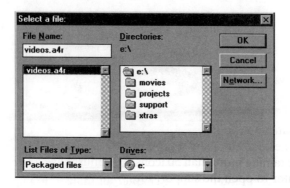

Windows 95 and Windows NT Users

Run the application titled RUNA4W32.EXE

Runa4w32.e...

At the dialog box, open the CD-ROM drive (in the illustration below, it's the "E:" drive), select the file titled *Videos.a4r* and click on the button labeled *Open*.

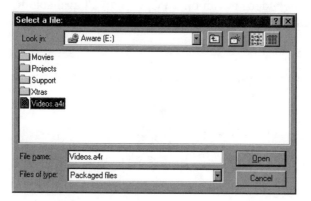

When the file opens:

1. Click once to exit the introductory screen.
2. At the Main Menu, select a chapter by selecting a navigation button.
3. Read the description of the content and press the button labeled *Video* to see a video on the topic.
4. You can replay the video by dragging the slide bar at the bottom of the video window.
5. Click once on the screen with the mouse to exit a video and return to the Main Menu.

Support Files

The CD-ROM contains support files that are linked closely to the content in the chapters. Use these files to follow the activities outlined in the text or open and examine the files at your leisure. One way to learn how to use Authorware is to manipulate these files and observe the results of your experimenting.

The CD contains both Macintosh and PC versions of Authorware 4.0 Working Model. The Working Model is a limited non-commercial version of Authorware. It can be used to open and examine the support files and to create mini-projects. However, you cannot use the Working Model to save files containing more than 50 icons. You must have a copy of Authorware 4.0 or higher on your computer to open the support files.

To install Authorware 4.0 Working Model:

If you are a Macintosh user, open the install program titled *Authorware 4 Working Model* and follow the installation instructions.

If you are a PC user, open the install program titled *AWWorkng.exe* and follow the installation instructions.

Project Files

A folder titled PROJECTS on the CD contains files used in the projects. The PROJECTS folder contains five folders named PROJECT1, PROJECT2, etc., which correspond to the projects in the text. Each folder contains one or more objects used in the projects.

The PROJECTS folder also contains a folder titled *Complete* that contains final versions of each of the project files. If you get frustrated, you can compare your work to one of these files.

Note: The files were created on a PC and may appear differently on a Macintosh.

THE WEB SITE

The third resource is an Internet Web site. You can connect to the Web site at :

    http://www.prenhall.com/Hooper/

The Web site includes three categories of resources: answers to exercises, development tools, teaching updates and discussion of common development problems. When appropriate, written answers to the problems at the end of each chapter will be given. However, where more complex solutions are needed, files are available for you to download to your desktop computer.

The development tools are designed to support all multimedia developers and include links to important development software that you can download without charge, connections to Authorware and other multimedia Listserv sites, on-line examples of Authorware and Shockwave files, and opportunities to post questions about development difficulties. Answers to these questions as well as discussions of updates and developing issues will form the foundation of a database of Authorware problem solving tools.

How Should You Use This Text?

There is no single best approach to learning to design multimedia using Authorware. However, my experience indicates that there are essentially two classes of Authorware students: Those who have and those who have not previously programmed computers.

One approach, commonly used by computer novices, focuses on learning rudimentary content covered in the early chapters before attempting more complex ideas presented later in the text. This approach "protects" users from the chapters on Variables and Functions that are often challenging for those who have never before programmed a computer.

Another approach seems to be more effective among users with programming backgrounds. These people may benefit from covering early in the learning process the chapters on Variables and Functions (Chapters 11 and 12). Learning how to integrate Variables and Functions into every phase of the design process is often critical to using Authorware effectively.

A third approach is also popular. This approach teaches Authorware within the context of an Instructional Design course. Instructors who follow this tack may wish to move rapidly through the first few chapters and emphasize the more complex concepts outlined in the chapters on the Interaction icon (Chapters 5, 7 and 8), Variables and Functions (Chapters 11 and 12), and Navigate and Framework icons, (Chapters 13 and 14). These chapters cover content that is most likely to be the focus of issues concerning human learning and interface design that are often emphasized in design courses.

ACKNOWLEDGMENTS

I am indebted to those who have provided their insight and guidance to this text. I am especially thankful to Jill Tuttle whose inspirational ideas and efforts accelerated the development process. Thanks also to the reviewers listed below for the thorough and timely efforts:

1. Luther Rotto, St. Cloud State University
2. Wilhelmina Savenye, Arizona State University
3. Cecelia Buchanan, Victoria University

1

Getting Started

CHAPTER OVERVIEW

In this chapter you will learn the basic structure of Authorware and how Authorware differs from traditional programming languages and other authoring tools. You will also examine the process of creating an Authorware lesson: adding icons to the course flow line; setting options within each icon; and placing lesson content into Display icons.

CHAPTER OBJECTIVES

After completing this chapter, you will be able to:

- Understand the difference between Authorware and other multimedia development tools.
- Open Authorware and create a new file.
- Learn the basic process of course development in Authorware.
- Navigate between the Presentation window and the Design windows.
- Open each icon's Properties dialog box.

KEY TERMS

Programming language
Authoring language
Course flow line

Icons
Display icon
Navigation
Design window
Presentation window
Icon Properties

CD-ROM VIDEO

On the CD-ROM disk, run the file titled **Videos.a4r**, and select the button labeled **Chapter 1** to examine how to place icons on the course flow line and to navigate between the Design and Presentation windows. If you are not sure how to run the file, refer to the section titled "To Run the CD-ROM Videos" in the Preface.

SOFTWARE DEVELOPMENT TOOLS

A Brief History

Before we start, it may be helpful to understand why Authorware is such a powerful tool for developing educational courseware. The tools used for computer-based lesson design have evolved considerably during the past twenty years. Educational software was originally developed using general-purpose programming languages. Although appropriate in a wide variety of technological, experimental, and industrial settings, these languages were often inappropriate for courseware design because they required developers to possess detailed computer-programming knowledge to create even simple lessons.

The beauty of Authorware is that it permits designers to develop sophisticated lessons without requiring deep programming experience or technical knowledge. Authorware is a powerful development tool that accelerates the design process by using icons to represent tasks that are usually created using programming languages.

How Do Programming Languages Work?

Computers understand several different levels of programming languages. At the most basic level, the language that a computer understands is machine code. Machine code is a stream of binary ones and zeros that correspond exactly to the electronic circuits within the computer. For example, the command to double a number might be 01100011. A human analogy involves stimulating specific portions of the brain with electric currents to cause predictable reflex actions.

Writing software in machine code would be a hopelessly tedious task. Instead, programmers sometimes use low-level, second-generation programming languages, such as Assembly, that employ brief commands to replace the streams of ones and zeros that control the machine. Instructions are translated by a tool known as a translator, which converts Assembly language into machine-readable ones and zeros. However, Assembly also is a labor-intensive and cryptic programming language that involves learning precise ways to communicate with the computer, and is inappropriate for educational software development.

Many programmers use higher-level, third-generation languages, such as PASCAL, BASIC, and C, to write software. Higher-level languages are generally easier to use than Assembly because they employ programming statements that are closer to human language and programming structures that are somewhat intuitive. Furthermore, programs written in these languages are generally portable. That is, they can be compiled and run on virtually any computer.

Programmers select programming languages to fulfill specific needs. For example, COBOL, a programming language that uses language-like instructions, was designed to be used by non-technical users in the business world. COBOL programs are commonly used by direct-mail advertisers to manage large databases and to sort and print mailing labels. FORTRAN, a more technical language, was created to be used in scientific environments, where processing speed is paramount.

In addition to fulfilling the programming roles for which they were originally designed, most higher-level languages can be used to develop educational materials. In the hands of sophisticated programmers, programming languages are very flexible and allow the designer to include virtually any option that is needed in a lesson. However, such flexibility comes at a price. All functionality must be programmed independently: Answer-judging routines must be designed and coded, text placement must be specified precisely, and graphics often must be laboriously defined. Similarly, every complete unit of programming code (known as a subroutine) created for a lesson has to be individually created and tested. The resulting programs produce webs of thousands of lines of interconnected computer code. Updating such programs is always difficult, and is often impossible when the original programmers are unavailable.

Despite their apparent flexibility, designing materials with traditional programming languages tends to limit design to activities that can be easily programmed and modified. In effect, designers are discouraged from employing the flexibility offered by programming languages because of the expertise and cost associated with implementing such features. Furthermore, most high-level programming languages do not include commands to access peripherals that are often used in educational software design. For example, commands to recognize and interact with a videodisk player usually are not incorporated into high-level programming languages.

What is Authorware?

Authorware is the state-of-the-art development tool for designing interactive multimedia. You can use Authorware to develop any combination of presentations, tutorials, simulations, tests, or educational games, as well as programs that interact with the World Wide Web. Multimedia software can be used in a variety of educational settings, including K–12, postsecondary, community, and corporate education.

What's more, you don't have to be a programmer to develop software with Authorware. Although technical expertise is a definite advantage for some of the more intricate details of the design process, non-programmers make excellent Authorware developers. In fact, many of the best developers are those individuals who cannot program, but are able to transfer their educational expertise onto the computer. Authorware encourages non-programmers by using an intuitive environment that is fun and relatively easy to learn.

Many readers will be aware of other authoring environments that can be used for multimedia development. Among the most popular are Hypercard, Hyperstudio, Supercard, Toolbook, and Web development tools such as HTML and Java. New developers often want to learn the "best" authoring tool and seek advice from current users. However, getting a straight answer to what appears to be a simple question isn't easy. Developers tend to promote the tool they know best. Indeed, proponents tend to be zealots about whatever computer operating system or programming language they use, in large part because of the expertise they have developed and the sheer time invested in learning to use the tool.

One of the main differences between Authorware and other systems is Authorware's use of two separate production environments: the Design window, featuring a "flow line" in which the structure of a file is created, and the Presentation window into which content is placed. Many of the other systems use a card metaphor to present information. File logic is controlled with a programming language that connects the cards and performs other functions.

In reality, each system has strengths and weaknesses. Authorware's strengths are considerable; in my mind, the following top the list: an intuitive development environment; sophisticated interaction capabilities; cross-platform development capabilities; and a vast array of system functions and variables that allow developers to customize applications. In contrast, its weaknesses include rather limited animation capabilities, the lack of a true built-in programming language, and some performance deficiencies that sometimes impact performance. I, too, am biased in my opinion; however, I believe that Authorware's strengths as an educational multimedia development tool outweigh its weaknesses, especially when compared to the limitations associated with other systems.

What Version of Authorware Do I Need?

You may have one of many different versions of Authorware. Over the past decade, Authorware has used several different names: Course of Action; Authorware Academic; Authorware Star; Authorware Working Model; Authorware Professional 2.0; Authorware 3 and 3.5; and, now, Authorware 4. Also, Authorware runs in both Mac and PC environments.

This book focuses on Authorware 4. However, you can use it to learn many features available in previous versions of Authorware. Readers who are familiar with earlier releases of the software will notice significant changes to the look of many dialog boxes. Macromedia changed the interface to bring the software in line with other products they distribute. This was done to try to provide users with greater consistency across Macromedia applications.

Moreover, this book is designed for both PC and Macintosh users. You may find some small differences between dialog boxes used for PC and Mac versions, however, most differences are superficial, and, apart from a few cross-platform differences that are addressed later in the text, functionality is almost identical on both platforms.

Mac or Windows?

Authorware is a cross-platform product designed for both PC and Macintosh users. Apart from cosmetic differences, the two versions of Authorware are practically identical. Also, files written on one platform are directly convertible to the other platform. In other words, if you have both Macintosh and PC editions of the software, you can create a file on a PC, save the file on a diskette or a network, and open and run the file on a Macintosh computer (or vice versa). Better still, applications will run across platforms. For example, an application created on the Macintosh can be used easily on either Mac or PC operating systems.

The cosmetic differences between the Mac and PC versions can be adjusted to quite quickly. Rather than having two different versions, the text incorporates graphics from both systems. Specifically, PC graphics are used to illustrate the Projects that appear at the start of many chapters. However, the rest of the graphics feature the Mac versions of the interface.

Although the functional differences across the two platforms are small, they are, important, nonetheless. The functional differences will not be addressed now. Instead, I will wait until later in the text, at which point the differences are likely to make more sense.

Note: Keyboards for Macs and PCs are different. One of the most important differences is that the Command key on the Macintosh is replaced by the Control key on the PC. Throughout this text, shortcuts are given in "Mac format." To obtain the PC equivalent, simply replace the word Command with the word Control.

How Does Authorware Improve Design?

Although other programming languages can be used to develop instruction, Authorware has been written specifically to stimulate courseware development. Not only is Authorware much simpler to learn and use, it has been created to include the types of tasks most commonly needed when developing course materials.

One obvious difference between Authorware and other programming languages is that designers do not need to know how to program to use Authorware. Instead, designers use several different icons that have been preprogrammed with built-in functionality. The task for the developer is to learn the role of each icon, as well as when each icon should be used and the options that can be employed. However, it should also be noted that previous programming experience does accelerate the learning curve. In particular, learning to use Functions and Variables (standard tools in the programmer's repertoire) is greatly facilitated with previous programming experience.

What's New in Authorware 4?

One of the key differences between this and previous versions of Authorware is a feature known as binary file compatibility. As many readers are aware, software authors usually consider two principal sets of computer users when developing multimedia: Macintosh and PC. Since its inception, Authorware has been a product that has allowed cross-platform development. That is, programs written in the traditionally friendlier Mac environment could be transferred to the PC, and more recently, vice versa.

If you worked with earlier versions of Authorware and developed for cross-platform delivery, you probably spent many hours transferring a file from one platform to the other, only to find that your carefully controlled text layout was destroyed by irregular fonts and other incompatibilities. Binary file compatibility means that you can create an Authorware lesson on either a Mac or a PC, and run the file on the other platform without having to perform a file conversion. The file you create on one system will automatically run on the other.

To reduce cross-platform font incompatibility problems, a special fontmap file is included. This file (which will be examined further in Chapter 16) can be edited to help ensure that the screen layout you use on one platform will be reproduced accurately on the other.

Another improvement is the addition of "digital asset management." The term *digital asset* refers to all the graphics, movies, and audio files that you use in a lesson. Until now, movies were the only digital assets that could be stored outside an Authorware file; all other assets had to be imported into the Authorware file. Now, digital files can be stored outside Authorware in an electronic repository.

Authorware 4 not only acts differently from previous releases; as soon as you start the application, you will notice that it also looks very different. Veteran users will notice that the pull-down menus have different titles and that the many features and tools have been reorganized.

How Do I Get Started With Authorware?

Before you can learn to use Authorware to create instruction, you must know how to open a new file, save your work, and quit the program. Then you must learn the basic structure of an Authorware lesson. This includes inserting icons on the course flow line, opening icons, and navigating between Presentation and Design windows.

To Open Authorware and Start a File

- Double-click the Authorware icon to open the application.

Authorware 4

- Authorware will start a new file and display its Design window. A window similar to the one below will appear.

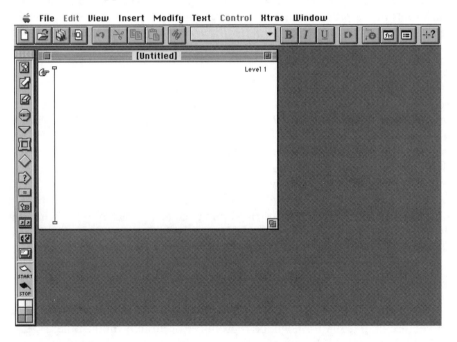

To Save a File

- Remember to save your work regularly. Select Save from the File pulldown menu. (Your program will be saved in the location you identify. If you have saved the program previously, the old program will be overwritten.) Incidentally, in the Authorware manuals, the word "piece" is used, instead of file or lesson. In this text, I will use the terms file and lesson interchangeably.

To Quit the Program

- If you want to quit the present file and work on another one, select Close > All from the File menu.

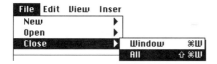

- If you want to quit Authorware, select the Quit option from the File menu.

Note: You may have noticed that many instructions use the "greater than" symbol to signify that the following terms appear in submenus (e.g., Close > All).

Creating Lessons

The design process involves selecting icons from a palette and placing them on the course flow line (the long vertical line with a finger pointing to it). When the lesson runs, the icons on the flow line are executed sequentially (with exceptions that you will learn about later).

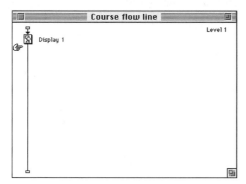

When the design process is complete, the file is converted into a standalone application that will run on any computer (assuming that the computer has the appropriate operating system and processing capabilities). After icons have been placed on the course flow line, the designer must open and set the options for each icon, and place lesson content or instructions in appropriate icons. Placing content into icons requires an understanding of the differences between Design and Presentation windows.

Design Windows

Authorware lessons are constructed within Design windows that include a course flow line and a menu of several icons.

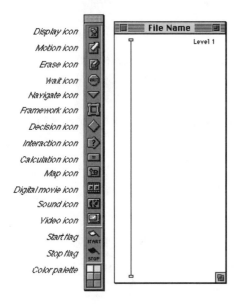

It may help to think of the icons in your lesson in the following way:

- *Display icons* are like transparent sheets on which you place objects. These objects can be text or graphics.
- *Motion icons* enable you to move the objects in Display icons in any direction.
- *Erase icons* remove objects in Display icons from the Presentation window. If you do not remove old displays as you add others, you will soon have text and graphic objects overlaying one another, and the screen will be unreadable.
- *Wait icons* control the speed at which information is displayed. Without them, Display icons would be inserted and removed so fast that the user would not have time to read them.
- *Navigate icons* allow users to link to icons attached to a Framework icon. Navigate icons can also be used to create "hypertext." Hypertext allows the user to navigate by clicking highlighted words in the lesson.
- *Framework icons* provide organized navigation structures. Framework icons allow the designer to create lesson segments that need not necessarily be completed linearly.

- *Decision icons* control the lesson flow. Icons attached to Decision icons form paths. These paths may be executed sequentially or randomly, or may be controlled by using variables.
- *Interaction icons*, like Display icons, can present text or graphic objects. However, they differ in one important respect: They require the user to respond. The designer can vary the lesson flow according to how the user responds.
- *Calculation icons* both control and monitor the file. Using Calculation icons is the closest an Authorware designer gets to traditional computer programming. Calculation icons can help you to control the lesson logic, update important lesson information, and perform a wide variety of other tasks.
- *Map icons* do not change the lesson content, but they help the designer to organize information. In a sense, Map icons are like file folders: They enable you to organize related objects. Map icons are necessary because there is limited room on a flow line.
- *Digital movie icons* control the presentation of movie files from applications such as Director and QuickTime.
- *Sound icons* play sound files. Digitized sound files can easily be incorporated into lessons.
- *Video icons* are used to control attached videodisk players and VCRs.

To Insert an Icon onto a Flow Line

- Place the cursor over the icon you want to use and click-hold the mouse.
- With the mouse button held down, drag a Display icon toward the flow line by moving the cursor with the mouse. Place the icon where you want to insert it on the flow line.
- When the Display icon is in place, deselect the mouse button. (The icon will snap into place on the flow line.)

- Notice that when an icon is placed on the course flow line, it is given the default name "Untitled." All icons are initially untitled, but, as will become apparent later, it is important to give every icon a unique name whenever possible. To name an icon, simply type a new name when the default name is highlighted. To highlight an icon's name, select the icon with the mouse (with a single click) or else press the Tab key. Pressing the Tab key highlights successive icons on the course flow line.
- To delete an icon on the course flow line, click the icon and press the Delete key on the keyboard.

Presentation Windows

Most of the "behind-the-scenes" design work is performed in the Design window. Here, the designer creates the lesson logic and decides how the user will interact with the lesson content. However, the end user never sees the Design window. It is available only to the designer and disappears when the final lesson is created. The designer enters lesson content into the Presentation window. The Presentation window displays the lesson content as the user will see it. This topic will be examined in detail in Chapter 2.

To Open a Display Icon and Go to Its Presentation Window

- Double-click the Display icon on the course flow line. (A presentation window for the icon will open and the toolbox will be displayed.) You may now enter text and graphics into the Presentation window.

To Close a Presentation Window and Return to the Design Window

One of Authorware's strengths is its ability to perform tasks in multiple ways. For example, listed below are five ways to navigate from the Presentation window to the Design window. It's important to learn how to navigate efficiently because you will be constantly testing your design in the Presentation window and then returning to the Design window.

- Click the Close box on either the Presentation window or the Toolbox. If the icon contains at least one object, selecting this option immediately closes the current window and returns to the Design window.

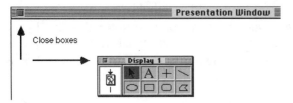

- Select Presentation from the Window pulldown menu.

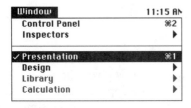

- Select a submenu from the Design menu to link directly to the level in which you want to work.

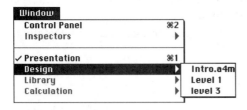

- Select Command-J from your keyboard.
- Click the Design window once if it is visible behind the Presentation Window.

Icon Properties

Every icon has an accompanying Properties dialog. From here, you specify which of the icon's built-in features you will use. To open an icon's Properties dialog window, select an icon on the flow line and choose the Properties pulldown menu (Modify > Icon > Properties). To use the shortcut to open an icon's Properties, press the Command key and double-click the icon.

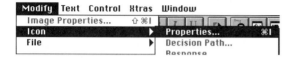

STUDY EXERCISES

1. Name each of the following icons and briefly describe the role that each one plays:

2. What is the difference between the Design and Presentation windows? List at least two different ways to navigate between the two windows.

3. Find someone with computer programming experience, and ask how difficult it would be to create an interactive lesson using a traditional programming language such as FORTRAN, PASCAL, or C.

4. Take some time to explore Authorware.

- Open Authorware and save a new lesson file.
- Place some icons on the course flow line.
- Try to drag the icons to different locations on the flow line.
- Double-click some of the icons on the flow line and examine the different options available for each icon.
- Find two different ways to navigate from the Design window to the Presentation window and four ways to navigate back.

2

Creating Displays

CHAPTER OVERVIEW

In this chapter you will learn how to use the Display icon to present text and graphics. You will also learn how to use the Authorware toolbox to create and manipulate graphic images and several features that facilitate the graphic design process.

CHAPTER OBJECTIVES

After completing this chapter, you will be able to:

- Use a Display icon to present text and graphic images.
- Name each tool in the toolbox.
- Understand the purpose of each tool in the toolbox.
- Create and modify graphic images using the toolbox.
- Manipulate text presentations, as well as font types and styles.
- Use several special effects to create visually exciting displays.

KEY TERMS

Toolbox
Display options
Select mode, Graphic mode, Text mode

Text fonts and sizes
Lines (thicknesses and fills)
Boxes and ovals (squares and circles)
Overlapping objects
Inspectors
Fills, effects, lines, and modes

SUPPORT MATERIALS

On the CD-ROM disk, run the file titled **Videos.a4r**, select the button labeled **Chapter 2**, and watch the video to see how to use the Authorware toolbox and other important tools. If you are not sure how to run the file, refer to the section titled "To run the CD-ROM videos" in the preface.

From the SUPPORT folder on the CD, open the file titled **CHP02.a4p**. The file contains graphic objects created with the toolbox. When you press the **Continue** button, an empty Display icon titled **You Try!!** will open. Try to reproduce each of the objects using only the Authorware tools. If you experience difficulties, examine the modes, fills, line thicknesses, colors, and other display attributes to help you discover how the objects were created (more on these terms later in the chapter).

PROJECT 1: CREATING A WELL-DESIGNED SCREEN

Materials Needed to Complete This Project

- Macromedia Authorware 4.0 for Macintosh or Windows
- PROJECT 1 folder

Time Requirements

Allow approximately 15 minutes to complete Project 1.

Project Description

In this project you will learn ways to navigate between the design and presentation windows, place icons on the course flow line, create an introductory or "splash" screen, import and position text and graphics into Authorware, and understand basic screen design principles.

Activity

Launch Authorware by double-clicking its application icon. In the Design window, drag a Display icon onto the flow line and label it **Background**.

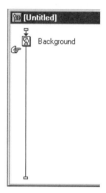

> *Note*: It is important to name icons with unique titles and to develop a logical icon-naming scheme, because you may need to refer to an icon by its name later in the development process.

Double-click the Display icon to open the Presentation window.

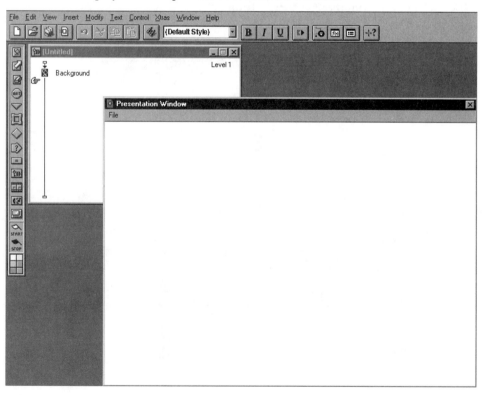

Next, import a background graphic. From the File pulldown menu, select Import...

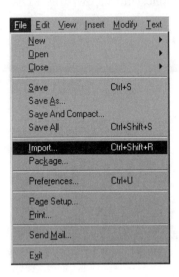

Select BKGRND.PCT from the PROJECT 1 folder.

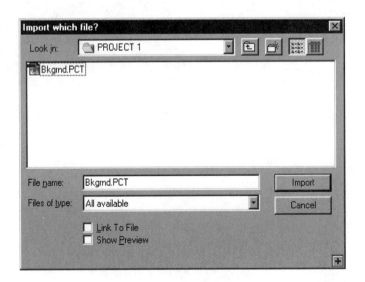

Click the Import button. Your screen should appear as follows:

Now save your file. Create a folder on your hard drive named PROJECTS. From the File pull-down menu, select Save. Name your file **PROJ1**, and, if you are a PC user, specify that it is an Authorware file. Click Save.

Drag another Display icon onto the flow line and name it **Title text**.

Background

Title text

Double-click the Display icon to open the Presentation window. From the toolbox, select the Text tool.

Click the Presentation window and type the following:

Select the text with the cursor. From the Text pulldown menu, select Font and Size to format the first line of text in 36-point (use 48-point, on a Macintosh) Arial Black and the second line of text in 14-point (use 18-point, on a Macintosh) Arial. (If you do not have the Arial font, substitute Helvetica.)

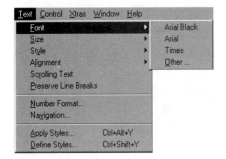

From the Inspectors pulldown menu, select Colors to bring up the color palette. (The Inspectors menu will be explained in detail later in the chapter.)

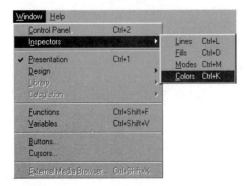

Click the box to the right of the pencil to change the text color. The boxes next to the paint bucket are for foreground and background colors. Click the top box to change the foreground color; click the bottom box to change the background color. Experiment with different color combinations for your title text. When you are finished, save your file.

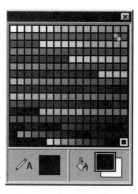

Close the toolbox to return to the Design window.

To view your file, select Restart from the Control pulldown menu.

The Presentation window should appear as follows:

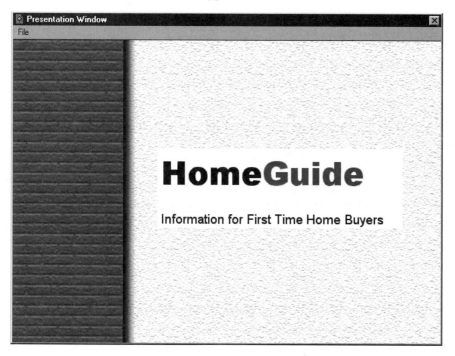

Notice that the title has a white background that does not match the rest of the screen. This can be changed by making the text transparent.

To make the text transparent, first navigate back to the Design window using one of the following techniques:

1. Click the flow line in the background, or select Quit from the File pulldown menu.

Next, open the Display icon that contains the text to be modified.

2. Double-click the text with the Selection tool. When the icon opens, the text will already be selected. From the Window pulldown menu, select Inspectors > Modes to access the Modes palette. Select Transparent to see through the text boundaries. Finally, use the Selection tool from the toolbox to move the text to its final destination; then Save and rerun your file.

Extending What You Have Learned

Screen design is an important, yet often overlooked, component of the multimedia development process. The quality of the screen and interface design can determine the success or failure of a project.

Many graphic design and cognitive psychology principles are at work in a well-designed screen. Discussing the subject in detail is beyond the scope of this lesson. (For more information, explore the section titled "For Further Information..." at the end of this chapter.) However, several simple rules can help you to improve screen design. When creating a display, heed the following guidelines.

Strive for Consistency

This rule of thumb applies to visual organization as well as functionality. For example, you should use the same fonts, color schemes, and naming conventions throughout a project. Remember that your screen design is actually teaching your end users how to navigate your project; do not change this information midstream. Consider how difficult interstate travel would be if every state had different shapes, colors, and placement rules for its highway signs.

Develop and Maintain Functional Screen Areas

Keep your related buttons (e.g., navigation tools) grouped together. If users must constantly hunt for information, they will waste valuable cognitive resources on what should become an automatic process—navigation. Consider how consistent functional areas help you navigate a book. You know exactly where to look for the table of contents, index, references, etc. This allows you to focus on the content, not on how to use a book.

Keep Font Sizes Large

The strength of a multimedia authoring program like Authorware is that you can (and should) provide information to your end users in several ways: through sound, color, motion, and text. Remember, however, that the computer monitor is not a good medium for reading text. Consequently, it is important to make text as legible as possible. Use medium to large font sizes for text. Try 18-point type for text and 24- to 36-point type for headlines. Font sizes may vary according to the font you select and the type of computer you use, so experiment to find the best combination.

Limit the Number of Fonts and Type Styles

Using too many fonts or the wrong style of font can quickly derail a project. Avoid the temptation to use decorative fonts. They can be difficult to read and often do not reproduce well on the screen. Try limiting yourself to two fonts—a sans serif font for headings and a serif font for body text. If you need variety (based on design and communication principles, not mere decoration!), try bold and italic variations on those fonts.

Use Color Wisely

Color can and should be an integral part of your design and navigation schemes. However, when used carelessly, color can detract from the visual impact of your project. Decide on a color palette at the beginning of a project and stick to it. A skillfully used palette of two or three colors will produce a much more sophisticated and cohesive impact than more colors used carelessly.

Form Should Follow Function

The form your project takes, visually as well as functionally, should relate directly to what the project needs to accomplish. Make your screens do what they need to do and no more. Unnecessary decoration distracts the user from the learning goals.

When working on multimedia projects, do not underestimate the power of well-designed screens. The points listed above are intended to stimulate you to think about screen design as part of the development process. You are encouraged to explore the resources listed at the end of the chapter to enhance your knowledge.

UNDERSTANDING THE DETAILS

Learning how to use Authorware begins with learning how to present information. Information is placed into Display icons. Initially, you will work with just one Display icon and learn this icon's attributes. Chapter 3 will explain how to use multiple Display icons to build presentations.

Working with Text and Graphic Objects: Using the Toolbox

When you double-click a Display icon, the toolbox opens automatically. To select a tool, single-click its icon with the mouse. Readers who are experienced with graphics and desktop publishing applications will probably be familiar with the toolbox tools, and may be able to skim the following section. It should also be mentioned that, in practice, little artwork is created with the toolbox. Instead, professional-quality graphics are usually imported into Display icons from clip art or created with graphics packages such as Adobe Photoshop. However, the toolbox is useful for creating simple graphics.

What Does the Toolbox Enable Me to Do?

The toolbox includes several tools that are used for creating, moving, and editing text and graphics. Although the toolbox enables you to create many different types of graphic objects, it is not usually used for complex graphic design. In practice, the graphics tools are used for simple tasks, such as drawing boxes, ovals, and lines. More complex graphics are usually created with specialized graphics applications and then imported into Authorware.

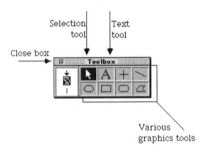

- Click the Selection tool to enter the Select mode. The Selection tool enables you to select text and graphic objects so that you can move them or change their characteristics.
- Click the Text tool to enter the Text mode. The Text mode enables you to type and edit text objects.
- Click the Oval, Rectangle, Rounded Rectangle, Polygon, or one of the line options to enter the Graphic mode. The Graphic mode enables you to create or change graphic objects.
- Click the Close box.
  - If you are *creating* the program, you will return to the course flow line.
  - If you are *running* the program, the toolbox will close.

The difference between creating and running a lesson will be explained later.

How Can I Control Where and When the Toolbox Is Displayed?

- If you are *creating* the lesson, the toolbox appears automatically when you open a Display icon; you cannot hide it.
- If you are *running* the lesson and reach a **Display** icon that you have not developed, the program will stop, and the toolbox will be displayed. After you develop the screen, click the toolbox's Close box. The toolbox will disappear and program execution will continue.

- If you are *running* the lesson and see a text or graphic object you want to edit, double-click the object to access the object's Presentation window. The toolbox associated with that Display icon will be displayed.
- To *move* the toolbox, click-hold the shaded area above the tools and drag the box to a different location.

How Do I Enter Text?

In this section we will enter text, position margins, and Set tabs. The Text tool works like a relatively simple word processor. You can control line length, font type and size, color, and Set Text and Decimal tabs.

To Enter Text

- Single-click the Text tool. (The lesson enters the Text mode.)

- Move the cursor off the toolbox. (The cursor becomes an I-beam.)
- Move the I-beam to where you want to create new text.
- Click once. (A paragraph ruler appears; small boxes identify the object's handles. Clicking and dragging a handle extends or shrinks the width of the object.)

- Type the text. (All text entered becomes a single text object that can be edited.)
- The triangles next to the handles control indentation and word wrap just like the controls on a word processor.

To Control the Width of the Object

- Move the cursor to the handle you want to move.

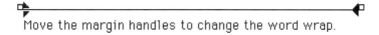

Move the margin handles to change the word wrap.

- Click-hold and then drag the handle to the desired position.

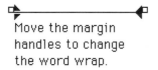

Move the margin
handles to change
the word wrap.

To Set Tabs

- Make sure that you are in the Text mode (i.e., the Text tool is highlighted).
- To insert a tab, click the paragraph ruler just above the point where you want to add the tab. (A solid triangle will appear at the tab location.)

- If you want to move the tab, drag it horizontally to the new location. (The Tab triangle moves to the new location.)

- If you want to create a Decimal tab, create a tab at the desired location and then single-click it. (The Tab triangle becomes an arrow.) Remember to type a tab before each word or number that you enter.

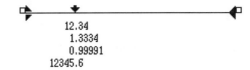

- If you want to remove a tab, drag it to a margin handle and release the mouse.

How Do I Set and Change Text Characteristics?

You can change the characteristics of a text passage at any time in the authoring process—before you enter text, while you are entering it, or after you've entered it. Changing text characteristics before entering text creates new default values. Set or change text characteristics by selecting options (Font, Size, Style, and Alignment) from the Text pulldown menu.

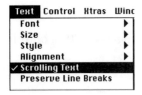

A fifth option, Scrolling Text, creates a scrolling text field that can be used to display more text than is usually possible in a window. Scrolling fields can be modified easily by dragging the text handles and a handle below the text field.

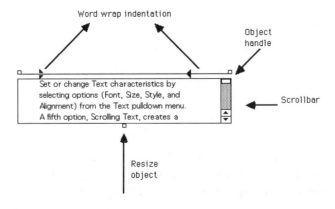

To Select Characteristics before Entering Text

- Enter the Select mode (click the Selection tool).

- Pull down the Text menu and select a new characteristic.
- Enter the Text mode and start entering text. This method creates new default values for the Text tool.

To Change Characteristics while Entering Text

- Enter the Text mode.

- Pull down the Text menu and select a new characteristic. As you continue typing, subsequent text will have new characteristics. Text entered before the change is not affected.

To Change Characteristics after Entering Text

For the Entire Text Object

- Enter the Select mode.
- Single-click the text object to highlight the object handles.

> Set or change Text
> characteristics by selecting
> options (Font, Size, Style, and
> Alignment) from the Text
> pulldown menu.

- Pull down the Text menu and select a new characteristic.

For a Portion of a Text Object

- Enter the Text mode.
- Highlight the text segment you want to change.
- Pull down the Text menu and select a new characteristic.

Text editing generally adheres to practices employed by word processing and other office utility programs. A summary of these conventions follows.

To Make a Small Change to Text

- Enter the Text mode.
- Move the I-beam to a position immediately to the right of the text you want to change.

- Click once.
- Use the Backspace or Delete key to erase the unwanted text.
- Enter the new text.

To Insert Text

- Enter the Text mode.
- Move the I-beam to the spot where you want to insert text.
- Click once.
- Enter the new text.

To Delete or Change a Single Word

- Enter the Text mode.
- Double-click the word to be deleted or replaced. (It will be highlighted.)

Set or change Text characteristics by selecting
options (Font, Size, Style, and Alignment) from the
Text pulldown menu. A fifth option, Scrolling Text,
creates a scrolling text field that can be used to
display more text than is usually possible in a window.
Scrolling fields can be modified easily by dragging the
text handles and a handle below the text field.

- To *replace* the word, start typing the new word.
- To *delete* the word, press the Backspace or Delete key.

To Make Large Changes to a Section of Text

- Enter the Text mode.
- Highlight the text you want to change.

Set or change Text characteristics by selecting
options (Font, Size, Style, and Alignment) from the
Text pulldown menu. A fifth option, Scrolling Text,
creates a scrolling text field that can be used to
display more text than is usually possible in a window.
Scrolling fields can be modified easily by dragging the
text handles and a handle below the text field.

- To *replace* the text, start typing the new text.
- To *delete* the highlighted text, press the Backspace or Delete key.

To Move a Section of Text

- Enter the Text mode.
- Highlight the text to be moved.

- Cut the text.
- Move the I-beam to the new location and paste the text.

To Duplicate a Section of Text

- Enter the Text mode.
- Highlight the text to be duplicated.
- Copy the text.
- Move the cursor (I-beam) to the spot where you want to insert the copy, and paste the text.

How Do I Create Graphics?

Use the Authorware toolbox to create ovals and rectangles, straight and diagonal lines, and various polygons.

To Create Ovals or Rectangles

- Select the Oval or Rectangle tool from the toolbox.

- Place the cursor at one corner of the location where you want the graphic to be placed.
- Click-hold and then drag the mouse diagonally until the object has the desired size and shape.
- Release the mouse key.

  Note: If you want a perfect circle or square, hold down the Shift key while you are dragging the mouse to form the graphic object.

To Create Straight Lines in Any Direction

- Select the Diagonal Line tool from the toolbox.

- Place the cursor where you want the line to start.
- Click-hold and then drag the mouse to draw the line.
- Release the mouse key.

To Create Horizontal, Vertical, or 45° Diagonal Lines

- Select the Straight Line tool from the toolbox.

- Place the cursor where you want the line to start.
- Click-hold and then drag the mouse to draw the line.
- Release the mouse key.

   Note: You can also create horizontal, vertical, and diagonal lines with the Diagonal Line tool by holding down the Shift key while dragging the line.

Using the Polygon Tool

- Select the Polygon icon from the toolbox.

- Place the cursor where you want the polygon to begin.
- Click the mouse to "drop anchor." An invisible anchor will mark the location of the beginning of the first side of the polygon.
- Move the cursor to the point where the first line will end.
- Click the mouse to drop a second anchor.
- Continue moving and clicking the mouse to create the number of anchors needed to create the desired polygon.
- Double-click the mouse on the final anchor to fill the polygon with the currently selected fill color and pattern.

How Do I Change the Size or Shape of Graphics?

You can change the length, direction, and attributes of a line, and you can change the size and shape of an oval or rectangle. To edit any graphic object, first identify the object that is to be edited by clicking it with the Selection tool. The object's margin handles will appear when it has been selected, indicating that the object is ready to be edited.

Margin handles

To Change the Length or Direction of an Existing Line

- Enter the Select mode.
- Select the line by clicking it. (Its margin handles will appear.)

- Place the cursor on a margin handle.
- Click-hold and drag the handle to the new location. (The line will be resized to fit the new margins.)

To Change the Size or Shape of an Oval or Rectangle

- Enter the Select mode.
- Select the oval or rectangle object by clicking one of its edges. (Its margin handles will appear.)
- To *increase the size* of the oval or rectangle, click-hold the cursor on a *corner* handle and then drag it to a new location. (The oval will be resized to fit the new margins.)
- To *change the shape* of the oval or rectangle, click-hold the cursor on a *side* handle and then drag it to a new location. (The shape of the oval will change to fit the new margins.)

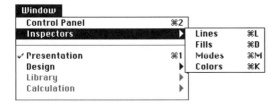

How Do I Change the Attributes of Graphics?

With the use of the Authorware toolbox, it is possible to control the following attributes:

- The thickness and style of a line
- The shade used to fill an object
- An object's mode
- The color of a line or internal shade

Each of these attributes is called an Inspector. You can access the Inspectors from the Window pulldown menu.

To Modify the Thickness and Style of a Line

- If the line is not selected, click the line with the Selection tool.
- Display the Lines dialog box by either:
  - Double-clicking either the straight line or diagonal line icon in the toolbox
    or
  - Selecting the Lines option from the Inspectors menu.

Lines	⌘L
Fills	⌘D
Modes	⌘M
Colors	⌘K

- Select the desired line thickness and style from the line palette.

- Line thickness can be invisible (indicated to the designer by a dotted line) or any of four widths.
- Line style can be plain, left arrowhead, right arrowhead, or double arrowheads.

How Do I Fill Rectangles and Ovals?

Rectangles and ovals can be colored black, white, transparent, or any of 33 patterns. To choose a transparent fill, select the box in the top left corner of the Fills option box.

To Fill in a Rectangle or Oval

- If the Rectangle tool or Oval tool is not selected, enter the Select mode and click the object.
- Display the Inspectors dialog box by either
  - Double-clicking the Rectangle, Rounded Rectangle, or Polygon tool from the toolbox or
  - Selecting the Fills option from the Inspectors menu.

- Click the desired pattern from the Fills palette with the mouse.

Changing Mode Effects

An object's mode determines how overlaid objects appear on the screen. Objects may be in Opaque, Matted, Transparent, Inverse, or Erase mode. This option is very important because it controls how objects appear when they overlap. By setting the mode of a text or graphic object, you can produce some unusual effects. To use mode effects, select Modes from the Inspectors menu or double-click the Selection tool.

Lines	⌘L
Fills	⌘D
Modes	**⌘M**
Colors	⌘K

- Opaque objects mask shapes on which they are placed. When overlaid on another graphic, an opaque object covers the lower object. Both objects shown below are opaque.

- Matted objects are similar to opaque objects. A major difference is that white space around imported graphics appears transparent when Matted mode is selected. This is very important, because graphics imported from other applications often include unnecessary white space. For example, in the figures below, the black cross appears on a white background when the Opaque mode is selected. Notice, however, how the white background disappears when the mode is set to Matted.

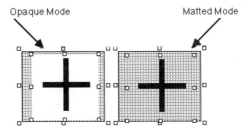

- Transparent objects are "see-through." When they are overlaid on another graphic, the bottom object shows through. The oval object below is set to transparent.

- The Inverse mode often produces unusual effects. White objects appear black when placed on a white background, and white when placed on a black background. The effects of the Inverse mode are unpredictable for colored and patterned objects.
- Objects drawn in the Erase mode assume the background color. The Erase mode is useful for masking objects in Display icons.

How Do I Color Objects?

Objects in Display icons (both graphic objects and text) can be colored using Authorware's color palette. However, the process of coloring objects can be confusing. To understand how to color objects, you need to know that it is possible to color three attributes of an object:

- The border
- The pattern used to fill the object
- The background of the object

To color an object, you must know which of the three attributes you will color. The following box has a thick border, a striped fill, and a solid background:

Authorware's color palette displays all three attributes.
    To assign a color:

- Use the selection tool to identify the object to be colored.
- Select the appropriate attribute (i.e., Border, Foreground, or Background).
- Select a color from the color palette.

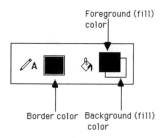

Note: Graphics have three color attributes: Border, Foreground, and Background. However, text has only two color attributes: Border and Background. Border defines the color of the font. Background defines the Background color. In the example below, the word "Text" has been created with a white border and a black background color.

How Do I Move Text and Graphic Objects?

To move an object, click-hold the object and drag it with the mouse.

To Move a Text Object

- Enter the Selection mode.
- Place the cursor anywhere within the text object.
- Click-hold the text.
- Drag the text to the new location.

To Move a Graphic Object

If in the Select Mode

- Select the object by clicking it with the mouse.
- Drag the object to a new location.

If in the Graphic Mode

- Move the cursor into the object until the cursor changes to a selection tool. (Stay away from margin handles.)
- Select the object.
- Drag the object to the new location.

  Note: If your keyboard has direction arrows, you can move a selected object in very small steps by pressing the arrow keys.

Tips for Selecting Objects

The procedure for selecting ovals and rectangles depends on whether the graphic objects are filled or empty.

- If an object is filled with white, black, or a pattern, you can select it by clicking the cursor anywhere inside the object.
- Empty graphic objects are sometimes difficult to move. If an object is empty, you must click the cursor along an edge of the object.

  Note: When selecting objects, be careful not to click-hold a margin handle. If you do, moving the mouse will drag the handle, and instead of moving the selected objects, you will resize them. If this happens, select Undo from the Edit menu (or hold down the Command key while you depress the Z key; hereafter this is indicated as "Command-Z").

To Move Several Objects at Once

When integrating text and graphics, you may want to move more than one object at a time. If more than one object is selected, moving one object moves all objects. To select multiple objects, press the Shift key while clicking successive objects with the mouse (using the Selection tool).

- Select the objects you want to move.
- Click-hold inside one of the selected objects.
- Drag the object, along with all other selected objects, to the new location.

How Do I Group Objects?

Sometimes, you will want to treat two or more objects as if they were a single image. Grouped objects are generally easier to manipulate than several individual objects. To do this, you can use the Group command from the Modify menu. The objects stay grouped until you ungroup them with the Ungroup command.

To Group Objects into a Composite

- Use the Selection tool and select the objects you want to be part of the group.

- Select the Group command by either
  - Selecting the Group option from the Modify menu
    or
  - Typing the shortcut, Command-G

To Ungroup a Composite Object

- Select the composite object you want to ungroup.
- Select the Ungroup command by either
  - Selecting the Ungroup option from the Modify menu
    or
  - Typing the shortcut, Shift-Command-G

The composite object is broken into the individual objects that were originally grouped.

How Can I Control How Text and Graphic Objects Are Overlaid?

You can place text and graphic objects anywhere on the screen. Sometimes graphics that are placed close to each other will overlay. In such cases it may be important to control which objects appear to be on top and which appear to be covered. In addition to using mode effects to control overlay, it is important to learn how to control overlapping objects and object selection.

Overlapping Objects

When objects overlap, they are said to be layered. In the example below, the oval appears to be placed on top of the square. To control the relative position of overlapping objects, use the Bring to Front and Send to Back options from the Modify pulldown menu.

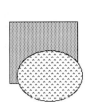

To Bring an Object to the Front

- Using the Selection tool, click the object. In the example below, the square has been selected.

- Select the Bring to Front option from the Modify pulldown menu. The object that was originally partially hidden appears dominant over other objects.

Sending an Object to the Back

- Using the Selection tool, click the object.
- Select the Send to Back option from the Modify menu.

Selecting Objects

When objects are overlaid, objects in front can restrict access to those behind. To select an object that is behind one or more other objects, you can either:

- Select the object that is in the way and drag the object out of the way

  or

- Select the object and send the object to the back

How Do I Access Graphics from Another Source?

Graphics created in other applications can be imported into Authorware and used in Display icons, or they can be imported by copying images from the clipboard or the scrapbook. The Insert command allows images to be stored internally or externally. Storing images internally is generally straightforward. Images may be cut from a graphics file or from the scrapbook and pasted into Display icons. Authorware is quite flexible in the file types it will recognize: In addition to the well-known PICT, TIFF, and JPEG file formats, Authorware now recognizes GIFs, Photoshop images, and several other formats.

Authorware will also permit the use of externally stored graphic images. Externally stored images have important benefits: First, they can be easily modified without editing within Authorware. Imagine, for example, that a file is to include current photographs of students or business personnel. If all the pictures are stored inside the original Authorware file, the file needs to be edited each time an image is modified. However, if files are stored externally, modifying images can be performed simply by editing the original externally stored graphic files. Second, storing images externally helps keep down File sizes. Storing images on a file server or network helps to keep the Authorware file smaller than if the images were imported. Maintaining a small file size can be an important design option to increase file portability.

Using the Import Command

The Import command allows you to access graphics to use in Display icons without leaving Authorware.

- Ensure that the toolbox is displayed.
- Select Image...from the Insert pulldown menu. Press the Import button from the dialog box.

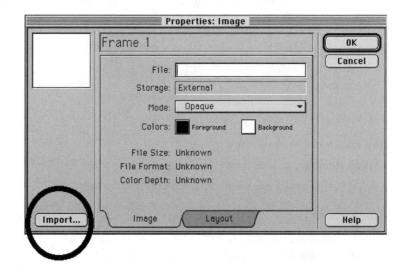

- Select the Link to File checkbox if you want to store images externally.

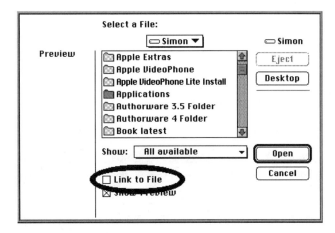

- Locate and open the document that contains the drawing you want to import.

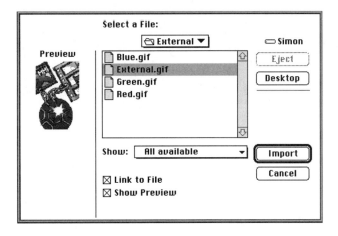

Linking with the Networks

One of the limitations of traditional courseware is that images remain rather static. The only way an image changes is when someone edits the file to make changes. In contrast, imagine the power of displaying images that change from moment to moment. One of Authorware's most exciting capabilities is its ability to import up-to-date images from a network such as an Intranet or the Internet.

How to Do It

The following sequence assumes that your end users will work at computers with active connections to the Internet or an Intranet.

- Place a Display icon on the flow line.
- Open the Display icon and select Image... from the Insert pulldown menu.

- From the dialog box, select the Image tab and enter the URL of your desired graphic. For practice, try using the following URL in the field labeled File:

    `http://www.macromedia.com/images/uberlogo.gif`

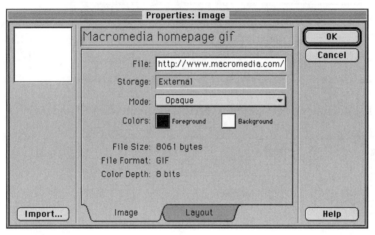

- Click OK.

You may have to wait a few seconds for your computer to make a connection and download the image, but the picture you specified will be placed onto your Display icon in the location indicated in the Layout menu.

Note: Authorware has the annoying habit of scaling images that it imports from the Internet. If this occurs, you may need to rescale the image by placing values of 100% in the Scale fields.

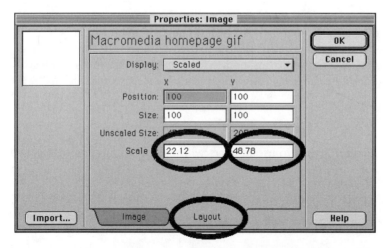

STUDY EXERCISES

1. Identify each of the following tools in the toolbox:

   - The selection tool
   - The text tool
   - The rounded rectangle tool
   - The straight line tool
   - The polygon tool

2. How do you make the toolbox disappear and reappear in a Display icon? How do you set default values for tools in the toolbox?

3. Open a Display icon and use the following features to control text layout:

   - Text tabs
   - Decimal tabs
   - Word wrap
   - Text justification

4. Type a paragraph in a Display icon. Change the size, color, and font of the following:

   - A complete sentence
   - A single word in a sentence
   - One character in a word

5. Open a Display icon and create the following:

   - An oval
   - A striped circle
   - A blue rectangle
   - A red square
   - A thick black line
   - A thin yellow line

6. Create a red circle, a green circle, and a yellow circle. Use the Bring to Front and Send to Back options to perform the following:

   - Place the red circle on top of the yellow circle
   - Place the yellow circle on top of the green circle
   - Place the green circle on the red circle on the yellow circle

7. Using the colored circles in the previous question, experiment with the following options:

   - Effects
   - Modes
   - Color

8. Import graphic images into an Authorware file from one or more of the following sources:

   - Clip art
   - The Internet
   - Scanned images
   - A digital camera
   - A graphics application

9. How do you group several graphic or text objects into a single object? How do you reverse the process?

10. Create a game board for a checkers game. Use only the toolbox to create all the graphics. Make sure that the game board contains the following:

    - 64 squares on a regular 8×8 grid

- 12 checkers on each side of the board
- Each set of checkers in different colors (or shapes)
- Alternating colors on successive squares

11. The following exercise is intended to encourage you to experiment with the toolbox:
Create a new Authorware file. Place a Display icon on the course flow line. Title the icon **Practice**.

- Open the display and use the Authorware drawing tools to draw a house.
- Use arrows to label the door, windows, and other parts of the house.
- Draw trees with leaves and flowers in a flower bed.
- Draw a path leading up to the front door.
- Use a variety of patterns, fills, and line thicknesses throughout your picture.

Save the file on a disk.

FOR FURTHER INFORMATION
ON THIS AND RELATED TOPICS

Listed below are books related to screen and graphic design, along with publisher addresses or Internet sites.

Designing Multimedia, by Lisa Lopuck
A good multimedia design guide with tips on project management, visual and screen design, and examples from real titles on the market. An excellent introduction for beginning and intermediate designers.
ISBN 0-201-88398-8
List price: $34.95 U.S.

Start With a Scan: A Guide to Turning Scanned Photos, Drawings and Objects into High-Quality Art, by Janet Ashford and John Odam
An excellent reference manual on how to capture, manipulate, and use digital images. Useful for both beginners and intermediate users, this book will provide invaluable assistance if you intend to create your own images.
ISBN 0-201-88456-9
List price: $34.95 U.S.

The Interface Design Wow! Book, by Jack Davis and Susan Merritt
Interface design explored fully, with real-world examples.
ISBN 0-201-88678-2
List price: $39.95 U.S.

Peachpit Press publishes excellent multimedia design texts. Its URL is:
http://www.peachpit.com/

Amazon.com is billed as the Earth's biggest bookstore. Its URL is:
http://www.amazon.com

One of the hundreds of available titles:
Making a Good Layout (Graphic Design Basics), by Lori Siebert and Lisa Ballard
This is a good starting point for novice graphic designers.
Published by North Light Books
ISBN 0-891-34423-3
List price: $24.99 U.S.

3

Creating Presentations

CHAPTER OVERVIEW

You have learned how to use the Display icon. In this chapter you will learn how to create and control presentations using several Display icons in combination with Wait and Erase icons. A presentation is the simplest task one can complete with Authorware. It is worth noting that several other applications can be used to create presentations, and generally do so more effectively. However, the presentations you learn to create in this chapter can be used as part of much larger hyperlinked and interactive files.

CHAPTER OBJECTIVES

After completing this chapter, you will be able to:

- Use the Wait options and Transition effects.
- Use the Erase options to remove displays.
- Use transitions to create special effects.
- Add new transitions to Authorware.
- Combine Display, Erase, and Wait icons to create presentations.
- Align objects in Display icons.
- Use layering to control overlapping objects in different Display icons.

KEY TERMS

Erase icons
Wait icons
Map icons
Erase options
Transitions
Wait options
Layers
Fields
Dialog box

SUPPORT MATERIALS

On the CD-ROM disk, run the file titled **Videos.a4r**, and select the button labeled **Chapter 3**. Watch the video to learn how to display information consistently on the screen and examine how to use Display, Wait, and Erase icons to create presentations. If you are not sure how to run the file, refer to the section titled "To Run the CD-ROM Videos" in the Preface.

From the SUPPORT folder on the CD, open the file titled **CHP03.a4p**. The file contains a simple presentation that you can examine.

PROJECT 2: CONSTRUCTING A BASIC PRESENTATION

Materials Needed to Complete This Project

- Your file from the previous project, **PROJ1.a4p**
- Macromedia Authorware 4.0 for Macintosh or Windows
- PROJECT 2 folder

Before You Begin

Allow approximately 20 minutes to complete Project 2.

Project Description

In this project you will learn to control how text and graphics are presented and removed from the screen by combining Display, Wait, and Erase icons. You will learn how to group icons into Maps and how to import and align text and graphic images.

Activity

Begin by opening the Authorware file from the previous project.

- Open your file from the previous project, **PROJ1.a4p**.
- From the File pulldown menu, choose Save As ... to rename the file **PROJ2**.

As you work on this project, remember to save your file often.

You are going to construct a presentation. Drag a Map icon onto the flow line and label it **Ads**. A Map icon creates a new flow line, allowing you to use additional icons. By using Map icons, you can use an unlimited number of icons in your file.

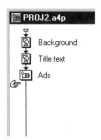

Double-click the Map icon to open a new flow line.

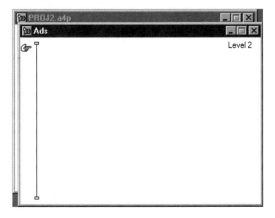

Drag a Display icon onto the flow line and label it **What they say**. Drag another Display icon onto the flow line and label it **What they mean**. The flow line should look like this:

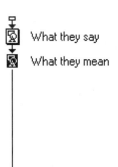

You will now add some preexisting text to your lesson. Switch back to the desktop of your computer, and locate and open the folder titled PROJECT 2. Double-click the file titled **AD1.TXT**.

The file should open in SimpleText (Macintosh) or Notepad (PC). Choose Select All from the Edit pulldown menu, and then select Copy. Return to your Authorware file and double-click the Display icon titled **What they say**.

When the Presentation window opens, click the Text Tool in the toolbox.

Click the Presentation window once to place the Text cursor. Select Paste from the Edit pull-down menu. Your screen should look like this:

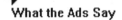

What the Ads Say

Real estate ads seem to be written in some sort of code:

Perfect Starter

Must see to believe! 2BR/2BA, mstr BR+BA, DR, LR, mod kit, hdwd flrs, lg pvt lot, dk, fam rm w/fplc, C/A, 2car gar. A real doll house. Low $80's. 124 Main, Sun O:3-5.

Use the Text tool to select text. Using Font and Size from the Text pulldown menu, and change the heading to 18-point (use 24-point, on a Macintosh) Arial Black and the body text to 14-point (use 18-point on a Macintosh) Arial. (Note: If you do not have the Arial font, substitute Helvetica.)

What the Ads Say

Real estate ads seem to be written in some sort of code:

Perfect Starter

Must see to believe! 2BR/2BA, mstr BR+BA, DR, LR, mod kit, hdwd flrs, lg pvt lot, dk, fam rm w/fplc, C/A, 2car gar. A real doll house. Low $80's. 124 Main, Sun O:3-5.

Choose the Selection tool from the toolbox and click the text once. You should see small boxes around the perimeter of the text.

What the Ads Say

Real estate ads seem to be written in some sort of code:

Perfect Starter

Must see to believe! 2BR/2BA, mstr BR+BA, DR, LR,
mod kit, hdwd flrs, lg pvt lot, dk, fam rm w/fplc, C/A, 2car
gar. A real doll house. Low $80's. 124 Main, Sun O:3-5.

By clicking and dragging these boxes, you can adjust and move the text box. Authorware has
a built-in grid that you can use to help place text and graphic objects consistently. To activate
the grid, go to the View pulldown menu and select Grid.

Use the grid to move and align text and graphic objects as follows:

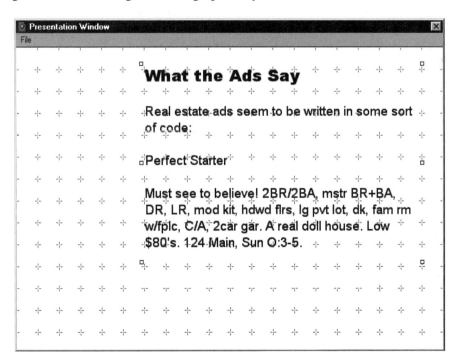

Repeat the process to place text in another Display icon. Double-click the Display icon titled **What they mean**. From the PROJECT 2 folder, double-click **AD2.TXT**. Choose Select All from the Edit pulldown menu, and then choose Copy.

Return to Authorware. Click the Presentation window once with the Text cursor. Select Paste from the Edit pulldown menu. Using the Text tool from the toolbox, reformat the text, changing the heading to 18-point (use 24-point, on a Macintosh) Arial Black and the body text to 14-point (use 18-point, on a Macintosh) Arial. Use the Selection tool to modify the text so that your screen looks like this:

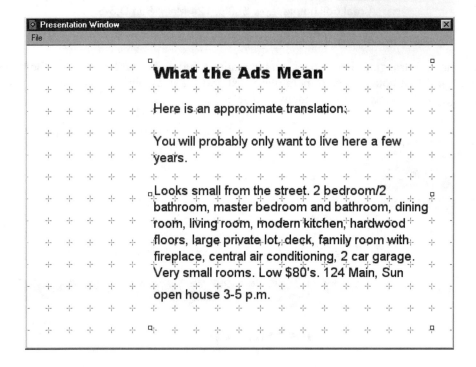

Now test your work. From the Control pulldown menu, select Restart.

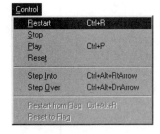

Your screen should look like this:

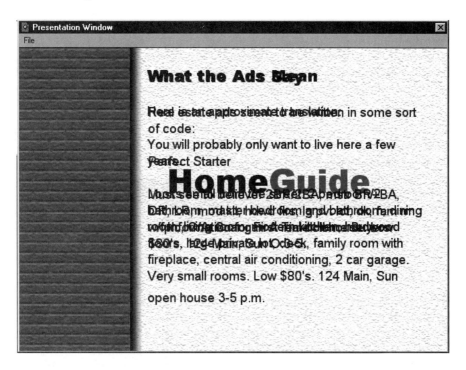

Obviously, there is a problem that needs to be fixed. The problem exists because several Display icons are presented simultaneously. To prevent information from piling up on the screen, you will need to insert some pauses and erase some text. First, reposition the **Ads** Map icon window so you can see the main flow line (Level 1) below:

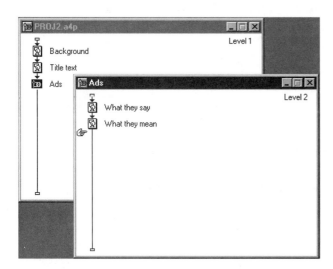

Now drag a Wait icon onto the main flow line between the icons labeled **Title text** and **Ads**

(notice that Wait icons are not usually labeled). Next place an Erase icon after the Wait icon and label it **Title text erase**.

Repeat the procedure on the Level 2 flow line, adding Wait and Erase icons after each Display icon. When you have finished, your screen should look like this:

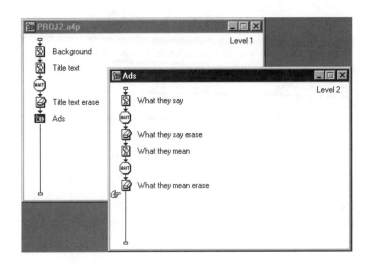

Select Restart from the Control pulldown menu and run your file. Notice that your lesson now pauses, and a button labeled **Continue** appears on the screen.

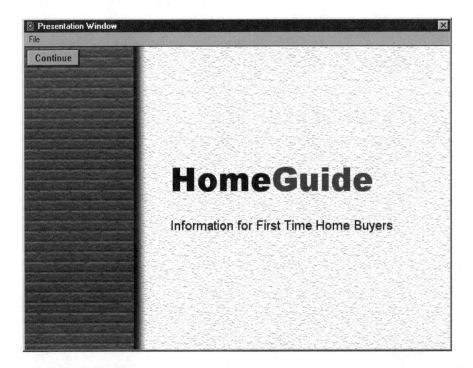

Clicking the Continue button once will bring up the Erase icon Properties dialog box. (Note that "Continue" is the default text assigned to the Wait icon.)

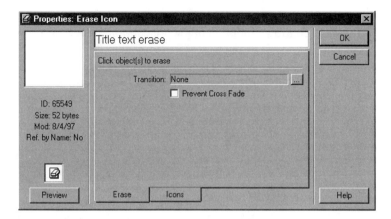

You must identify objects to erase. For now, you will erase only text. The background image will appear throughout the lesson. Place the Selection Tool over one of the words in the Presentation window and click once: The text should disappear.

Click OK in the Properties dialog box to advance to the next screen. Once again, click the Continue button to access the Erase Icon Properties dialog box. Move the Selection tool onto the text in the Presentation Window and click once. Click OK in the dialog box. Repeat this procedure for each Continue button that you encounter.

You will now add another Map icon and import more text. Click the main flow line. Drag a Map icon onto the flow line and label it **Features**. Double-click the Map icon. Drag a Display icon onto the **Features** flow line and label it **Features 1**. Drag another Display icon onto the flow line and label it **Features 2**.

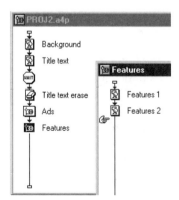

Next we will copy some preformatted text from a word-processing file and place formatting instructions into a Display icon. From the PROJECT 2 folder, double-click **FEATURES1.TXT**. Choose Select All from the Edit pulldown menu, and then choose Copy. Return to Authorware. Double-click **Features 1** to open the Display icon. From the toolbox, select the Text tool and click once in the Presentation window to place the paragraph ruler. Place three Tab stops by clicking with the mouse on the top of the paragraph ruler.

Select Paste from the Edit pulldown menu. Your screen should appear as follows:

Home Features by Price

As a home's price increases, so do the features. Consult the guide below to see what's available in your price range:

Price	Bedrooms	Living Room	Dining Room
to $50,000	1+	Yes	No
to $75,000	2+	Yes	Maybe
to $100,000	3+	Yes	Yes
to $150,000	4+	Yes	Yes

Use the Text tool to reformat the text so that the screen looks like this:

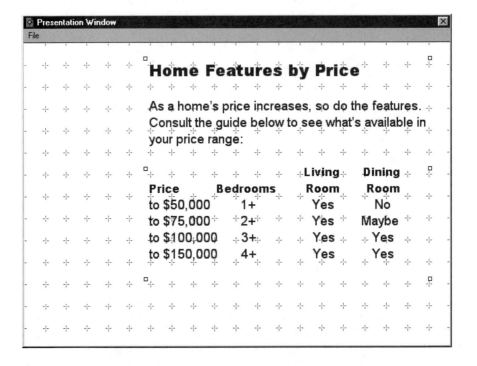

Repeat the process by placing the contents of **FEATURES2.TXT** into the Display icon titled **Features 2**. When you are done, the screen should look like this:

Presentation Window		
File		

Home Features by Price

As a home's price features, so do the amenities. Consult the guide below to see what's available in your price range:

Price	Baths	Garage	Other
to $50,000	1	1 car	fenced yard
to $75,000	1 ½	1 car	3 season porch
to $100,000	2 ½	2 car	central air, deck
to $150,000	3+	2+ car	pool, large rooms

Now add Wait and Erase icons to control the information flow.

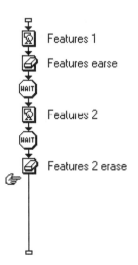

Features 1

Features earse

WAIT

Features 2

WAIT

Features 2 erase

Run the file from the beginning and make sure that you have placed and erased information appropriately. Finally, run the file again; you should be able to view the screens by clicking the Continue button.

You will now import two graphics files into your lesson. Return to the main flow line. Drag a new Map icon onto the flow line and label it **Mortgage**. Open the Map icon titled **Mortgage**. Drag a Display icon onto the flow line and label it **Mortgage chart**.

Open this Display icon. From the File pulldown menu, select Import.

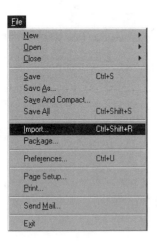

Using the Text tool, type the heading **Mortgage Payment Chart** in 18-point (use 24-point, on a Macintosh) Arial Black. Using the Selection tool, position text and graphics as follows:

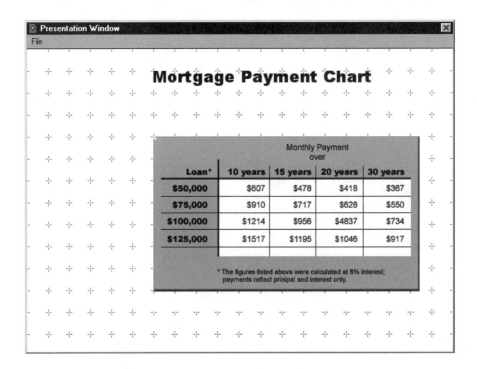

Now add Wait and Erase icons to the flow line.

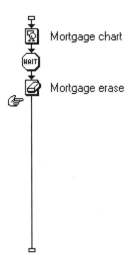

Mortgage chart

Mortgage erase

Run the lesson to access the new Continue button Properties dialog box.

Return to the main flow line. Drag another Map icon onto the flow line, label it **Interest**, and repeat the steps listed above to import the graphic titled INTEREST.PCT. Title the heading **The Impact of Interest Rates**. Reformat the text; then use the Selection Tool to position text and graphics as follows:

Presentation Window

File

The Impact of Interest Rates

You Borrow	Monthly Payment	Interest Rate	Duration	You Pay Back
$50,000	$594	7.5%	10 years	$71,280
$50,000	$464	7.5%	15 years	$83,520
$50,000	$350	7.5%	30 years	$126,000
$100,000	$1188	7.5%	10 years	$142,560
$100,000	$928	7.5%	15 years	$167,040
$100,000	$700	7.5%	30 years	$252,000

The figures listed above reflect principal and interest only.

Add Wait and Erase icons to the flow line; then save and run the file to test the lesson.

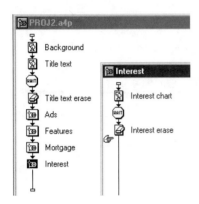

UNDERSTANDING THE DETAILS

In Chapter 2, you learned to create screens using a single Display icon. In practice, presentations are created by combining several Display icons. Think of your lesson as a stack of transparent sheets on which you have created text and graphic objects. Each transparent sheet corresponds to a Display icon on the flow line. As your program develops, these transparent sheets/Display icons are inserted into your lesson to build presentations. Display icons can also be removed to erase parts of the presentation.

You will often want to display or erase text or graphic objects individually. For example, imagine a screen containing two paragraphs and a related graphic. At some point, you may want to remove the graphic and replace it with another picture. Unfortunately, this apparently routine task cannot be completed if all the objects on the screen are placed on the same Display icon.

Wait and Erase Icons

Two Authorware icons help to create presentations: Wait and Erase.

- Wait icons insert pauses into the lesson. Pauses may be either for a set time period or until the learner acts by pressing a key or clicking the mouse button.
- Erase icons remove one or more Display icons and their contents from the screen.

How Do I Use Wait Icons To Pause Between Display Icons?

While a lesson executes, the contents of successive Display icons are displayed in rapid succession. Without pauses, the lesson would execute so quickly that you would not have time to read anything. Therefore, it is necessary to slow the lesson to give the user time to read the screen. The lesson flow can be stopped in two ways:

- By inserting a Wait icon in the program.
- By asking the user to respond with an Interaction icon (see Chapters 5, 7, and 8).

This section will focus on using the Wait icon to temporarily stop the program. When inserted, this icon causes the lesson to pause. The lesson continues when one of the following events occurs:

- A certain amount of time passes.
- The user presses any key.
- The user clicks the mouse.
  or
- The user activates a button on the screen.

To Use Wait Icon Options

- Place a Wait icon on the flow line at the point where you want the program to pause.
- Double-click the icon. The Wait icon properties will be displayed.

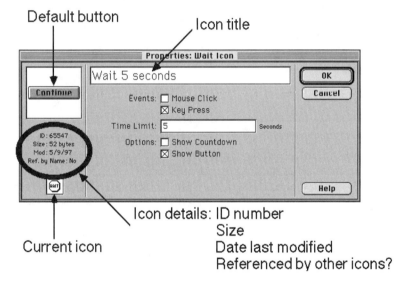

Default button   Icon title

Icon details: ID number
                Size
Current icon   Date last modified
                Referenced by other icons?

- Use the mouse to select the options that are appropriate for your needs. The meanings of the options are generally clear from their titles:
  - Mouse Click waits for the user to click the mouse once.
  - Key Press waits for the user to press any key on the keyboard.
  - Time Limit waits for the given time to expire before proceeding. (Show Countdown places a small clock on screen to show the user the time remaining.)
  - Show Button places the default "Continue" button on the screen.

You often will want to select several Wait options to make it easy for users to navigate. The Wait option box in the figure above is set to pause until the learner either presses a key, clicks the Continue button, or waits for 5 seconds.

- Click OK when you are done.

Note: Boxes that display messages or seek input from the designer are called *dialog boxes*. Many dialog boxes include spaces, known as *fields*, where designers can type information. For example, in the illustration above, you can type a time limit in the Time Limit field. It is important to know that many fields in Authorware allow you to enter variables instead of specific values. Using a variable instead of a specific value can save many hours of editing when programs need to be modified. Don't worry if the term *variable* is unknown to you. At this time, only readers with programming experience are likely to understand this term. Variables are covered in detail later in the book.

To Move Wait Buttons

Selecting the Show Button option in a Wait icon causes a button (with the default title **Continue**) to appear on the screen.

The "Continue" button is automatically placed in the top left corner of the screen. Many designers move this button to a different screen location, because objects in the top left corner of the screen tend to be overlooked by users. Make an early decision about where this button will be placed: After moving a Continue button, all subsequent buttons will automatically be placed in their new "home."

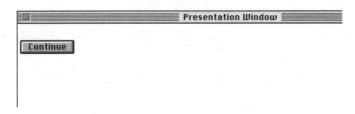

Note: To move the button while running the lesson, it is necessary to pause the lesson. To do this, use the Command-P shortcut on the keyboard to switch from Play mode to Pause mode. Pressing Command-P at any time immediately switches from Play mode to Pause mode, or vice versa; however, notice that you remain in the Presentation window.

When the lesson is paused, use the mouse to click and drag the button to its desired location. The new location is now the default location for subsequent buttons. Select Play from the Control pulldown menu to resume the lesson.

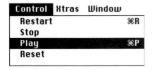

Another quick way to pause the lesson is to press Command-1. The result is similar to Command-P; the difference is that Command-1 not only switches from Play mode to Pause mode, but also switches between the Design and Presentation windows.

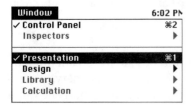

Note: The default button title (i.e., **Continue**) is set in the dialog box accessed from the File > Properties pulldown menu. You will learn more about setting file properties in Chapter 6.

How Do I Erase Icons?

Remember that Display icons are like transparent sheets that are stacked on top of each other. If Display icons are not removed, the screen will soon become a mass of unreadable text and graphic objects. To prevent this from occurring, you must remove Display icons when you no longer want their contents to appear. An Erase icon can be used to erase one display or multiple displays.

It is important to remember that the objects in an icon cannot be displayed or erased separately. During program execution, icons, not individual objects, are displayed and erased. If you want an object to be displayed or erased separately from other objects, you must put that object in a separate Display icon.

To Erase Objects

- Insert an Erase icon on the flow line where you want one or more icons to be erased.
- Title the Erase icon with a name that hints at the name(s) of the icon(s) to be erased.

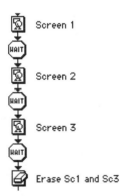

- Double-click the Erase icon. (All Display icons that are currently active—that have been displayed but not yet erased—are shown along with the Erase option box.)
- Transitions are special effects used when displaying or erasing Display icons. You may select a Transition effect that will be applied to all the objects you erase (see below). When you are done, click the Icons tab.

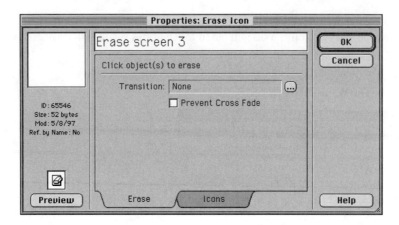

- Select the Display icon that you want to erase. To select an icon, use the mouse to click an object from its Display. Continue to select Display icons if additional objects are to be erased. All selected icons will appear in the Erase icon's options box. If you select the wrong icon, highlight and remove the icon from the list of icons to be erased.

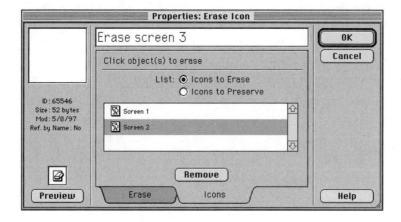

How Can I Display and Erase Objects Using Special Effects?

Authorware provides many options for displaying and erasing objects. These options, known as transitions, create exciting special effects to present and erase information. If transitions are not used, objects are displayed and erased from the screen without any special effects.

Note: Many companies are developing transitions that you can use in Authorware. Add new transitions by placing them into the Xtras folder, which is found in the same folder as the Authorware application. The Xtras folder contains files that add functionality to Authorware or ensure that media are incorporated smoothly.

To Display Objects With Transitions

- There are several ways to access transitions. A quick way is to highlight the icon for which you want a transition (i.e., single-click the icon), and select Icon > Transitions from the Modify pulldown menu. The shortcut for this is Command-T.

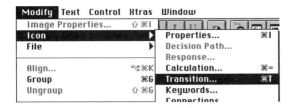

Select a transition by combining options from the Categories and Transitions windows. Spend some time experimenting with transitions to find out how each works and which ones you like best. Note also that you can change many transitions by modifying the values in the Duration and Smoothness fields. Press the **Apply** button to view each change you make. You may need to drag the dialog box to one side to view a transition.

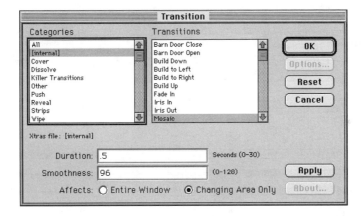

- Select the option you want. Authorware demonstrates each effect as soon as it is chosen.
- If you like the effect, click the OK button; if not, try another option or click Cancel.

You can also access transitions by way of an icon's **Properties** dialog box.

- Select Icon > Properties from the Modify pulldown menu.
  or
- Press the Command key and double-click the icon.

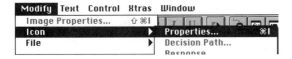

- Several icons include a link to the Transitions dialog box. For example, the illustration below shows links from the Framework and Display dialog boxes. Select the button to access the Transitions dialog window.

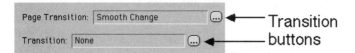

To Erase Icon Objects With Transitions

- Select an Erase icon. Select the Erase tab and open the Erase Transition dialog.

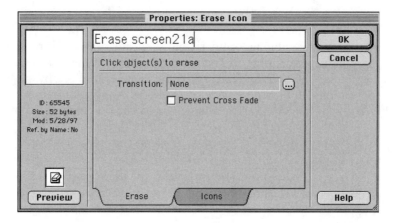

- Select the Erase effect you want. Click the Apply button to view the transition that you have selected.

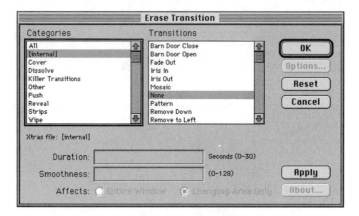

- If you like the effect, click the OK button; if not, try another option or click Cancel. Experiment with Duration and Smoothness options to vary effects and decide whether to apply a transition to the entire screen or simply to the changing information.

Use transitions wisely. Transitions can greatly enhance the visual appeal of your work. For example, using the Push: Push Down transition to remove old information and present new information can greatly improve the look of your screens. However, transitions should be used skillfully and sparingly to gain maximum effect.

How Can I Add New Transitions to Authorware?

In addition to the standard transitions available in Authorware, you can add transitions developed by third-party vendors. To use a new transition, you must first add the transition file to the Xtras folder, which is located in the same folder as the Authorware application. The folder contains files that expand Authorware's capabilities, and will be examined later.

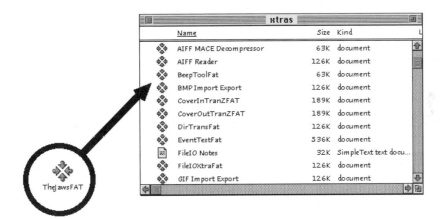

How Do I Run My Lesson?

Test your lesson often and early in the development process. Do not create large chunks of your lesson without checking to see that the lesson works properly. It is better to find problems or errors early in the development process before debugging becomes too onerous a task.

Run the lesson from the Control pulldown menu. You can run a lesson at any time. It doesn't matter whether you are in the Design window or the Presentation window.

There are four ways to run a lesson: from the start to the end of the program, from the start to a point within the program; from a point within the program to the end of the program; and from a point within the program to a later point within the program.

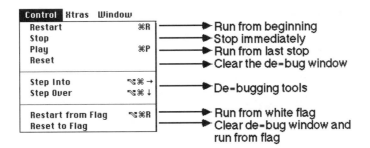

To Run the Entire Lesson

- Select Restart from the Control menu or the tool bar.
  or
- Press Command-R.

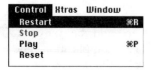

Your program will run from first icon to last icon.

To Run from a Point within the Lesson

- Find the point on the flow line where you want to begin.

- Drag a Start flag to where you want to begin.   sTART
- Execute the Restart from Flag command by selecting the Restart from Flag option from the Control menu or the tool bar.

Your program will run from the Start flag to the end of the program.

To Run to a Point within the Lesson

- Find the point on the flow line where you want the lesson to stop.
- Drag a Stop flag to a position immediately after the last icon that you want.   sTOP
- Execute the Run command by:
  - Selecting Restart from the Control menu or the tool bar
    or
  - Pressing Command-R

Your program will run from the beginning to the Stop flag.

To Run between Two Points within the Lesson

- Identify a starting point on the flow line.
- Drag a Start flag to where you want to begin.   sTART
- Identify an ending point.

- Drag a Stop flag to where you want to end.   STOP

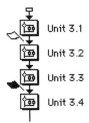

Unit 3.1

Unit 3.2

Unit 3.3

Unit 3.4

- Execute the Restart from Flag command by:
  - Selecting the Restart from Flag option from the Control menu or the tool bar

Your program will run from the Start flag to the Stop flag.

How Do I Temporarily Stop a Running Lesson?

While running a lesson, the file will stop whenever it reaches:

- A Wait icon (with user input rather than a time option)
- An Interaction icon, which requires a response from the user
- A Stop flag

To Stop a Lesson

- Wait until the program reaches the point at which you want to pause.
- Enter the Pause command by:
  - Pressing Command-P

To Resume a Lesson

- Enter the Proceed command by:
  - Selecting the Play option from the Control menu
    or
  - Pressing Command-P

You can also use the Play command to bypass a Stop flag. After the program stops at the flag, press Command-P and the lesson will ignore the flag.

Note: The same key sequence is used for both Pause and Play (Command-P). If the lesson is running, Command-P stops it. If the lesson is paused, through a pause or a Stop flag, Command-P causes it to continue.

How Do I Edit a Lesson While It Is Running?

One of Authorware's strengths is that you can edit text and graphics "on the fly." Your screen layout need not be perfect before you run a lesson; in fact, you don't need to develop any lesson content before you run the lesson.

First, place icons on the flow line; then run the lesson. The lesson will stop at each empty icon and wait for you to enter text and graphics, or set other options. When you are more familiar with Authorware, you may find this a quick and efficient approach to lesson development.

To Edit Display Icons That Contain at Least One Object

- You must be able to stop the lesson at the point where you want to begin editing. Do so by:
  - Inserting a Wait icon after the icon is displayed, but before it is erased
    or
  - Inserting a Stop flag after the icon has been displayed, but before it is erased
    or
  - Being ready to execute the Pause command
- Run the program.
- When the program stops, the contents of one or more icons will be displayed.
- Double-click the object you want to edit. (Margin handles and the toolbox for the selected icon will be displayed.)
- Check the icon name in the toolbox to be sure that you are working on the correct icon.
- Edit objects in the displays.

To Enter Text into an Empty Display Icon

- Run the program. When the program reaches the empty icon, the program will stop and the toolbox for the empty icon will be displayed.
- Create desired text and graphic objects.
- Click the toolbox's Close box. The toolbox will disappear, and the lesson will resume until the next empty Display icon is reached.

All icons except the Wait icon can be created and their options set during program execution. For Wait icons, settings are predetermined and must be reset for each icon (with the exception of the placement of the Continue button).

Selecting Objects While Running a Lesson

Using the Pause option to interrupt a lesson can cause confusion. Pausing does not cause the toolbox to appear. Consequently, the handles that are used to move and edit graphic objects also do not appear, making it impossible to edit individual graphics. Instead, handles appear around the perimeter of all the objects in the selected Display icon. For example, in the figure below, three individual rectangles are surrounded by "grayed" handles These gray handles indicate that a Display icon has been identified, but the objects cannot yet be edited.

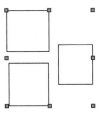

To select an individual object in the display, double-click the object to be edited with the mouse to reveal the editing handles. This will reveal the handles for each of the objects in the display.

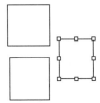

Next, single-click with the mouse the object you want to edit. The editing handles will appear around the desired object only.

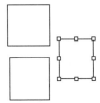

How Do I Duplicate an Icon or an Icon's Name?

When working in the Design window, you will often want to reproduce an icon that you have used elsewhere. To do so, first copy the icon and then paste it onto the flow line. To copy the icon, use the Selection tool to highlight the icon you want to duplicate, and select Copy from the Edit pulldown menu. To paste the icon, click the flow line at the location where you want to paste the icon. A small hand with a pointing finger will appear, indicating where the icon is to be pasted. Select Paste from the Edit pulldown menu to duplicate the icon.

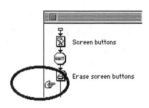

Often, you will want to copy an icon's name without copying the entire icon. Copying and pasting an icon's name is often faster than typing the name, and helps prevent potentially important typos. To copy an icon's name, first use the Selection tool to highlight the icon whose name you want to copy.

Now use the mouse to click the icon's name. The Selection tool will change to an I-beam when it enters the icon's name field. Click the icon's name with the mouse and highlight the text you want to copy.

To copy the text, select Copy from the Edit pulldown menu. To paste the text, place the cursor where you want the text to appear and select Paste from the Edit menu.

How Can Authorware Create Icons For Me?

The title of this section may sound like a joke, but it isn't! Authorware can create Display icons for the designer. The trick to this approach is to use Authorware's capability to import what are known are Rich Text Format (RTF) files. RTF files keep the text formatting applied in a word processor.

To create an RTF file, create your display in a word-processing file and save the file in RTF format. (Check the manual that accompanies your word processor for more information on this topic.)

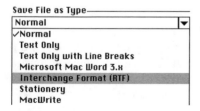

Next, go to your Authorware lesson file and open a Display icon into which you want to place the text. Select Import from the File menu.

Authorware will prompt you to locate the file you want to import. After identifying the file you want to import, the following dialog box will appear:

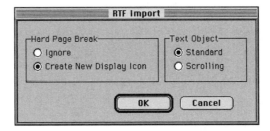

clicking OK tells Authorware to open the selected file, fill the screen with the first page of text from the word-processing file, and create additional Display icons containing subsequent pages from the file. The illustration below shows an original Display icon titled **Import data file** and two additional displays. The icons titled **data.rtf: 2** and **data.rtf: 3** were created automatically when Authorware encountered a page break in the imported RTF file. The titles of the new icons come from the name of the data file that was imported into Authorware, which, in this case, was **data.rtf**.

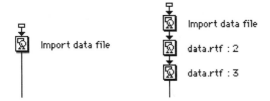

Note: To create new Display icons, it is important to place hard page breaks into your work-processing file rather than accepting the usual pagination created by the word-processing application.

How Do I Organize Icons?

As you have already seen, creating lessons in Authorware involves navigating between Design and Presentation windows. As you add icons to the flow line to create presentations, you will soon run out of space to add more icons. When the flow line is full, it is necessary to use Map icons to group icons.

Map Icons

You will need to group icons because there is a limit to the number of icons that can be placed on a flow line. This limit is determined by the size of your computer's monitor. The following techniques can be used to place icons into Maps:

- You can add icons to an existing Map simply by dragging and dropping icons into the Map. First open the Map icon. Drag an icon onto the flow line in the open Map icon.
- Highlight two or more adjacent icons on the flow line, and then select Group from the Edit pulldown menu.

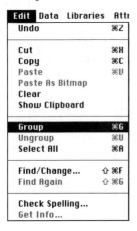

The highlighted icons will be placed into a new Map icon on the flow line. Try to group icons logically to help you edit and troubleshoot your lesson.

Several levels of Design windows can be created by grouping icons into Maps. The level of the Design window in which you are working is displayed in the upper right corner of the Design window. There is no limit to the number of levels you can have. Just remember that the deeper the level, the more time it will take you to access it.

In the figure below, the first flow line (Level 1) has three Map icons. Opening the first Map icon displays its contents—the flow line designated as Level 2. In turn, opening the Map icon in Level 2 gives you its contents—the Level 3 flow line.

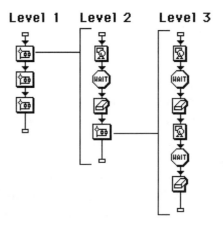

How Do I Align Objects Located on Different Display Icons?

Because presentations often consist of several Display icons, it is often necessary to align objects in separate displays to ensure that they don't overlap and are well spaced. For example, objects in displays are often carefully placed to maintain a sense of balance and spaciousness among the objects. Aligning objects requires you to select and move objects to desired positions. There are two main ways to align objects: by jumping from icon to icon, or by aligning objects while running a file.

To Align Objects by Jumping from Icon to Icon

- Access the flow line that contains the Display icons you want to align.
- Double-click the first Display icon in the series of icons.
- After the icon opens, return to the flow line by selecting Current Icon from the View pull-down menu or clicking on the Close box of the toolbox.

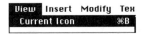

- While holding down the Shift key, double-click the second Display icon in the icon series. The selected icon will open, and the contents of both the first and second Display icons will be displayed.
- Continue this process of Shift-opening icons until the contents of all icons in the series you want to align are displayed.
- To select a specific icon, double-click an object from that icon. Margin handles will be displayed, along with the toolbox for the selected icon.
- Move the contents of the selected icon to the desired location.

You can also edit while running a lesson. In fact, this is often the most efficient way to make small changes and align objects.

To Align Objects While Running the Lesson

- Be sure that you can stop your lesson at the end of the series of icons that you want to align. Do this by:
  - Inserting a Wait icon at the end of the icon series
    or
  - Inserting a Stop flag at the end of the icon series
    or
  - Being ready to execute the Pause command
- Run the lesson.
- When the lesson stops at the end of the icon series, the contents of all icons in the series you want to align will be displayed.

- To select a specific icon, double-click an object in that icon. (Margin handles will be displayed, along with the toolbox for the selected icon.)
- Move the contents of the selected icon to the desired location.

Note: Object alignment, discussed here, concerns objects in different icons. Aligning two or more objects in a single icon is performed using the Align Objects command, and is discussed in Chapter 6.

How Do I Hide Displays?

Sometimes it is important to ensure that information in one display is always dominant over information in another display. However, this can be difficult to guarantee. When Authorware draws text or graphic objects, the newly presented information is dominant over the old.

One solution to ensure that information is presented as intended involves layer effects. Layering establishes a dominance hierarchy that controls how displays appear: Displays that appear higher in the hierarchy are dominant over others.

To set a Layer level, either highlight (with the selection tool) or open a Display icon. Select Icon > Properties from the Modify pulldown window, select the Display tab, and enter a number into the Layer field. Higher layer numbers result in dominance over displays with lower layer numbers.

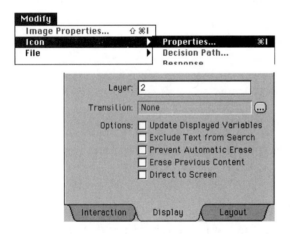

Use layering effects cautiously. They can provide "quick fixes" to irritating design problems; however, Display icons with changed layer numbers can also prove difficult to hide, and are sometimes used when designers don't understand how other icons operate. Layering effects can come back to haunt you!

How Do I Design Effective Presentations?

Several techniques are easy to learn, but make the difference between sloppy, amateur designs and attractive, professional-looking presentations. The guidelines outlined below are intended to build on those presented in previous chapters.

1. Use consistent layout plans. The following approach involves establishing specific locations for placing text on the screen. The example uses a heading in 48-point text, an underlined subheading in 24-point text, and 24-point tab-indented text with bullets to display main
points.

 Screen 1

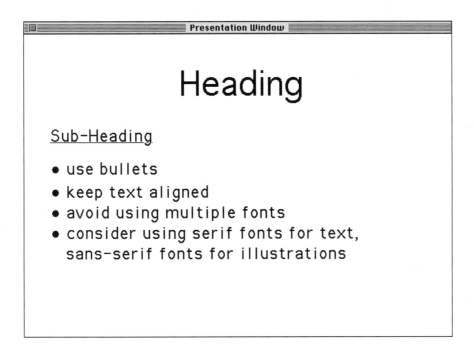

After creating a master Display icon, copy and paste the icon whenever similar text layout is
needed. In the illustration below, the Display icon titled Screen 1 has been copied and pasted
onto the flow line and then renamed Screen 2. Screen 2 can now be opened and the text edited,
thereby ensuring that the look of the first Display is maintained.

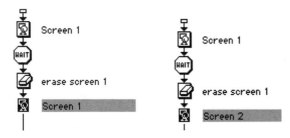

Presentation Window

Using Color

Use Color Combinations

- use complementary colors for contrast
- avoid using reds and blues for text
- avoid over-using color
- don't combine the following colors:
 --red with green
 --green with blue
 --red with blue

---

2. Use the Grid to control layout. The Grid and Snap to Grid options from the View pulldown menu help to ensure that text and graphic objects are placed consistently. The grid aligns objects on the screen and nearly always is more precise than using your judgment. When objects are even one pixel out of alignment, screens can look unpolished. Snap to Grid works like Grid, but places what appear to be little magnets into the grid hash marks. When you place a graphic on the screen, it appears to be attracted to one of the hash marks.

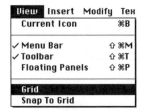

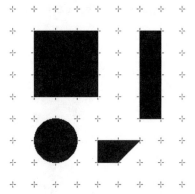

STUDY EXERCISES

1. How can you control where Authorware places the "Continue" button in the Presentation window?

2. Use Wait icon options to create presentations in which the user moves to the next screen:

   - By clicking the mouse
   - By pressing a key on the keyboard
   - By waiting 10 seconds before moving on automatically

3. Create a blackboard to display a class lecture. On the blackboard, build a presentation that gradually unfolds several steps that together complete an activity.

4. Use at least three Display icons to build an electronic resume:

   - Display parts of the resume sequentially (i.e., one line at a time) by placing words in different Display icons.
   - Use transitions (fade in, dissolve, push, strips, etc.) to make the presentation visually interesting.
   - Create special effects by drawing objects in one pattern and changing the fill to make objects appear to shimmer.

5. Use Display, Wait, and Erase icons to build an outline for a speech, a plan for a lesson, or a description of a sequential process. For example, a mathematician might outline the steps for solving quadratic equations using the quadratic formula. Use Start and Stop flags to test subsets of the presentation.

Multimedia

CHAPTER OVERVIEW

One of Authorware's greatest strengths is its ability to incorporate multimedia into files. Multimedia lessons—those that use animated objects, sound files, and video, as well as text and still graphics—not only are possible, but are relatively easy to create with Authorware.

CHAPTER OBJECTIVES

After completing this chapter, you will be able to:

- Animate objects between two points.
- Animate objects on a path or along a curve.
- Use animation as a navigation tool.
- Incorporate sound files into lessons.
- Incorporate QuickTime digital video files into lessons.

KEY TERMS

Animation
Sound
Digital Movie

SUPPORT MATERIALS

On the CD-ROM disk, run the file titled **Videos.a4r** and select the button labeled **Chapter 4** to examine how to play sound files. If you are not sure how to run the file, refer to the section titled "To Run the CD-ROM Videos" in the preface.

From the SUPPORT folder on the CD, open the file titled **CHP04.a4p**. The file demonstrates how to incorporate sound files and animation into your lessons.

PROJECT 3: IMPORTING MEDIA INTO AUTHORWARE

Materials Needed to Complete This Project

- Your file from the previous project, **PROJ2.a4p**
- Macromedia Authorware 4.0 for Macintosh or Windows
- PROJECT 3 folder

Before You Begin

Allow approximately 30 minutes to complete Project 3.

Project Description

In this project, you will import and manipulate graphics, use a Sound icon to play a sound file, and use a Library file to store icons that are used repeatedly.

Activity

Begin by opening the Authorware file from the previous project. From the File pulldown menu, choose Save As... and rename the file **PROJ3**.

You are going to add some graphics to your presentation. Double-click the **Ads** Map icon. Double-click the **What they say** Display icon. From the File pulldown menu, choose Import. Select **Man.pct** and click the Import button:

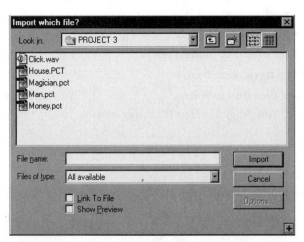

Using the Selection tool from the toolbox, position the graphic like this:

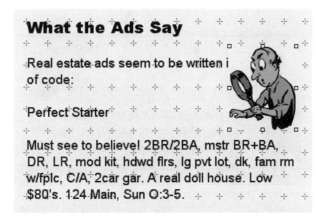

Notice that the graphic has a white background and overlaps some of the text. From the Window pulldown menu, choose Inspectors > Modes:

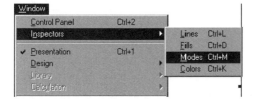

Click the graphic with the Selection tool; then select Transparent from the Modes palette to eliminate the white background:

Select the Text tool from the toolbox. Click the text and place the cursor to the left of the word "in." Press the Return or Enter key on the keyboard to move the text to a new line. Your screen should look like this:

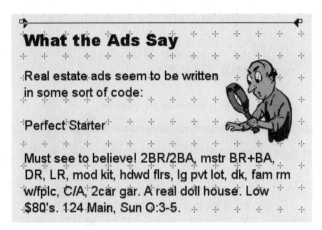

Next, place the same graphic in the Display icon titled **What they mean**. Using the Selection tool, click the graphic once. From the Edit pulldown menu, choose Copy:

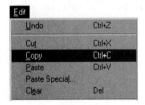

Click the **Ads** Map icon once to bring the flow line to the front. Double-click the **What they mean** Display icon. From the Edit pulldown menu, choose Paste. This will place the graphic in the same location as it appears in the Display icon labeled **What they say**. Use the Text tool from the toolbox to manipulate the text block. Your screen should look like this:

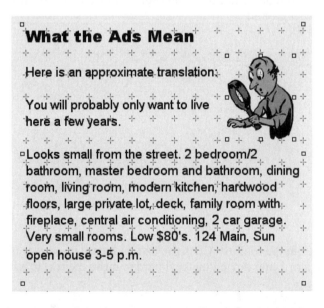

To check your work, choose Restart from the Control pulldown menu. Make sure that your new graphic doesn't jump between screens.

Return to the Level 1 flow line and double-click the Map icon titled **Mortgage**. Double-click the Display icon titled **Mortgage chart** and import the graphic titled Money.pct. Make the background transparent and move the chart to make room for the new graphic. Your screen should appear as follows:

Mortgage Payment Chart

Loan*	10 years	15 years	20 years	30 years
$50,000	$607	$478	$418	$367
$75,000	$910	$717	$628	$550
$100,000	$1214	$956	$4837	$734
$125,000	$1517	$1195	$1046	$917

Monthly Payment over

* The figures listed above were calculated at 8% interest; payments reflect prinipal and interest only.

Return to the Level 1 flow line. Open the Map icon titled **Interest** and open the Display icon titled **Interest chart**. Import the graphic titled Magician.pct, change the background to transparent, and place the graphic as follows:

The Impact of Interest Rates

You Borrow	Monthly Payment	Interest Rate	Duration	You Pay Back
$50,000	$594	7.5%	10 years	$71,280
$50,000	$464	7.5%	15 years	$83,520
$50,000	$350	7.5%	30 years	$126,000
$100,000	$1188	7.5%	10 years	$142,560
$100,000	$928	7.5%	15 years	$167,040
$100,000	$700	7.5%	30 years	$252,000

The figures listed above reflect principal and interest only.

Return to the Level 1 flow line. Open the Display icon titled **Title text**. Import the graphic titled House.pct. Format and place the graphic as follows:

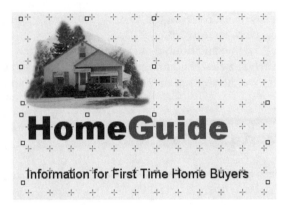

Run your lesson to check alignment.

Next you will add a sound that will play whenever you click the Continue button. Return to the Level 1 flow line, place a Sound icon above the Erase icon titled **Title text erase**, and label the icon **Click**.

Double-click the Sound icon to access the Properties dialog box.

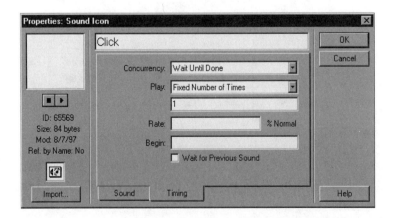

Click the Import button.

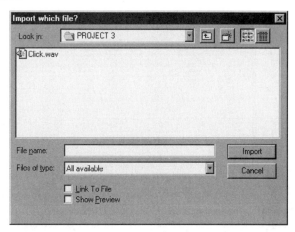

Select the file titled **Click.wav**. Click the Import button, and then click the OK button.

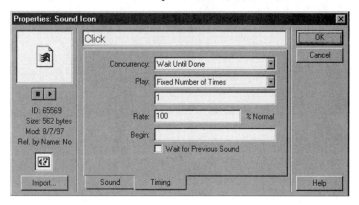

Run your file to check your work.

Authorware supports the use of libraries, allowing you to import a file once and use it many times. Creating and using libraries can significantly reduce the size and efficiency of your lesson file. To create a library, select New > Library from the File pulldown menu.

The following Library window will appear:

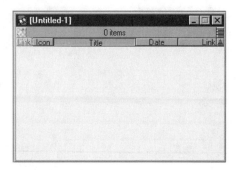

Drag the Sound icon titled **Click** onto the Library window. This moves the sound file titled **Click** into the Library and replaces the original icon with an alias on the Level 1 flow line. This alias appears in italic type.

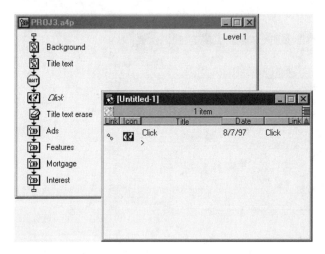

You need to save your Library. From the File pulldown menu, choose Save.

You will see the following dialog box:

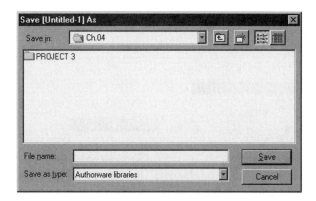

Title your Library **Home**. Click the Save button. Authorware will add the suffix .a4l to the name of a Library file.

Double-click the **Ads** Map icon. Position the **Home.a4l** Library window next to the **Ads** flow line.

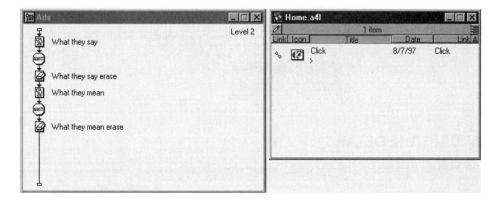

To use an icon from the Library, select the icon and then drag copies from the Library window to the flow line.

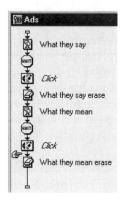

Repeat this process to replace all other references to the Sound icon titled **Click**; then run your lesson:

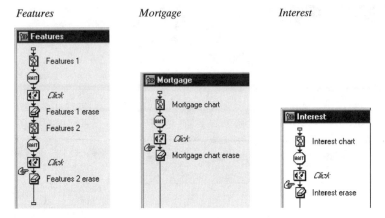

Features   *Mortgage*   *Interest*

Extending What You Have Learned

Running a lesson to test changes and additions is a standard part of the development process. To save time, you can place a control panel on your desktop. The control panel makes it easier to run, back up, and replay lesson segments. To access the control panel, select Control Panel from the Window pulldown menu. The following should appear on your desktop:

UNDERSTANDING THE DETAILS

Managing File Size

To work effectively with multimedia (i.e., sounds, images, and video), you should understand the factors that influence multimedia quality. As the quality of a graphic, sound, or movie improves, the space needed to save the file increases. Managing this balance between file size and quality is an important skill for any multimedia designer.

Working effectively with media files involves understanding how files are stored. The basic storage unit on the computer is the binary digit, or bit. A bit is a single digit written in base 2. We can write numbers in virtually any base, but we generally count in base 10 because we have ten fingers and thumbs. Consequently, to represent twenty-six different objects, we write 26 (i.e., two sets of ten and six digits). However, if humans had only one hand with five digits, we would most likely represent those twenty-six objects as 101 (i.e., one set of twenty-five, zero fives, and one digit). That is, we would write numbers in base 5. Computers function by sending electricity along circuits, and control flow through these circuits by using gates that are in one of two states: open or closed. In a sense, computers have two digits; consequently, base 2 is used to represent information in the computer.

Sets of two-digit numbers (ones and zeros) can be interpreted by computers as characters, numbers, operations (such as multiplication), colors, sounds, or graphic images. Files are stored on disks, and the size of a file is limited only by the capacity of the storage medium. For example, floppy diskettes have a storage capacity of slightly more than 1 MB. In contrast, a standard CD-ROM disk can store approximately 650 MB of information. A small project containing just a few color images and sound files will quickly fill a floppy disk beyond its capacity.

In recent years, computer-file storage capacity has skyrocketed, while costs have plummeted. Together, these developments have created the potential to store large color graphics, sounds, and movies that used to be too large or too expensive to store on most computers. However, it is still important to keep files as small as possible to preserve storage space and to ensure high performance—larger files take longer to reproduce than do smaller files. To understand how to keep file sizes small, it is important to understand the concept of bit depth. A discussion of bit depth is presented in Appendix A.

Working with Sound Files

One of the most important issues in multimedia development is interface design. An interface is the visual illusion used to help the user interact with the computer. Images on computer monitors are, of course, simply electronic pulses. Sound can add a degree of realism to a lesson. By helping users to believe that the environment in which they are interacting is real, sound can make the interface easier to use. For example, adding a sound to a button often helps to persuade the user that the object being clicked is really a button, not simply an electronic image!

Sound can also help fulfill other important goals. Sound can create vivid mental pictures that help the audience remember events. Sound can also accompany or replace text to transmit information. The effects of sound are important because spoken messages are often remembered by the audience for a long time. Sound effects such as screeching tires, breaking glass, and gunshots also have a strong motivational impact. They add excitement and drama and help instill a belief that the audience is present at an event.

Ambient sound can help create a desired mood. For example, the sound of waves breaking on the seashore, wind blowing, or the distant cries of birds can help people relax. When used carefully, sound can help transport users' minds from the cold environment of the computer to more conducive mental settings.

Carefully chosen music can also evoke emotional responses from an audience. Faster, rhythmic music creates excitement, whereas slower, fluid music creates a sense of calm and contentment. Similarly, music can stimulate emotions such as pride, fear, and compassion. One other dimension of sound should be considered. Just as the presence of sound or noise can evoke emotional responses, silence can be dramatic and can be used to encourage reflection or to dramatize events.

Sound is highly motivating, but don't get carried away! If used sparingly, sound files can help to focus learners' attentions and motivate them to work. However, when overused or used carelessly, sounds tend to lose their impact.

What Are Sound Files?

The process of digitizing audio involves transforming a continuous soundwave into discreet ones and zeros. The final representation of the soundwave in digital form can never contain exactly the same information stored in the soundwave, but in many cases, the missing information will never be perceived by the human ear.

The size and quality of a sound file is determined by three factors:

- Sampling rate
- Bit depth
- The number of channels (one for mono, two for stereo)

Sampling rate is the number of times per second that a computer digitizes a soundwave. Sampling rates are reported in hertz (Hz). Higher sampling rates result in higher quality (and higher file size). A typical sampling rate for speech is 11,000 samples a second, or 11 kilohertz (kHz). The recording industry uses 44.1 kHz or higher to create audio CDs.

Bit depth refers to the amount of information used to describe a sound. Larger bit depth allows the computer to replicate a sound with greater precision than does smaller bit depth. Using 8-bit sound, the computer can distinguish among 256 different sounds. However, with 16-bit sound, the computer can distinguish among 65,536 sounds. If you think that the difference in sound quality between 8-bit and 16-bit sound must be noticeable, you're right—it is!

Many computers can record and play stereo files. The main difference between a mono file and a stereo file is that mono records one soundtrack, but stereo records two. Hence, stereo records twice the amount of information and requires twice as much storage space.

Where Do Sound Files Come From?

Sound files are available from many sources. Commercial CDs containing sound files that can be used in lessons are available from bulletin boards and the Internet. However, if the exact sound for your needs is unavailable, you may have to create one yourself.

Sounds are not created with Authorware. Instead, sound files are created with an application, such as SoundEdit 16, that converts voice or sounds from a tape, CD, or other medium from analog signals into digital formats. Once created, the sound can be loaded into, and saved as part of, an Authorware file. This chapter assumes that you either know how to create your own sound files or have access to a library of digital sounds.

Sound files, like graphics, can be created in many formats. However, Authorware recognizes only certain types of files. The most common formats are probably AIF, SoundEdit, and WAV files. The range of file formats tends to change, so check your manuals to determine which file formats will work.

How Do I Play a Sound File?

Playing a sound file involves the use of a Sound icon. To play a file, drag a Sound icon onto the flow line and label the icon.

Scream!

Open the Sound icon by double-clicking its icon. Opening the Sound icon produces a dialog box with two tabs. The tabs are labeled Sound and Timing.

To load a sound file, select the Sound tab and press the Import... button to locate the file you want to play. The process is virtually identical to that used in loading a graphic image. Sound files, like graphic files, may be stored internally or externally. The benefit of storing files externally is that they can be edited without modification of the Authorware file. Alternatively, you can load a file into Authorware to become a permanent part of the lesson file. In the illustration below, the Link to File box has been checked, indicating that the audio file will be stored externally.

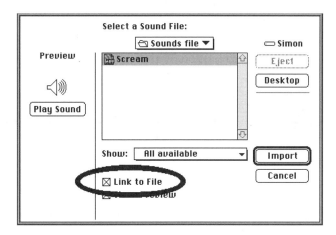

The effect of selecting Link to File is illustrated below. Here, the fact that the file is stored externally is indicated, along with the path to the folder where the file is located.

The dialog box also contains important information about the file. Most of this can be interpreted with ease, assuming that you have a general understanding of how computers create and store files. For example, in the illustration above, the dialog box indicates that the file is approximately 110 KB in size, is stored in AIFF format, contains mono rather than stereo sound, and was recorded at a bit depth of 16 bits and a sampling rate of approximately 44 kHz. In addition to understanding Sample Size and Sample Rate, it is important to consider the potential impact of Data Rate. A discussion of Data Rate is presented in Appendix B. Selecting the Timing tab brings up the following dialog box:

Several decisions must be made every time a Sound icon is used. These include:

- *Concurrency*: Concurrency controls whether a sound is played before or while other events occur. This decision is important. Sometimes it is necessary to play a sound before another event occurs. For example, you may want students to listen to corrective feedback completely before proceeding with a lesson. In such cases, select the Wait Until Done option. However, at other times, simultaneous events are important. For example, a sound file may be used to introduce a concept that unfolds visually in front of users. In such cases, select the Concurrent option.

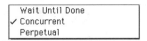

- *How many times the sound file will be played*: This determines whether a file is played a fixed number of times or whether it is to be controlled by a variable. Most sounds are played only once. However, creative use of this option can save time and storage space. For example, a cuckoo clock striking midnight might involve playing a sound file twelve times in rapid succession. The Until True option involves variables. In this case, a sound file will continue to play until the value of a variable becomes true.

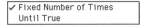

- *The rate at which the files will be played*: Playing a sound file at over 100% increases the pitch of the sound. Many cartoon characters' voices are created by increasing the actor's voice pitch. In contrast, playing sounds under 100% slows the sound and deepens tone. Sometimes, files are stored at high speed to save disk space, and must be slowed for playback in Authorware.

- *When a file is played*. The field labeled Begin allows you to control a file with a variable or expression. The relevance of this feature may not become apparent until you have read Chapter 11, "Calculation Icons: Variables."

How Do I Play a Digital Movie?

Digital movies are files that play multiple graphic images each second to convey the illusion of motion, and have the capability of delivering a concurrent sound track. Videos are usually created by digitizing brief clips from videotape or by developing animations. The processes of creating a digital movie from video and creating an animated movie are quite complex and will not be addressed here. However, it should be noted that the process of creating digital video is usually very expensive. Also, it is important to know that digital movies may be of several different types. For example, movies may be created in Director or captured using protocols such as QuickTime, AVI, or MPEG.

Playing a movie is similar in operation to playing a sound file. However, unlike sound files, digital movies are not usually loaded into the lesson file. Instead, they are stored on a disk alongside the Authorware file. The most common way to play a movie involves placing a Digital Movie icon on the flow line and setting several options that control how the movie will be displayed.

First place a Digital Movie icon onto the flow line and label the icon.

 Running horse

Opening the Movie icon produces a dialog box with three tabs. The tabs are labeled Movie, Timing, and Layout.

To load a movie, press the **Import**... button and locate the movie.

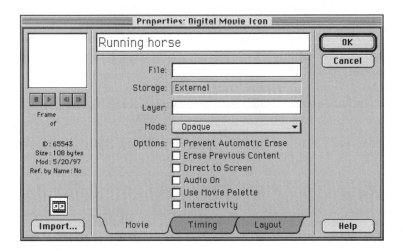

Authorware will now ask you to identify the movie that you want to play.

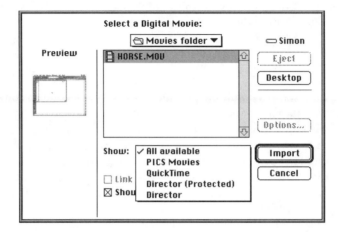

After locating a movie, press the tab labeled Timing to produce a dialog box similar to the one below.

As you can see, several options can be controlled. Often, files do not need to be adjusted. However, if you wish, you can modify which frames are displayed, the presentation rate, and the number of times the movie shows.

   Also, as was possible with the Sound icon, you can control the Concurrency. That is, you can decide whether Authorware stops and displays the entire video before proceeding (Wait Until Done), continues with the lesson while the movie is playing (Concurrent), or is available as a Perpetual option.

The relevance of Perpetual options will not become apparent until that topic is addressed in Chapter 8.

You can also control where the movie will be shown. To do so, check the Layout tab and select one of the four options from the Positioning dropdown menu.

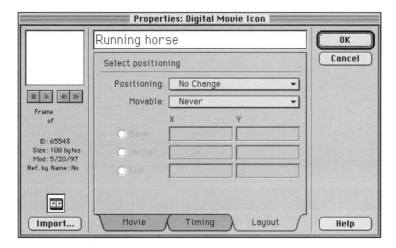

Selecting one of these options then allows you to enter x- and y-coordinates to control where the movie appears on the screen.

How Do I Create an Animation?

By using the Motion icon, you can create, in just a few minutes, animations that might otherwise take many hours. Designing animation with a traditional programming language is often a complex and tedious process. It involves creating subroutines that systematically and repeatedly draw, erase, and move objects on the computer monitor to create the illusion of motion. Creating animation with Authorware is much simpler. Simply identify the object to be animated and trace the path along which the object will move.

It should be noted that Authorware's animation capabilities are limited. When faced with the need for sophisticated animation, Authorware designers often use tools such as Director. Animations created with other programs can often be imported into Authorware and displayed via the Digital Movie icon.

The first step in creating an animation is to place an object by itself into a Display icon. This object is the one that will be animated. Next, place a Motion icon below the Display icon on the flow line.

Opening the Motion icon reveals a dialog box with two tabs: Motion and Layout.

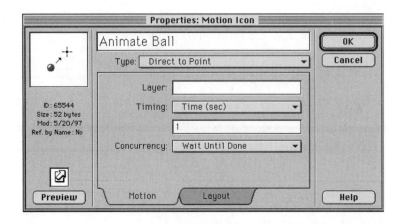

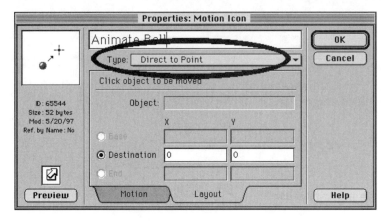

The Type dropdown menu indicates the animation type, which in this case is Direct to Point. Authorware offers five classes of animation, although only three will be addressed in this text.

```
    Direct to Point
    Direct to Line
    Direct to Grid
  ✓ Path to End
    Path to Point
```

Those classes we will examine here are Direct to Point and Path to End. Direct to Point is the simplest class of animation. It moves objects from one screen location to another in a straight line. Linear animation can be useful when you want to show relationships between objects. For example, imagine that you are attempting to illustrate how equations are manipulated to produce a formula. Using animation, you can literally take apart and regroup pieces of the original equation to help students understand how to decompose an equation.

Path to End is more sophisticated. It allows you to specify a path along which an object will be animated, as is indicated by its icon. This path is essentially unlimited in length or the number of turns. Path animation is often used to move objects along nonlinear paths, such as the orbit of an object in space.

Direct to Line may be the animation you use most in Authorware, because it helps you create intuitive interfaces. For example, you could use Direct to Line animation to create a slide bar showing time remaining in an experiment. Similarly, you could use an animation to mark a navigation menu. However, you'll have to jump ahead to Chapter 11 to see this animation illustrated, because it uses variables that you may find confusing now.

Note: Authorware animates Display icons. That is, when an object is animated, all objects that exist in the same Display icon will also be animated. If you want to animate a single object, then the object must exist in its own Display icon.

Guiding Activities: Motion Icons

Complete the following activities to learn how to create simple animations:

Task 1: Animate a ball moving across the computer screen in a straight line.

- Create an object in a Display icon. Label the icon **Ball** and place an oval object into the Display.

Note: Filled, solid objects are easier to animate than empty or shaded objects.

- Place a Motion icon on the flow line below the Display icon. Label the icon **Animate Ball**. Run the file.

- Authorware will run until it encounters the undefined Motion icon. The dialog box for the Motion icon will open and appear as in the illustration below.

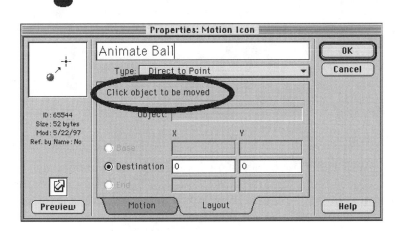

- The default animation type is Direct to Point.

- Complete the instruction to "Click object to be moved" by clicking the object to be animated.
- Notice how the instruction changes after you have selected an object. Drag the object to its ending location.

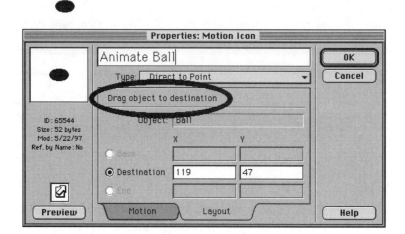

- Click Preview to test the animation you have just created.
- Press the Motion tab and adjust the Timing selection to meet your needs. You may select either Time or Speed for the animation timing. If you select Time, the animation will be completed in the number of seconds specified. If you select Speed, the animation moves at the rate of one inch per number of seconds specified. If you want objects to move at identical speeds, select Speed as the option and set a common rate for both animations.

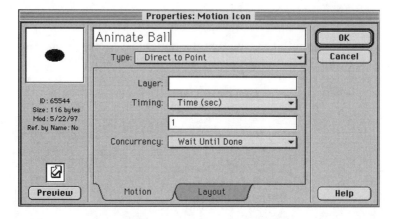

- Select the Wait Until Done or Concurrent option for concurrency.

Note: Selecting Wait Until Done pauses the lesson until the animation has been completed. Selecting Concurrent causes the next icon on the flow line to be executed immediately. If you want two or more Display icons to be animated simultaneously, you must select the Concurrent option.

- Click OK when you are satisfied with the animation.

- Restart the file to test the animation.

Task 2: Animate two or more objects moving across the screen simultaneously but in different directions.

- Place two solid objects in two Display icons (one object in each icon). Remember to label each Display with a different name.
- Place two Motion icons, one for each object to be animated, on the flow line.
- Run from the flag to set each Animation.
- Follow the instructions that appear for each object to be animated.
- Set Timing to Concurrent for the first Motion icon.
- Run the file to test the animation.

Task 3: Animate an object moving around the perimeter of the monitor.

- Place a solid object in a Display icon.
- Place a Motion icon on the flow line.
- Run the lesson. At the Motion icon, select Path to End as the animation type.

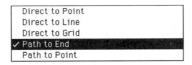

- Notice the instruction "Click object to be moved." Authorware needs to know which object (that is, which Display icon) will be animated. Identify the object by clicking it once with the mouse.

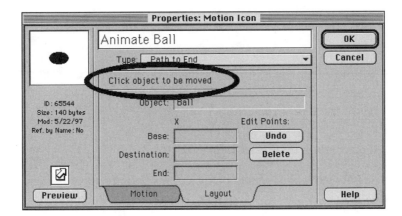

- Clicking an object drops a triangular anchor onto the screen in the center of the object. (Sometimes the anchor may be hidden behind the object to be moved.)

- Notice how the message in the Animation dialog box changes to "Drag object to extend path."

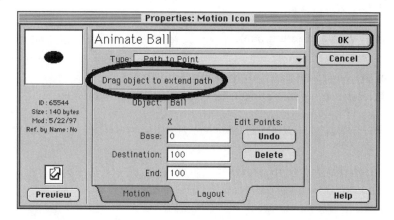

To create the path along which the object will be animated, click the object with the mouse and, with the mouse button still depressed, drag the object to a new screen location. When the object is in the desired location, deselect the mouse. Deselecting the mouse button places a new anchor on the screen. Each time you drop the object (by releasing the mouse button), you will create another anchor. The anchors define the path along which the object will be animated. Repeat this process of selecting–dragging–deselecting until the desired path has been created.

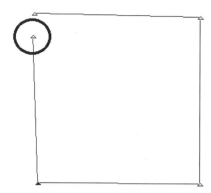

- Press the Replay button to test the animation.

Note: You may need to move the Animation dialog box to place anchors. Also, be careful not to accidentally move the anchor (the small triangle located at the center of the object to be moved) instead of the object.

Task 4: Animate an object "orbiting" the screen (i.e., create a curved path rather than a linear one).

- Place a solid object in a Display icon.
- Place a Motion icon on the flow line.
- Run the lesson. At the Motion icon, select Path to End as the animation type.
- With the mouse, click once the object to be animated, as in the previous example. Once again, clicking an object drops a triangular anchor onto the screen in the center of the object. Create at least five animation anchors.

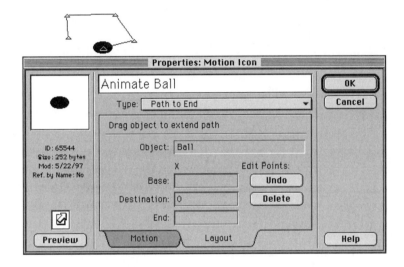

- Move the anchors with the mouse for more accurate placement. Shift-click and drag an anchor to move it.
- You must now change the straight-line animation to curved animation. To do this, double-click each of the triangular anchors. Notice that the triangles change to circles to indicate curved animation. Be careful with curved animation. Some paths are very unusual!

- Click OK in the animation box when you are done. Run the animation to test it.

STUDY EXERCISES

1. What is the difference between the Wait Until Done and Concurrent options in the Motion dialog box?
2. Place one or more Sound icons onto the flow line to deliver music or speech. If you have access to a microphone, you may be able to create your own sound files to create a narrated presentation.

3. Use a Digital Movie icon to play a movie in a file. Include several icons that explain the content of the movie for the user. (Note: You need a digital movie file, such as a QuickTime movie, to complete this exercise.)

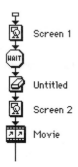

4. Animate an object around the perimeter of a rectangle.
5. Create three planets orbiting simultaneously around a static sun. The icon sequence for this exercise is illustrated below.

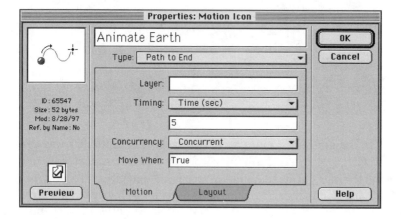

Notice that the field titled "Move When:" contains the value True. Setting this field to True assures the user that the animation will never stop. That is, the Earth icon will continue to orbit the Sun icon for as long as the file is running.

6. You may need to read Chapters 5, 7, and 8 before attempting the following exercise.
Use the Interaction icon to ask a question and Sound icons to deliver feedback. The illustration below shows how Sound icons can be used for feedback.

Note: You will need to have two sound files available to complete this exercise.

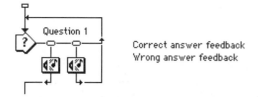

Correct answer feedback
Wrong answer feedback

5

The Interaction Icon:
Part 1

CHAPTER OVERVIEW

You have learned how to use Authorware to create presentations. Although presenting information is often an important task in the educational process, simply displaying content to users rarely results in deep or lasting learning, and barely scrapes the surface of the types of activities that can be created within Authorware.

Effective instruction engages students with lesson content. In this chapter, and in Chapters 7 and 8, you will learn how to create interactive lessons that ask users to type, move objects, select hot spots with the mouse, use pulldown menus, and perform other tasks that require thought. Creative use of these options can result in more active and engaging learning.

The Interaction icon is probably the most complex of all the Authorware icons. In addition to learning how the Interaction icon operates, it is important for you to learn each of the interaction types that accompany Authorware. In this chapter, you will examine the basic structure of an interaction and three interaction types. In subsequent chapters you will examine the other types of interactions.

CHAPTER OBJECTIVES

After completing this chapter, you will be able to:
- Understand the general structure of an Interaction icon
- Construct questions that require the following types of responses:
  - Keypress
  - Button
  - Hot spots

KEY TERMS

Interactions
Interaction structures
Feedback icons
Response options
Judging
Branching
Erasing
Keypress responses
Button responses
Hot spot responses
Hot spots
Wildcard

SUPPORT MATERIALS

On the CD-ROM disk, run the file titled **Videos.a4r** and select the button labeled **Chapter 5**. **Chapter 5** includes three videos that examine the basic structure of an Interaction icon and show how to create Button, Keypress, and Hot spot responses. If you are not sure how to run the file, refer to the section titled "To Run the CD-ROM Videos" in the Preface.

From the SUPPORT folder on the CD, open the file titled **CHP05.a4p.** The file demonstrates Keypress, Button, and Hot Spot interactions.

PROJECT 4: CREATING A BUTTON INTERACTION

Materials Needed to Complete This Project

- Your files from the previous project, **PROJ3.a4m** and **HOME.a4l**
- Macromedia Authorware 4.0 for Macintosh or Windows
- PROJECT 4 folder

Before You Begin

Allow approximately 30 minutes to complete Project 4.

Project Description

In this project you will use the Interaction icon to create buttons that control a navigation screen. Rather than scrolling through screens sequentially, you will create a menu that allows users to select topics according to their needs and interests.

Activity

Begin by opening the Authorware files from the previous project. From the File pulldown menu, choose Save As... and rename the design file **PROJ4**. (*Note*: If you create a new folder for this file, you will need to save a copy of the library file, **HOME.a4l**, in the folder.)

Place an Interaction icon on the Level 1 flow line, beneath the icon titled **Title text erase**. Label this Interaction icon **Menu**.

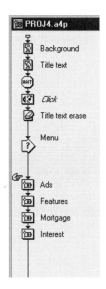

Drag the **Ads** Map icon to the right of the **Menu** Interaction icon. You will see the following dialog box:

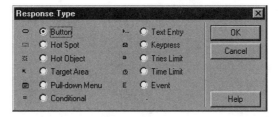

Select Button as the response type, then click OK. The flow line should look like this:

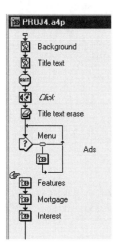

Place the other three Map icons to the right of the **Ads** Map icon. When you are finished, your screen should look like this:

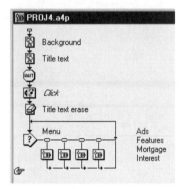

Run your file to check your work. After clicking the Continue button on the splash screen, you should see the following buttons:

Clicking each of the buttons should take you to the contents of the specified Map icon. Notice that the labels on some of the buttons are cropped. To resize the buttons, pause the lesson, either from the Control pulldown menu or from the control panel on your desktop. (You can access the control panel from the Window pulldown menu.)

Holding down the Shift key, use the Selection tool to select all four buttons.

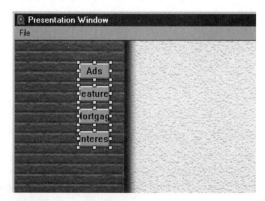

You may now release the Shift key. Grab one of the center handles on the left edge of one of the buttons:

Drag the handle to the left. This will resize all the buttons at the same time. Reposition the buttons on the left side of the screen.

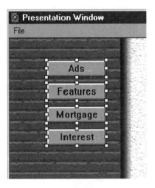

Run the lesson again. Each time you encounter a Continue button, pause the lesson and move the button beneath the button titled **Interest**. After repositioning the buttons, rerun your lesson to check button alignment. When you are finished, your screen should look like this:

You will now add some text to the Menu screen. Open the file titled **MENU.txt** from the PRO-JECT 4 folder. Select all of the text, and then copy it. Return to Authorware. Double-click the **Menu** Interaction icon. You will see the following:

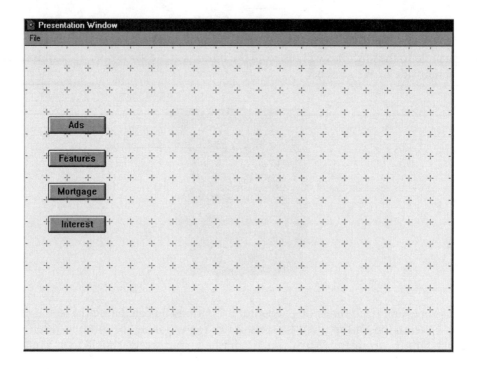

Select the Text tool from the toolbox. Click the Presentation window once, then select Paste from the Edit pulldown menu.

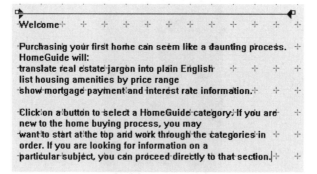

Format the text using 18-point (use 24-point, on a Macintosh) Arial Black for the heading and 14-point (use 18-point, on a Macintosh) Arial for the body text. Your screen should look like this:

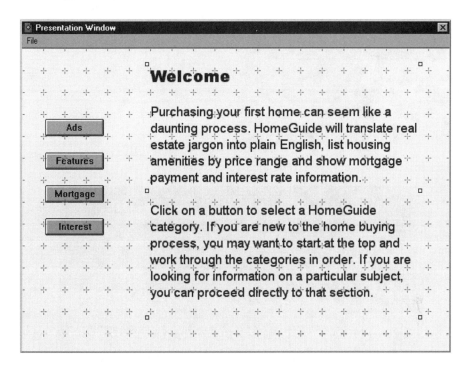

Run your lesson to check your work. When you click on the Ads button, you will see the following:

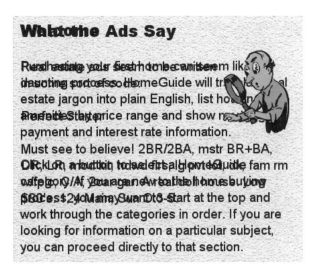

You must erase the menu text to prevent it from appearing beneath all subsequent screens. Pause the lesson and return to the Level 1 flow line. Select the **Menu** Interaction icon. From the Modify pulldown menu, select Icon > Properties….

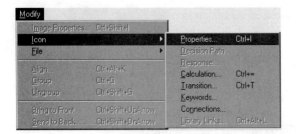

A dialog box will open. Select the tab labeled Interaction.

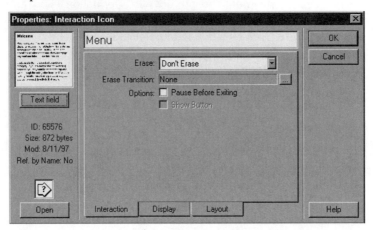

From the Erase: dropdown menu, choose After Next Entry.

Click OK and run your lesson to check your work.

Extending What You Have Learned

Modifying Buttons

In this activity, you learned to modify buttons by selecting them and altering their size in the Presentation window. You may also modify or customize buttons with the Button Editor. You will be exploring some features of the Button Editor in the next project.

Placing Continue Buttons

In this project, you manually repositioned each Continue button in your lesson. You can do this "automatically" if you follow these steps:

- Delete the first Wait icon in your lesson.
- Replace it with another Wait icon.
- Run the file.
- When you get to the new Continue button, place it at its new location on the screen.
- From the Design window, delete all existing Wait icons and replace them with new Wait icons.
- When you run your file, all of the new Continue buttons should conform to the placement of the first Continue button.

UNDERSTANDING THE DETAILS

The process of creating interactions may seem complex at first, but with practice it soon becomes straightforward. You will learn about the Interaction icon in three phases.

- First, you will follow a series of steps to give you some first-hand experience on which you can build.
- Second, you will learn the general process of creating an interaction.
- Finally, you will apply the process to three different response types.

What Is an Interaction?

In Project 4 you used an Interaction icon to create a navigation aid. Interaction icons are often used as ways of asking questions. In the following example, you will create a simple question in which you ask the user to identify a correct answer by pressing the appropriate button.

- Place an Interaction icon on the flow line. Label the Interaction icon **Question 1**.

Question 1

- It is often important to place a pause onto the flow line before exiting an Interaction structure. Failing to do so may cause information to "flash" on the screen. Fortunately, such an option is built into the Interaction icon and is found in the Interaction icon **Properties**. To access this option, highlight the icon with the mouse and select Icon > Properties from the Modify pulldown menu.

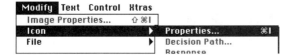

A dialog box will appear. Check (i.e., ✕) the box titled Pause Before Exiting. This dialog box controls how information is erased from the screen and several options associated with Text Entry interactions. It will be examined later.

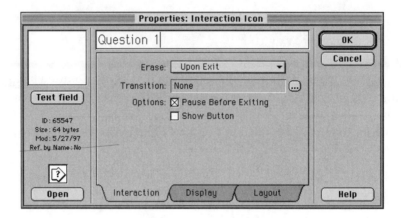

- Click the button titled **Open** to open the Presentation window associated with the Interaction icon. This Presentation window is typically used to display questions or provide instructions. Enter the following text into the window:

How many days are in a year?

Click on the button of your choice.

- Navigate back to the Design window and drag a Display icon to the right of the Interaction icon. The icon attached to the Interaction icon is known as a Feedback icon, because it contains the information or other activity(ies) that is (are) a consequence of selecting this option.

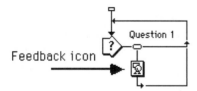

Immediately, a dialog box will appear. The dialog box asks you to identify how the user will respond to the question. Select Button and click OK.

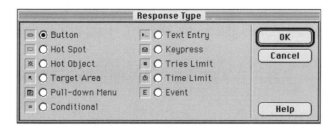

- Notice that immediately above the Feedback icon is a small button. The button is a window to the response options for this anticipated response. The response options contain many settings that you can modify.

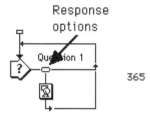

- Double-click the Response Options button to access a dialog box with two tabs titled Button and Response. The Button tab contains settings that control where and how the button will appear. In the title field, replace the word "Untitled" with "365". The title will appear in the button on the screen. Click OK to continue.

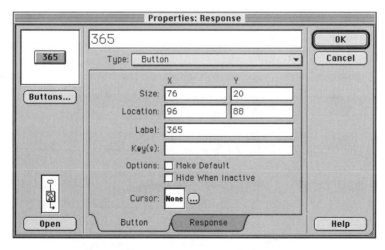

- Now add another Display icon to the right of the icon titled **365** and label this icon **366**.

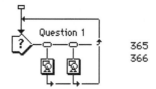

- Open the Display icon titled **365** by double-clicking its icon. The information entered here will appear if the user selects this button. Type the following text:

That's right. Well done!

- Open the Display icon titled **366** and enter the following text:

Sorry, but you must be thinking about a leap year.

- Navigate to the Design window when you are done.
- Double-click the Response Options icon **365**.

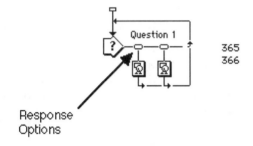

- Select the Response tab and set the Erase, Status, and Branch options to match those below. These options determine when feedback will be erased from the screen; whether this answer is correct, incorrect, or not judged; and the path that will be followed next.

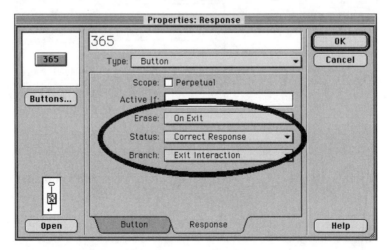

- Select OK to close the window, and repeat the steps for the Display icon titled **366**. Use the following three settings:

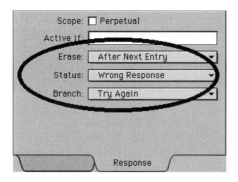

- Select OK to return to the flow line. The icons should now appear as follows:

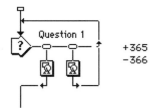

- Save your file and run the lesson. Notice that two buttons appear in the upper left corner of the screen. To place the buttons, pause the lesson, and then move each button by clicking and dragging.

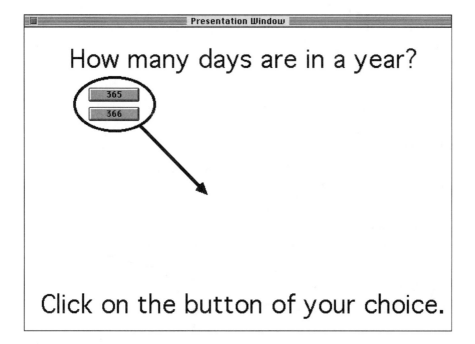

- Run the file again and answer the question by clicking first on the incorrect answer, and then the correct button. Notice the feedback associated with each response. Also, notice that the question repeats when you click the incorrect answer, but ends on a correct response.

The General Process

You have created an interaction. How did it work?

Although Authorware permits many different response types, the design process is similar for each. Once you have learned the process of creating an interaction, you can apply it to all response types. The following section explains this process. Subsequent sections examine additional options specific to each interaction type.

Creating interactions involves building interaction structures. Interaction structures include:

- An Interaction icon that presents a message (a question or instructions to the user) and controls when the message is erased from the screen.
- One or more icons that are used to match users' responses against predicted responses. These are called Feedback icons. Once matched, Feedback icons present additional information to the user or initiate other actions.
- Response options for each Feedback icon. Each response type offers different choices, but three options—Judging, Branching, and Erasing—must be set for every Feedback icon.

How Do I Create an Interaction Structure?

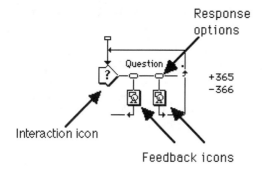

The Interaction Icon

The Interaction icon usually contains a message and controls how the message is erased. To enter information into an Interaction icon:

- Place an Interaction icon on the flow line and label the icon.
- With the icon highlighted, select Icon Properties from the Modify pulldown menu.

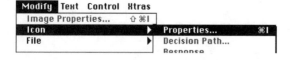

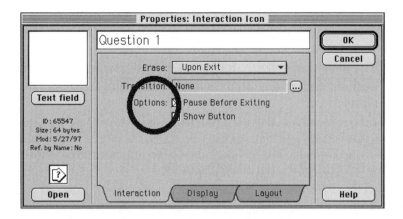

Notice the Erase: pulldown menu. It is important that you clearly understand how and when the message is removed from the screen. The menu offers three options that control when the message is erased.

```
  After Next Entry
✓ Upon Exit
  Don't Erase
```

The default Erase setting (Upon Exit) ensures that the message remains on the screen until the interaction is completed. The message is removed when the user exits the question and returns to the flow line.

After Next Entry removes the message from the screen as soon as the user responds. This option is frequently used for pulldown menu interactions and whenever it is important to remove the message from the screen. The final option, Don't Erase, ensures that the message remains on the screen until it is removed with an Erase icon.

Notice the box titled Pause Before Exiting. Checking this option helps prevent feedback from being erased from the screen before the user has had a chance to react. In effect, this option places a Wait icon onto the flow line when the question is finished.

- Clicking the button labeled **Open** opens a Display within the Interaction icon. This is where the designer enters the text and graphics that form the instructions on how to interact. You will usually include at least one text or graphic object in an interaction icon; however, in some cases you may have entered a question stem and instructions on preceding icons. In these cases, you can leave the interaction icon empty. It does not demand an entry.

Feedback Icons

Feedback icons provide distinct responses to different user input. In other words, they allow the designer to customize feedback. Response options must be set for each Feedback icon. These options vary for different response types, but give the designer considerable flexibility.

- Before using a Feedback icon you must decide how the user will interact. In other words, will the user type a response, move an object, select from a pulldown menu, or use another interaction type?

- Next, decide what type of feedback you will use. Initially, it is easiest to use Display icons for feedback. However, with experience you will recognize that your options are almost unlimited. For example, a Sound icon can be used to play a sound file, or a Motion icon can be used to animate an object. More complex feedback can be put into Map icons.

- To add a Feedback icon, drag an icon from the Icon palette and drop it to the right of the Interaction icon.

- Add one Feedback icon for each anticipated response. Anticipated responses are the different ways that you believe the user will respond to the interaction. When the first Feedback icon is added, a dialog box will prompt you for a response type. Subsequent response types follow the first choice, but can be modified.

- To enter text into a Feedback icon, double-click each Display icon and enter the relevant information.

Setting Response Options

Three options are common to all Feedback icons: Judging, Branching, and Erasing. Judging refers to whether an answer is correct or incorrect. Branching controls whether the user will repeat a question or continue with the lesson. Erasing controls when feedback is erased from the screen. Although the options for each response type differ, all include the same menus for judging answers, branching, and erasing feedback.

To Set Judging

Three judging options facilitate tracking of correct and incorrect responses:

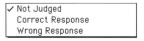

Setting judging is important because this updates system variables that are used to track the number of correct and incorrect responses. When you set answer judging, Authorware keeps track of the number of correct and incorrect answers made during the lesson. This information is often used by designers to help decision making later in the lesson. For example, sometimes users are allowed to exit a lesson only when they have answered a given number of questions correctly. Selecting Not Judged turns off the system variables. (System variables will be examined in Chapter 11.)

To Set Branching

Three branching options control whether the user repeats a question or lesson segment. A fourth option (Return) is available only for perpetual responses, which will be introduced later (see Chapter 8). In general, set branching to Exit for a correct response and Try Again for an incorrect response.

```
✓ Try Again
  Continue
  Exit Interaction
  Return
```

- *Try Again*: Authorware repeats the current Interaction icon. Try Again is often used for wrong answers and is particularly useful when you want the user to repeat a question.
- *Continue*: Authorware checks whether the learner's response matches more than one anticipated response. Continue is used when more than one response or condition could be true.
- *Exit Interaction*: Authorware exits the interaction and returns to the next icon on the flow line. Exit Interaction is typically used for correct answers.

Branching options for each Feedback icon are indicated by arrows attached to the Feedback icons.

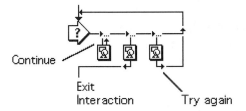

Note: To change the branching, you do not need to access the response options for each anticipated response. By holding down the Command key (i.e., the Control key on a PC) while clicking the arrowhead of the branching symbol (immediately above or below the Feedback icon), you can change the branching type (the arrow will change direction). Continue clicking until the branching is set to the desired option.

To Set Erasing

You can control when feedback is erased from the screen. As is true for erasing the question from the screen, understanding how feedback is erased is very important. Four options exist for erasing feedback:

```
✓ After Next Entry
  Before Next Entry
  On Exit
  Don't Erase
```

- *After Next Entry*: Feedback for the current answer stays displayed until the learner enters another response. This is the standard option to use when an answer is wrong and Try Again branching is used.
- *Before Next Entry*: This option erases feedback for the current answer before the learner enters another response. Be careful with this option. The lesson needs some way to pause to ensure that the user has time to read the feedback.
- *Upon Exit*: Feedback is erased when the Interaction icon is exited. This is the standard option to use when an answer is correct and Exit Interaction branching is used.
- *Don't Erase*: Feedback remains displayed. If you select Don't Erase, you will need to use an Erase icon to remove feedback.

The illustration below shows the components of an Interaction Structure for a Text Entry response.

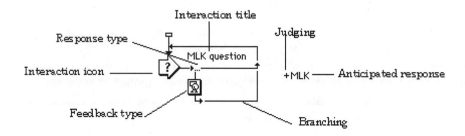

What Are Response Types?

The Interaction icon supports eleven response types. Although the process of creating an interaction is essentially the same for each, their response options are quite different. In the remainder of this chapter we will examine three commonly used response types: Keypress, Button, and Hot Spot.

◉ Keypress

Keypress Responses

Keypress responses are the simplest to create and use. To use a Keypress response, the user presses a key on the keyboard. Authorware responds if the designer has anticipated that response. Keypress responses are often associated with multiple-choice questions, but may be used for a wide range of interactions. For example, the designer can use Keypress responses to control navigation. The numbers on the numeric keypad can correspond to menu options, the Return or Control key can move the user to the next page, pressing "H" can access Help, and so on. The following exercise constructs a multiple-choice question with four anticipated responses: three possible answers and a wildcard.

The Following Exercise Demonstrates How to Create Keypress Interactions.

- Place an Interaction icon on the flow line. Title the interaction **Keypress Interaction**.
- Open the Interaction icon **Properties**.

Mark the Pause Before Exiting option and Show Button.

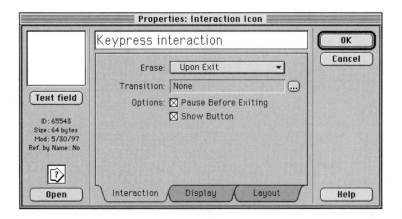

Click the button labeled **Open** and use the Text tool to place an interaction in the Presentation window. For example, you might enter the following multiple-choice question:

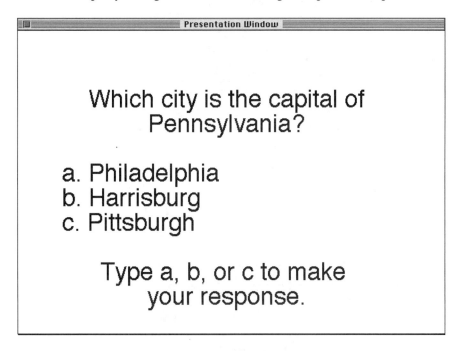

- Navigate to the flow line and attach four Display icons to the interaction structure for feedback.
- At the prompt, select Keypress for the response types, and enter appropriate icon names. For a Keypress response, the icon names specify the keys that the user will select. For this multiple-choice question, the icon names will be **a**, **b**, **c**, and **?** for Philadelphia, Harrisburg, Pittsburgh, and a wildcard, respectively. The key for the wildcard (which catches any unexpected entries) is **?**.
- Open each Feedback icon and type appropriate feedback for each anticipated response. For the wildcard, explain that the user pressed the wrong key.

- Open the response options to modify judging, branching, and erasing.
  For the correct answer (b):

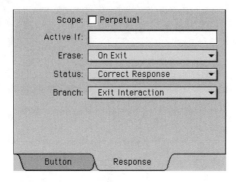

For the wrong answers (a and c):

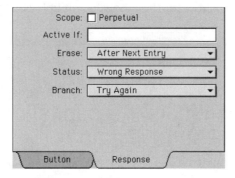

For the wildcard (?):

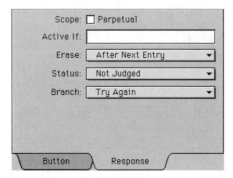

- The icons should now appear as follows:

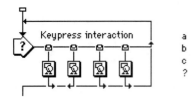

- Run the file to test the interaction.

Things You Should Know about Keypress Options

- Keypress responses are case specific. Therefore, if you want to allow the learner to enter either an uppercase letter or a lowercase letter, you must include both in the list of anticipated responses, separating them with a vertical bar.
  - *Example*: A|a
- To use special-function keys as anticipated responses, type their names; do not just press their keys.
  - *Example*: CmdQ requires the user to press Command-Q

⊖ ⊙ Button

Button Responses

A Button response was used earlier in the chapter to introduce the Interaction icon, and is probably already familiar to you. The following activity gives you a chance to see how the previous question used for the Keypress response can be redesigned for a Button response. Button responses place buttons on the screen that can be used to answer questions, make selections, or navigate. Button responses tend to be popular because they provide users with visual clues about how to enter responses. The following exercise reconstructs the multiple-choice question used above, but uses Button responses instead of keypresses.

The Following Exercise Demonstrates How to Create Button Interactions.

- Place an Interaction icon on the flow line. Title the interaction **Button Interaction**.
- Open the Interaction icon **Properties**. Mark the Pause Before Exiting and Show Button options. Click the button labeled **Open** and use the Text tool to place the following interaction in the Presentation window.

Presentation Window

Which city is the capital of Pennsylvania?

Click on a button to make your response.

- Navigate to the flow line and place a Display icon into the interaction structure for feedback.
- At the prompt, select Button for the response type.
- Type "Philadelphia" for the title of the Feedback icon.
- Add two more Display icons to the right of the first Feedback icon. Title the icons **Harrisburg** and **Pittsburgh**. The icon names will appear on the screen in the buttons.
- Open each Feedback icon and type appropriate feedback for each anticipated response.
- Open the response options to modify judging, branching, and erasing. For the correct answer (Harrisburg):

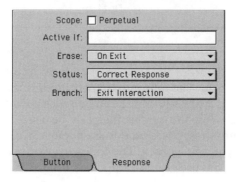

For the other answers:

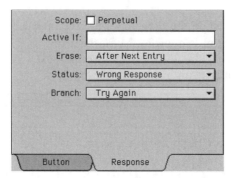

- The icons should now appear as follows:

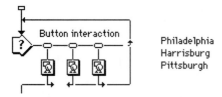

- Authorware places buttons in the top left corner of the screen. You will need to move them to their appropriate locations. To access the buttons, either reopen the Interaction icon and edit the display or run the lesson and pause at the interaction. Select and drag with the mouse to move the buttons.

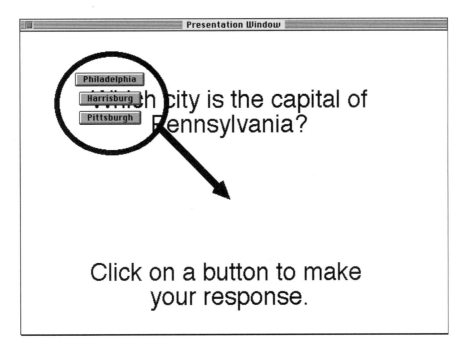

- Select Run to test the interaction.

Things You Should Know about Button Options

- Selecting the option titled Make Default enables the user to press Return to select the button. Only one feedback icon can have a Default button.
- You may want to make all the buttons the same size. To move or resize a button, first pause the lesson, then select and drag the button to its desired location. You can also modify a button's size and location from the Response Options dialog. With the lesson paused, double-click the button you want to modify, then select the Button tab. This window allows you to control button placement by specifying a location and size in pixels. You can also use variables in the Size and Location fields to determine button placement.

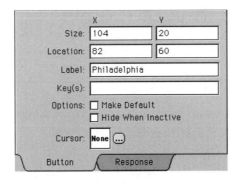

Hot Spot Responses

When a hot spot is created, rectangular areas of the screen become sensitive to the location of the mouse. When the user clicks inside the rectangle (or, sometimes, when the mouse enters the area), the lesson provides feedback. In a sense, hot spots are like invisible buttons, and can be used to provide feedback when a user expects something to happen onscreen, or to surprise the user with hidden information. Computer game players tend to expect hot spots; games often include hidden clues that are "buried" behind invisible hot spots. The following exercise reconstructs the multiple-choice questions used above, but this time uses Hot Spot interactions.

The Following Exercise Demonstrates How to Create Hot Spot Interactions.

- Place an Interaction icon on the flow line. Title the interaction Hot Spot Interaction.
- Open the Interaction icon **Properties**. Mark the Pause Before Exiting option and Show Button. Click the button labeled **Open** and use the Text tool to type the following message:

Presentation Window

Which city is the capital of Pennsylvania?

Philadelphia
Harrisburg
Pittsburgh

Click on the correct answer with your mouse.

- Navigate to the flow line.
- Place a Display icon into the interaction structure for feedback.
- At the prompt, select Hot Spot for the response type.
- Type "Philadelphia" for the title of the Feedback icon.
- Add two more Display icons to the right of the first Feedback icon. Title the icons Harrisburg and Pittsburgh. The icon names will label the hot spots, making them easy to identify.
- Open each Feedback icon and type appropriate feedback for each anticipated response.

- Open the response options to modify judging, branching, and erasing. For the correct answer (Harrisburg):

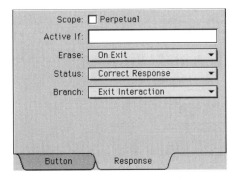

For the other answers:

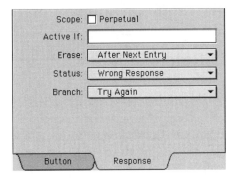

- The icons should now appear as follows:

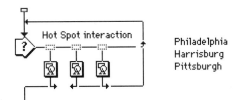

- You will need to move the hot spots to their appropriate locations. In this case, each hot spot should cover the name of a city. To access the hot spots, run the file from the Interaction icon and pause at the interaction to reveal the hot spots.
- Use the mouse to move and resize each hot spot. Make sure that the hot spot completely covers the appropriate area of the screen, but don't allow hot spots to overlap (unless you are creating a wildcard).

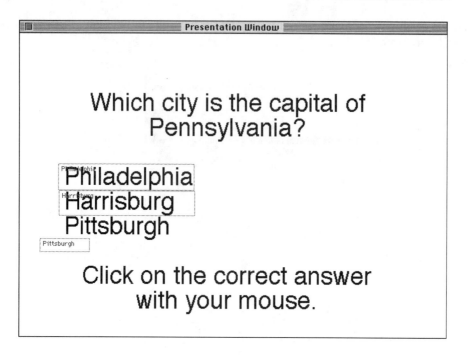

- Select Run to test the interaction.

Things to Know about Hot Spot Options

- For each Hot Spot Feedback icon, Authorware sets aside an area called a hot spot. Double-clicking a hot spot opens the response options for that icon.
- Each hot spot is represented by a dotted rectangle. Hot spots are not visible to the learner.
- You can overlap hot spots to trap for clicks that are out-of-bounds (like wildcards). This is a useful technique to provide feedback when the user clicks the mouse in the wrong location. To do this, create a hot spot for out-of-area clicks; make the hot spot for this icon cover the entire screen. Any mouse click that misses the other feedback hot spots will be caught by the large one. You must place this icon to the right of any other hot spots in the interaction structure; otherwise, Authorware will always match the wildcard.

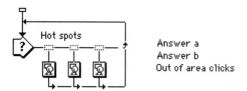

- Optional keys can be used as an alternative way to select a hot spot. Specify special optional keys by typing the key name in full.

EXAMPLES

Return

Tab
Left Arrow
Backspace
Esc

- Don't use the Active if True and Perpetual options yet. They are more complex and will be dealt with later. The Active if True option causes the hot spot to be active only when a variable is true. This option is especially useful for hiding options. For example, hot spots and buttons can be active during some lesson sections (e.g., when the variable is true) and inactive during other lesson sections (c.g., when the variable is false).
- In addition to setting the response options, you must place a hot spot for each anticipated response. Like buttons, Authorware places hot spots in the top left corner of the screen. There are two ways to place or resize the hot spots:

1. Open the response options. A hot spot will appear in the Presentation window. Modifying the hot spot involves clicking and dragging inside the hot spot or dragging the gray handles that appear in the Presentation window. Moving or resizing the hot spot modifies the location and dimensions of the hot spot.

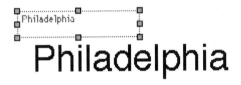

2. Run the lesson and pause at the interaction to highlight the hot spots. Resize the area where you want the learner to click. Resize or move the hot spots as necessary for each anticipated response.

What Is a Wildcard?

The title given to a Feedback icon often is important because it can be used to compare user input with an anticipated response. However, sometimes it is important to accept any response that the user enters. For example, the question "What is your name?" has no correct response, but can be used to collect data from a user. In such cases, you can use a wildcard to match a user's response. Wildcards are so named because they match any entry, as a wildcard does in a card game.

Wildcards are used for several different response types, but the processes used for their creation varies. For Text Entry and Keypress responses, special keys are used to recognize the wildcards: The key for a Text Entry wildcard is an asterisk (i.e., *), and the key for a Keypress wildcard is a question mark (i.e., ?). Other wildcard entries can be constructed. For example, it's possible to create wildcard entries for Hot Spot and Target Area response types.

STUDY EXERCISES

1. Examine the response options for Keypress, Button, and Hot Spot responses to find answers to the following.
Name which response types offer the following features:

- Custom cursors.

- Mark the area after matching a response.

- Permit use of the Perpetual option.

- Allow the designer to control button placement.

- Match a response by placing the cursor within a "hot" area.

- Require the designer to move "touch-sensitive" areas.

2. Experiment with the following Hot Spot options to discover how each operates.

   - Optional Keys

   - Custom Cursor

   - Auto Highlight

   - Match with: Single-click or Double-click or Cursor in Area

3. Use a Keypress interaction to create a multiple-choice or true/false test. Include approximately five questions in the test. Allow users no more than one chance to answer each question. Include a wild-card for "out-of-bounds" responses, but do not count this as an answer (i.e., allow the user another chance to answer the question).

4. Create another multiple-choice test, this time using Hot Spot response. Allow users to repeat questions that they answer incorrectly. Use the Mark After Match option to indicate past answers. Create a Help button that pops up when the user places his or her mouse in a specific screen area.

5. Use Button responses to create a navigation system that leads to two or more sets of multiple-choice questions. Use the tests you created in questions 3 and 4 for the test content. Include a Quit button that allows the user to escape from the tests and to continue with the lesson. Experiment with the Button Types option in the response options to find buttons that you like.

6. Create an entertainment center with a sliding door. Include a button on the front. When the button is pressed, the door should open to reveal a TV and a radio. Click the TV to play a movie. Click the radio to play a sound file.

6

Odds and Ends 1

CHAPTER OVERVIEW

Learning to use Authorware to develop instruction can be a daunting task at first. The volume of information that must be learned to complete even modest tasks may be overwhelming. However, with practice, it becomes much easier, and even the most complex structures become clear!

Up to now, the focus of this text has been to learn the features essential to using Authorware effectively. Along the way, you have probably noticed that several options have been ignored. The reason these options have been ignored is not because unimportant; rather, it is an attempt to prevent you from experiencing the type of mental overload often experienced when one is learning new information.

In this chapter you will examine some of those options we skipped in earlier chapters. These options are important. In some cases, you will learn to use time-saving tools. Other options will make you a more effective designer. For example, the ability to customize buttons enables you to animate navigation links. Hopefully, the mental picture you have developed while studying the first five chapters of the book will place you in a much better position to understand these new concepts.

CHAPTER OBJECTIVES

After completing this chapter, you will be able to:
- Use the Tool Bar to execute actions quickly.
- Understand and control the options in the File Properties dialog box.
- Edit and import custom buttons.

- Use Grid to place objects accurately on the screen.
- Use the Align Object option to balance objects or align two or more objects in horizontal or vertical planes.
- Define and apply styles to text.
- Use the Trace window to debug lessons.

KEY TERMS

Tool Bar
File Setup
Show Grid
Snap to Grid
Align Objects
Define Styles
Apply Styles
Trace window

SUPPORT MATERIALS

On the CD-ROM disk, run the file titled **Videos.a4r** and select the button labeled **Chapter 6**. This video shows how to create custom buttons. From the SUPPORT folder on the CD, open the file titled **CHP06.a4p**. The file demonstrates how to control several important options available in the File Properties dialog box.

PROJECT 5: CUSTOMIZING BUTTONS

Materials Needed to Complete This Project

- Your file from the previous project, **PROJ4.a4p**
- Macromedia Authorware 4.0 for Macintosh or Windows
- PROJECT 5 folder

Before You Begin

Allow approximately 30 minutes to complete this module.

Project Description

In this project you will learn how to use the Button Editor to customize buttons and create "animated" or "rollover" buttons.

Activity

Begin by opening the Authorware file from the previous project. From the File pulldown menu, choose Save As… to rename the file **PROJ5**.

To customize the Continue button, select File > Properties… from the Modify pulldown menu to open the dialog box that controls the default setting.

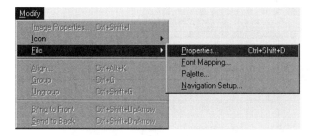

You will see the following dialog box:

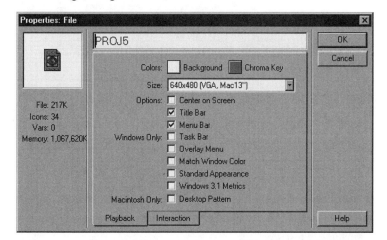

Select the Interaction tab at the bottom of the dialog box. You will see the following:

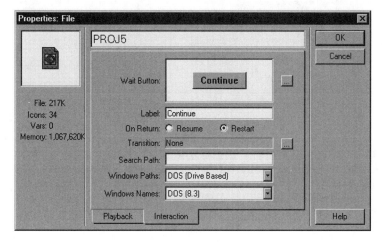

Click the Continue button in the window labeled Wait Button. You will see the following dialog box:

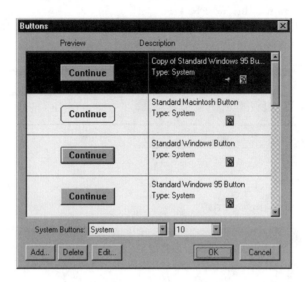

Click the button labeled **Add**... to access the Button Editor.

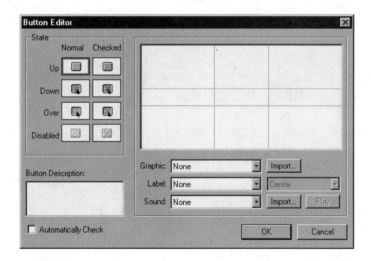

Here you will import and customize a button with three different states: an Up state, a Down state, and an Over state. Click the button labeled **Import**... to the right of the popup menu labeled Graphic.

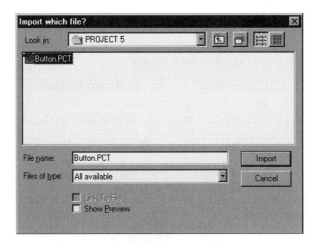

Select **Button.pct** from the PROJECT 5 folder. Notice that the button has no text or "label" when it first appears in the editing window. From the popup menu titled Label in the Button Editor, select Show Label.

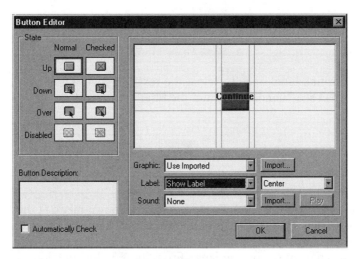

You should now see the word Continue on the imported button. The left side of the Button Editor allows you to specify different conditions for each state of the button. You will now customize the text for each of the first three states. Select Normal/Up from the State portion of the Button Editor.

A button can be in one of four states: Up, Down, Over, and Disabled. The Up state is the normal state of a button. When the user clicks a button once, it is in its Down state. When the user moves the cursor onto a button, it is in its Over state. When a button is turned off (discussed in Chapter 11), it is in its Disabled state.

Notice that you can also select from two other states: Normal and Checked. The Normal state is relevant for all types of buttons. However, the Checked state can be used only with check boxes and radio buttons.

☐ **Check Box**   ○ **Radio Button**

The checked state shows how the button will appear when it has been selected.

☐ **Check Box "Checked"**   ◉ **Radio Button "Checked"**

The checked options are not available when you select a standard button for editing because standard buttons can't be checked.

Next, click the Continue label once to select the text. You will know that the text has been selected when you can see "handles" around the title.

First, set the font for the button label. From the Text pulldown menu at the top of the screen, select Font > Arial Black. From the Text pulldown menu, change the font size to 12-point (use 18-point text on a Macintosh).

Next, change the color of the button label. From the Window pulldown menu at the top of the screen, select Inspectors > Colors. (*Note*: If the text is not selected, this will not work.)

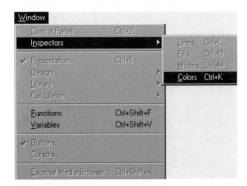

Select white, then click OK. You have now defined the button in its Normal/Up position.

Next, you will change the Down state of the button to make the text color change when the user presses the button. Select the Normal/Down state. Select Show Label from the popup menu titled Label on the right side of the Button Editor, and select the text over the button.

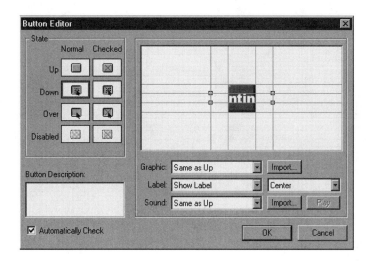

From the pulldown menu titled Windows, select Inspectors > Colors and change the text color to pink.

Next, you will change the Over state of the button to make the text color change when the user places the cursor over the button. Select Normal/Over state. Select Show Label from the popup menu titled Label and select the text. Change the size of the text to 14-point (use 24-point text on a Macintosh) and the color to gold. Close the Button Editor; close the Button dialog box; and close the Properties: File dialog box.

Run your lesson to see the results. The Continue button should "animate" when you roll over it with the cursor. The button should also change color when it is selected. You can now apply this custom button to the navigation buttons.

Pause the lesson. Return to the Level 1 flow line. Double-click the Response Option button above the **Ads** Map icon to the right of the **Menu** Interaction icon.

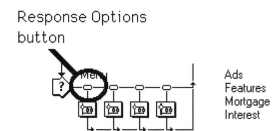

Response Options
button

You will see the following dialog box:

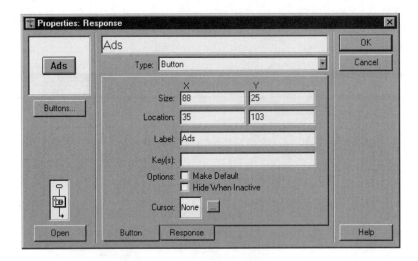

Click the **Ads** button on the left side of the dialog box. You will see the following dialog box:

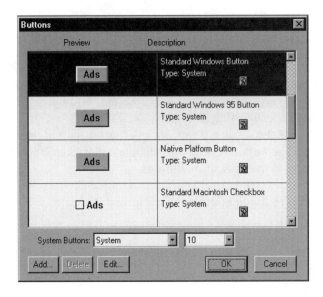

Using the scroll bar on the right side of the dialog box, select the custom button you created earlier in this activity.

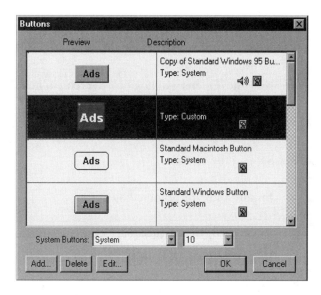

Close the dialog box; then repeat this procedure to add the new customized button for the Buttons responses titled Features, Mortgage, and Interest. Run your lesson to check your work.

Suggestions for Applying What You Have Learned

You can use custom graphics, specify typefaces, styles and colors, and assign sounds to buttons in the Button Editor. You can then use customized buttons throughout your lesson.

Notice that the Button Editor includes five other states. A navigation button can be disabled, but still show on the screen after it has been used. Also, two types of buttons (radio and check box) have checked or used states. Each time a check box or radio button is selected, a check mark is added or removed (according to its previous state). Adding or renaming a check mark is an excellent visual technique for showing whether a button is on or off.

UNDERSTANDING THE DETAILS

In the following sections you will examine several Authorware tools that are designed to enhance effectiveness and improve productivity.

Tool Bar

Have you noticed a menu with several icons close to the top of the screen in the Design window? This menu is the Tool Bar. The Tool Bar allows you to activate several commands with a single mouse click. Many of the tools will be familiar to users who have worked with other word-processing, spreadsheet, or similar applications.

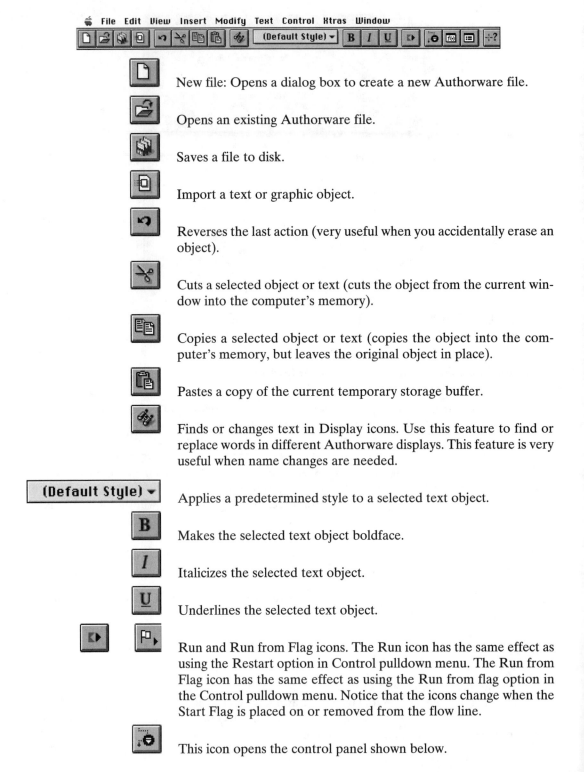

New file: Opens a dialog box to create a new Authorware file.

Opens an existing Authorware file.

Saves a file to disk.

Import a text or graphic object.

Reverses the last action (very useful when you accidentally erase an object).

Cuts a selected object or text (cuts the object from the current window into the computer's memory).

Copies a selected object or text (copies the object into the computer's memory, but leaves the original object in place).

Pastes a copy of the current temporary storage buffer.

Finds or changes text in Display icons. Use this feature to find or replace words in different Authorware displays. This feature is very useful when name changes are needed.

Applies a predetermined style to a selected text object.

Makes the selected text object boldface.

Italicizes the selected text object.

Underlines the selected text object.

Run and Run from Flag icons. The Run icon has the same effect as using the Restart option in Control pulldown menu. The Run from Flag icon has the same effect as using the Run from flag option in the Control pulldown menu. Notice that the icons change when the Start Flag is placed on or removed from the flow line.

This icon opens the control panel shown below.

Show Trace

The control panel provides several tools to run and debug files. The Show Trace tool helps the debugging process. Debugging is the process of finding and fixing errors (known as bugs) in courseware. As the lesson executes, the Trace window maintains a list of the precise order in which icons are executed. This list can be used to follow the lesson's logic and to identify precisely where the actual lesson flow deviates from the intended flow. Items in the Trace window indicate the flow line depth, the icon types, and icon titles.

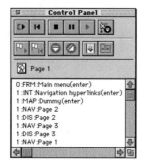

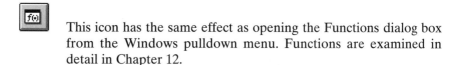

This icon has the same effect as opening the Functions dialog box from the Windows pulldown menu. Functions are examined in detail in Chapter 12.

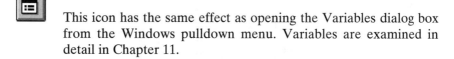

This icon has the same effect as opening the Variables dialog box from the Windows pulldown menu. Variables are examined in detail in Chapter 11.

Help: Use this button to access the help system. The help system is a detailed online reference source that provides information on a broad range of Authorware topics. The system is usually installed on your computer at the same time that Authorware is installed. To activate Help, click the Help icon once and then click the item with which you need help.

Setting File Properties

The File Properties dialog box contains important options that must be set before completing a lesson. Although it is not prominent in the menu structure, the File Properties dialog box contains several very important features.

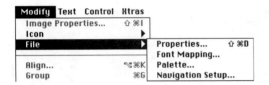

Selecting File > Properties brings up a dialog box with two tabs: Playback and Interaction. There are many options, some of which are quite detailed. We will describe only the more commonly used options.

Naming Your Files

The names you choose for your lesson files are important for at least two reasons:

- The names help you manage files on your computer.
- The names you pick will appear on the end users' computers.

When you save a file, Authorware automatically adds a suffix if you don't create one of your own. For example, if you name a file **Lesson**, Authorware will add the suffix .a3r and rename the file **Lesson.a3r**. However, if you create your own suffix, Authorware will not overrule your decision.

The name you choose for your lesson appears in the File > Properties dialog in the lesson title field, and will also appear in the title bar of the completed file. If you wish, you can change the name in this field without changing the lesson name.

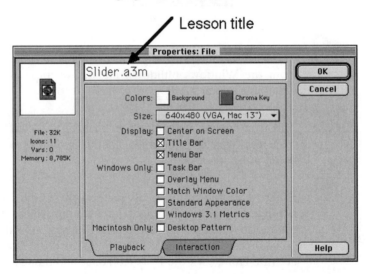

The Lesson Title dialog box allows you to control the name that appears in the Title Bar. The Title Bar contains the text that appears at the top of the Presentation window of the packaged file. While designing the course, "Presentation Window" appears in the Title Bar. Once the file has been packaged, the user sees only the Presentation window and the title given in this Lesson Title dialog. The default title is the name given to the design file, and often needs to be changed. For example, you would probably want to change the title of a file on fractions from **fctns5.a3m** to one that reflects the lesson content more accurately.

Background Color

The default background color for your lesson is white. To change the default color, select the Background Color button and choose from the color palette. The color you choose will appear in the File Setup window and immediately will fill all Display icons.

Changing the default background color can cause problems, because the color cannot be erased. An alternative approach to creating a color background—and a strategy that permits greater design flexibility—involves using a Display icon that contains a background color. This Display icon is simply left on the flow line until it is no longer needed, at which point it is erased with an Erase icon.

To create a new background color in a Display icon:

- Place a Display icon on the flow line. Label the icon.
- Double-click the Display icon to open its Presentation window.
- Select the Rectangle tool from the Authorware toolbox and draw a large rectangle.
- Select Lines and Color from the Inspectors pulldown menu to display their palettes.

- Select the desired color for the background color.
- Select transparent lines from the Lines palette.
- Use the Selection tool to stretch the rectangle across the entire Presentation window. To completely cover the window, it may be necessary to move the rectangle and resize it. To do this, select and drag the rectangle to a corner of the Presentation window. Now, stretch the rectangle before moving it so that it covers the entire window.

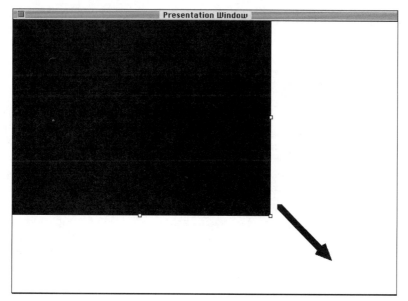

Note: You may have noticed that when you work with a colored background text appears on a white background, rather than on the desired background color. To make the text background the same color as the default background, you must change the background color for the text object.

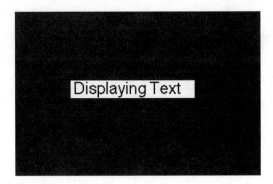

- Click the text object with the Selection tool or drag over the text with the Text tool.
- Select Inspectors > Colors from the Window pulldown menu.

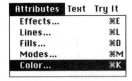

- Click the Background color box.

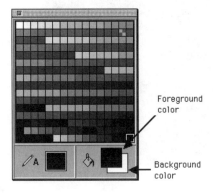

- Select the desired background color.

Selecting a Monitor Size

Determining the monitor size that will be used to run the completed lesson is an important task that must be determined early in the needs-assessment phase of any design project. The Presentation window size refers to the size of the monitor that will be used to present the lesson.

```
 Variable
 512x342 (Mac 9")
 512x384 (Mac 12")
 640x350 (EGA)
 640x400 (Mac Portable)
✓ 640x480 (VGA, Mac 13")
 640x870 (Mac Portrait)
 800x600 (SVGA)
 832x624 (Mac 16")
 1024x768 (SVGA, Mac 17")
 1152x870 (Mac 21")
 Use Full Screen
```

It is important to carefully examine the equipment that will be used to present the lesson, because Authorware does not automatically scale content in Display icons to fit the user's monitor. If you select a large monitor (c.g., a 16" color monitor) on which to design a lesson and the lesson file is used on a laptop computer with a small monitor, lesson content may be masked or navigation buttons may be missing.

The Wait Button

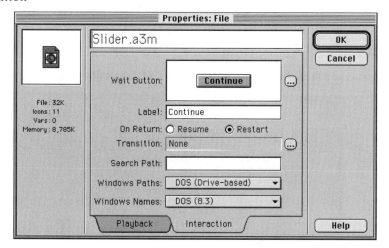

The Wait icon places a button on the Presentation window. The default text in the button is Continue.

You can modify the message on the button by changing the contents of the field titled **Label**.
You can also edit the button style or import your own buttons created in a graphics program.

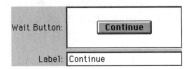

Customizing Buttons

Authorware provides a set of buttons to create different designs. However, you can also modify these buttons or import new buttons. Perhaps the easiest way to create a button is to open
the Button Editor through the Window pulldown menu.

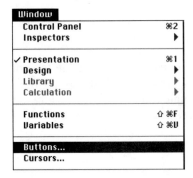

From here, select an existing button to edit or press the Add button to open the Button Editor
in which you will create a new button.

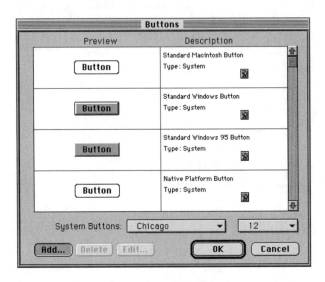

To create a new button, import an image from a graphics file or else paste a graphic from the
clipboard into the image window. You will need to spend some time learning all the options

available in this window. However, learning how to use the Button Editor effectively is a wise time investment, because it provides a flexible way to manage screen presentations.

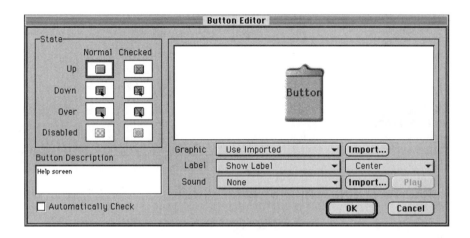

Setting the On Return: Option

As the designer, you control where the lesson begins each time a user quits and restarts a lesson. The default value is to restart the lesson each time from the beginning.

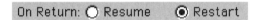

Sometimes it is beneficial to allow the user to restart a lesson from the point at which the user left off. In such cases, check the Resume button. This feature should be used with caution, however. Unless an option is included for the user to restart the lesson from the beginning or to navigate easily through the lesson file, the lesson may be unusable after it has been completed once! The usual strategy to circumvent this potential problem is to include the Restart Function in a Calculation as the final icon on the flow line. Functions will be examined in detail in Chapter 12.

You can use transitions to display a special effect each time the user returns to the lesson from the Return Effects menu. These transitions are the same options that exist for Erase icons.

Other Features

Show Grid and Snap to Grid

One design feature that quickly separates professional-looking designs from those created by beginners is the ability to arrange text and graphics consistently on the screen. Authorware provides three tools (Grid, Snap to Grid, and Align) that greatly facilitate screen layout. Selecting Grid from the View pulldown menu creates a series of grid marks on the monitor. The designer can use these marks to help align objects on the screen.

Closely related is the Snap to Grid command. Snap to Grid encourages consistency by limiting where objects can be placed. When Snap to Grid is on, objects cannot be moved in increments of less than 16 pixels.

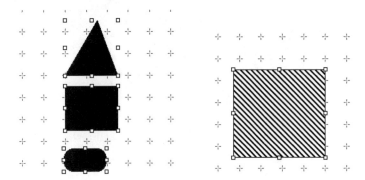

Note: Show Grid does not need to be ON in order to use the Snap to Grid option.

Align Objects

The Align objects option allows the designer to organize two or more objects in the same horizontal or vertical plane. Alternatively, it can be used to space three or more objects horizontally or vertically. Spaced objects generally appear more balanced on the screen, and balance is often cited as a factor that makes attractive presentations.

To align or space objects, you must be in the Presentation window (i.e., open a Display icon). Select the Align... option from the Modify pulldown menu. This brings the Alignment palette to the forefront.

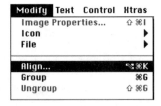

The operation of this palette is clear from its visual appearance. For example, the top left option is used to align objects along their left edges. To align objects, first select two or more objects to be aligned by Shift-clicking. Next, use the mouse to select the appropriate option from the alignment grid.

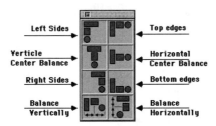

Define and Apply Styles

Have you noticed that you are spending a lot of time formatting text? When Authorware starts up, it reads a file to determine the default text font and font size. Any variation from the default style requires a manual change. Over the course of a project, this may result in hundreds or even thousands of modifications. Worse, it is not unusual to change type specifications late in the development process, requiring every text object in the file to be modified. Luckily, a feature is available to resolve such problems. The feature is called Style. You can apply a specific font, font size, or text formatting by selecting from a list of available styles. Moreover, text styles can be edited, resulting in immediate changes throughout a file. Later, in Chapter 13, on Framework icons, you will learn that styled text can also be used to create hyperlinks.

Before applying a text style, the style must be defined. Defining styles is generally performed in one of two ways:

- Copying styled text from other Authorware files and pasting the copied text into the current file. Pasting styled text not only places new text onto the Display icon, it also places a copy of the style sheet into the current lesson. The new style sheet can now be applied to any other text objects, as described below.
- Selecting Define Styles from the Text pulldown menu and setting options in a dialog box.

To create a new style:

- Select the Add button. The default name New Style will appear.
- Type the desired name for the new style.
- Select the text-formatting options from the dialog box.

- Select Modify to complete the new style.
- Select Done to return to the lesson.

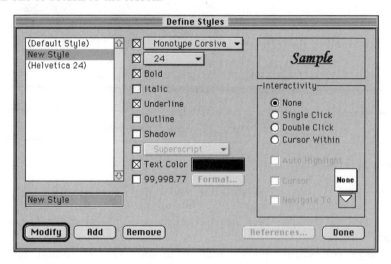

Applying Styles

To apply a style, highlight text with the mouse and choose the appropriate style from the Apply Styles pulldown menu or from the Tool Bar.

In the following example, a style is applied to text in a Display icon by selecting a style from the Tool Bar. First, the text is selected.

Next, a style is selected from the Tool Bar. In this case, a style titled New Style is selected.

The text reappears in the desired style.

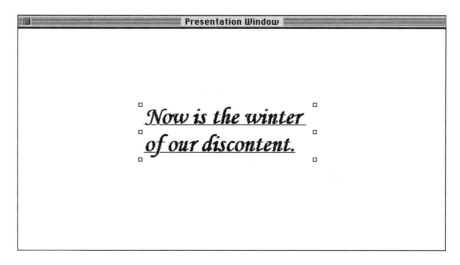

STUDY EXERCISES

1. Name the keyboard equivalent for each of the following commands.

Example: *Command*   *Keyboard equivalent*
          Run the File   Command-R

- Show Variables
- Pause
- Jump to Presentation Window
- Show Lines Palette
- Show Current Icon
- Proceed
- Show Fills Palette
- Show Functions
- Show Color Palette
- Jump to Design Window
- Left-Justify Text
- Center-Justify Text

2. The default name given to the button for a Wait icon is **Continue**. How can you change the default name to **Next**?

3. Create a lesson with the following default settings:

- A blue background
- The pulldown menu bar and Title Bar removed when you run the lesson
- A Wait button that reads Press the Spacebar to Continue.

4. Create three different objects in a Display icon (e.g., a rectangle, an oval, and a hexagon). Align the three objects as follows:

- Vertically along their left borders
- Horizontally along their top borders
- Vertically along their center axes

5. Define and name a Text style with the following attributes:

- Times or Arial font
- 30-point text
- Bold text
- Red text
- Underlined text

Create a presentation and apply the style to several words or phrases in the display.

6. Run a file by selecting the Run option from the Tool Bar in the Design window.

Place a flag on the flow line and rerun the file from the flag by selecting the Run from Flag button in the Tool Bar.

Rerun the file using the Trace window in the control panel. Observe the entries in the Trace window while the file is running. When the lesson stops, try to follow the lesson logic by observing each line in the Trace window.

7

The Interaction Icon: Part 2

CHAPTER OVERVIEW

In Chapter 5, you learned the basic structure of an interaction and three response types. In this chapter, you will learn how to use four more response types: Hot Objects, Text Entry, Target Area, and pulldown Menus. Hot objects are similar to hot spots, but they allow you to specify an entire object as "hot" without defining a rectangular target area around the object. Text Entry responses require the user to type text into the computer. Whatever the user types can be stored, analyzed, and manipulated to reuse later. Target Area responses create interactions in which users must move objects to specific screen locations. Target areas can be particularly useful when learning steps to complete procedural tasks. For example, you can use a Target Area response to test whether a user knows how to operate machinery. Lastly, pulldown menus allow you to create navigation structures that control lesson flow.

CHAPTER OBJECTIVES

After completing this chapter, you will be able to create interactions using the following response types:

- Hot objects
- Text entry
- Target areas
- Pulldown menus

KEY TERMS

Hot Object responses
Text Entry responses
Target Area responses
Pulldown menus
Feedback icons
Response options
Judging
Branching
Erasing
Wildcard

SUPPORT MATERIALS

On the CD-ROM disk, run the file titled **Videos.a4r** and select the button labeled **Chapter 7**. **Chapter 7** includes four movies that show how to create Hot Objects, Text Entry, Target Area, and Pulldown Menu responses. From the SUPPORT folder on the CD, open the file titled **CHP07.a4p**. The file demonstrates Hot Objects, Text Response, and Pulldown menu interactions.

PROJECT 6: CREATING A DEVELOPMENT SHELL

Materials Needed to Complete This Project

- Your file from the previous project, **PROJ5.a4p**
- Macromedia Authorware 4.0 for Macintosh or Windows

Before You Begin

Allow approximately 1 hour to complete this module.

Project Description

In this project you will build a "shell" that will function much like a flow chart for the rest of the project. You will develop the logic for an interactive real-estate planner that will house a homebuyer's worksheet, a mortgage calculator, and a glossary.

Activity

Begin by opening the Authorware file from the previous project. From the File pulldown menu, choose Save As… to rename the file as **PROJ6**.
    To begin, place a new Map icon on the Level 1 flow line, next to the Map icon titled **Interest**. Title the Map icon **Planner**.

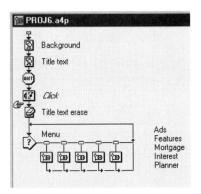

Open the Map icon titled **Planner**. By now you probably know enough to place icons onto the flow line without detailed instructions. Consequently, some of the following instructions will be briefer than those described in earlier chapters. For the next step, place the following icons onto the Planner Level 2 flow line (choose Button responses when the Response Type dialog box appears):

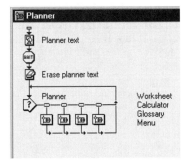

Open the Map icon titled **Worksheet**. Add and title the following icons:

You will now copy and paste the contents of the Map icon titled **Worksheet** into two other Map icons. Select and copy the Display, Wait, and Erase icons from the Map icon titled **Worksheet**.

Open the Map icon titled **Calculator**. Click the flow line, and then select Paste from the Edit pulldown menu. Retitle the Display and Erase icons to match the following:

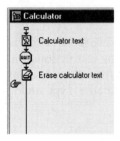

Now paste the same icons into the Map icon titled **Glossary**, and again retitle the Display and Erase icons. When you are finished, the Glossary flow line should look like this:

Place an Interaction icon on the flow line under the Erase icon titled **Erase glossary text**, and title the Interaction icon **Glossary**. Add and label three Display icons and a Map icon to the right of the Interaction icon titled **Glossary** as follows (choose Button when the Response Type dialog box appears):

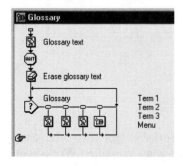

You will now add text to the Display icons. Return to the Planner Level 2 flow line. Double-click the Display icon titled **Planner text**. Using the Text tool from the toolbox, type the following:

HomeGuide Interactive Planner

Do you need answers to these questions:

Can I afford to buy a home?
How much will my mortgage payments be?
What do all these terms mean?

Use the Interactive Planner to find out...

Disclaimer: The HomeGuide Interactive Planner is intended for educational and demonstration purposes only. For information concerning an actual home purchase or mortgage financing, please consult a real estate professional or mortgage banker.

Use 18-point Arial Black for the heading (36-point, on a Mac), 14-point Arial for the text (18-point, on a Mac), and 10-point Arial Italic for the disclaimer (14-point, on a Mac). Double-click the Interaction icon titled **Planner**. Using the Text tool, type and format the following text:

Interactive Planner

Features:

Use the **Worksheet** to determine whether or not you can afford a home.

Use the **Calculator** to figure mortgage payments.

Use the **Glossary** to decode the language of real estate.

Open the Response Options dialog box for the icon titled **Worksheet**. Click Buttons… and select the customized button that you created in a previous project. Repeat the process for the other three buttons. When you are finished, your screen should look like this:

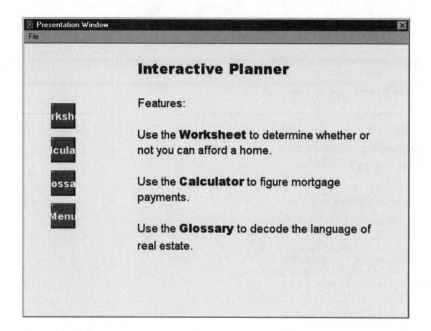

You will now create "placeholders" to help you check your logic as you develop the content. Open the Map icon titled **Worksheet** and the Display icon titled **Worksheet text**. Type and format the following:

Worksheet text will go here.

Now open the Map icon titled **Calculator** and the Display icon titled **Calculator text**. Type and format the following:

Calculator will go here.

Open the Display icon titled **Glossary text** and type the following:

HomeGuide Glossary

Reading real estate ads can be a real challenge. If you "know the code", you are better equipped to evaluate the many homes in the newspaper **before** you call a real estate agent.

The HomeGuide Glossary is designed to help you translate standard real estate abbreviations into plain English.

Open the Interaction icon titled **Glossary** and type the following:

Glossary

Click on the buttons to view common real estate abbreviations and their defintions.

Next, replace the default buttons with the custom button. When you are finished, your screen should look like this:

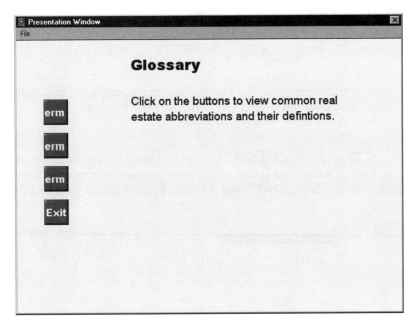

Return to the Glossary Level 3 flow line. Change the titles of the Display icons to the right of the Interaction icon titled **Glossary** as follows:

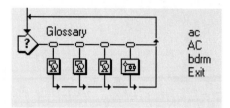

In the following three examples, to avoid overlapping text, be sure to type beneath the text you entered in the Interaction icon titled **Glossary**. Open the Display icon titled **ac** and type the following:

= acreage

Double-click the Display icon titled **AC** and type the following:

= air conditioning

Double-click the Display icon titled **bdrm** and type the following:

= bedroom

Now run your lesson. At the Welcome screen, click the Planner button and check the icons you have just constructed. In particular, check and correct any errors to the following:

- Placement of new Continue buttons
- Erasing problems: For the Interaction icon titled **Planner**, you need to change the erasing options from Upon Exit to After next Entry: (Select the Interaction icon, and from the Modify pulldown menu select Icon > Properties. Change Erasing from Upon Exit to After Next Entry)

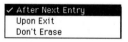

- Navigation problems
- Custom buttons

Notice that the Exit button does not work when you enter the Glossary. To activate this button, you must change the branching for the **Exit** Map icon. Pause the lesson and return to the

Glossary Level 3 flow line. Open the response options for the **Exit** Map icon. In the Response Options dialog box, select Exit Interaction from the Branch dropdown menu.

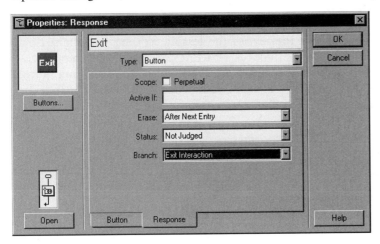

The flow line should now look like this:

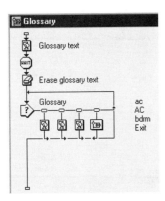

Repeat this operation for the Planner Level 2 flow line, clicking the button above the Map icon titled **Menu**. The Planner flow line should look like this:

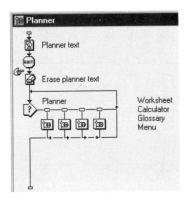

Run your lesson to check the navigation.

Extending What You Have Learned

In this project, you created the logic for the rest of the lesson. You have "roughed out" screens, assuming that you will return later to check text formatting and placement. However, you can streamline this process and ensure better placement of your text and buttons with careful use of the Cut and Paste options. Try rebuilding your lesson using the following sequence:

Step 1

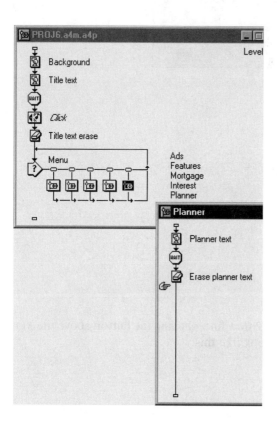

- Place a Map icon titled **Planner** on the Level 1 flow line.
- Open the Planner Map icon.
- Add Display, Wait, and Erase icons to the Level 2 flow line.
- Title the icons.
- Type text into the **Planner text** Display icon.

Step 2

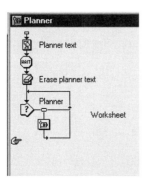

- Place an Interaction icon titled **Planner** on the Level 2 flow line.
- Add a Map icon titled **Worksheet**.

  Note: Use Map icons whenever you need more than one icon for feedback. Map icons can be used to store an unlimited number of icons.

- Select Button as the response type.
- Double-click the Response Options button above the Map icon titled **Worksheet**.
- At the Response Options dialog box, click the **Worksheet** button and select the custom button from the choices presented.

Step 3

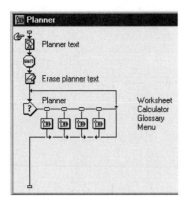

- Copy the **Worksheet** Map icon.
- Paste three copies next to the **Worksheet** Map icon.
- Retitle the three copied Map icons.
- Double-click the button above the **Menu** Map icon and redirect the branching.

Step 4

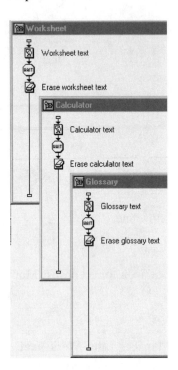

- Select the **Planner text** Display, Wait, and Erase icons.
- Copy and then paste them onto the flow lines in the **Worksheet**, **Calculator**, and **Glossary** Map icons. Remember that duplicating and modifying existing icons is a great timesaver.
- Retitle the icons in each Map icon.

Step 5

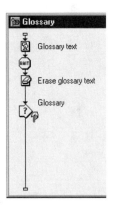

- Double-click the **Glossary** Map icon.
- Copy the **Planner** Interaction icon, and paste and relabel it on the **Glossary** Map icon flow line.

Step 6

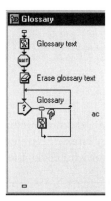

- Copy the **Glossary text** Display icon.
- Paste this copy next to the **Glossary** Interaction icon and retitle it.
- Select Button as the response type.
- Double-click the small button above the **ac** Display icon.
- At the Response Options dialog box, double-click the **ac** button and select the custom button from the choices presented.

Step 7

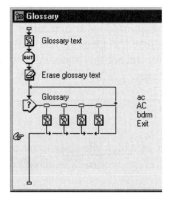

- Copy the **ac** Display icon.
- Paste three copies next to the **ac** Display icon and retitle it.
- Double-click the button above the **Exit** Display icon and redirect the branching.

Step 8

- Run the file.
- Each time you click a new button, pause the lesson, select the existing text, and type in the appropriate copy for that icon.
- Remember to check your Navigation, Button Placement, Content, and Erase functions.

UNDERSTANDING THE DETAILS

The following sections examine Hot Object, Text Entry, Target Area, and Pulldown Menu responses.

✳ ◉ Hot Object

Hot Object Responses

Have you noticed that hot spot interactions accept any response within a defined rectangular area? This may cause problems when hot spots overlap: The user may click one object, but receive feedback associated with another. In the illustration below, a user who clicks the circle may receive feedback intended for the star.

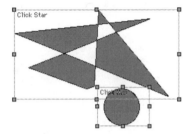

One solution to this problem involves using Hot Object interactions. Hot objects are particularly useful when you want to activate irregularly shaped objects. Hot objects are like hot spots: They require the user to interact with the computer by clicking an area on the monitor. However, hot objects use entire objects instead of rectangles to define the target areas. Although the physical action involved in using Hot Object and Hot Spot interactions is essentially identical, different processes are employed in creating the interactions.

The Following Exercise Demonstrates How To Create Hot Object Interactions

The goal of this exercise is to create a Hot Object interaction in which the user must use the mouse to click one of two objects (a triangle or a square). Different feedback is given for correct and incorrect responses.

- Place two Display icons on the flow line. Title the icons Triangle and Square. Open each display and use the graphics tools to create a triangle and a square in their respective icons.

  Note: Fill each object with a solid fill to make it easier to click the objects.

- Place an Interaction icon on the flow line. Title the interaction **Hot Object response**.
- Open the Interaction icon **Properties**. Mark the Pause Before Exiting option and Show Button.

Click the button labeled **Open** and type the following statement:

Click on the Triangle with the mouse

- Navigate to the flow line.
- Select a Display icon for feedback, and place it into the Interaction structure.
- At the prompt, select Hot Object for the response type.
- Type Click Triangle for the title of the Feedback icon.
- Open the Feedback icon by double-clicking it.
- Enter appropriate feedback for a correct response, and jump back to the flow line.
- Open the Response options and select the options illustrated below:

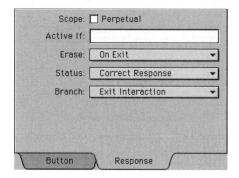

Click OK to return to the flow line.
- Add a second Display icon to the right of the first Feedback icon.
- Type Click Square for the title of the Feedback icon.
- Enter appropriate feedback for a wrong response, and jump back to the flow line. Appropriate feedback could be:

No, that's a square. Click on the Triangle.

- Open the Response options and select the options illustrated below:

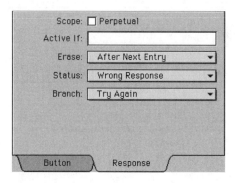

Click OK to return to the flow line.

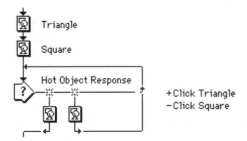

- Run the file. The lesson will stop at the Response options for you to identify the appropriate object. The title of the object to be selected (in this case, "Triangle") will appear in the Icon Name window.

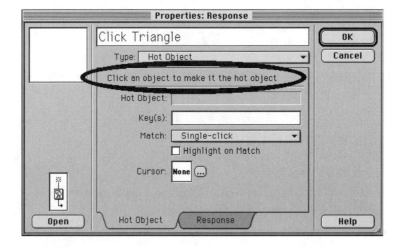

- Click the appropriate object with the mouse. The name of the selected object will appear in the window titled Hot Object, and a thumbnail picture of the image will appear in small window in the top left corner of the dialog box:

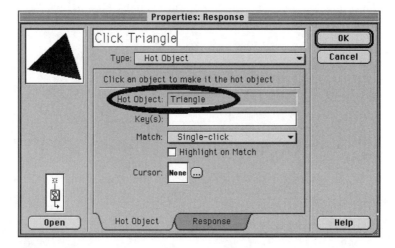

- Press the Response tab to set other options, or click OK to proceed. Repeat the exercise for the second object.
- Run the file again and test the lesson by entering both the correct and incorrect responses.

Things to Know about Hot Object Options

- Match: Allows you to select an object with a single click or double click, or by placing the cursor over the hot object.

- ◉ Text Entry

Text Entry Responses

In Chapter 5, you learned how to construct a Keypress response that responds to the pressing of a single key on the keyboard. Use Text Entry responses whenever you want the user to type more than one character into the computer. Text Entry interactions can be used in many different settings, and the text that the user types can be judged for accuracy. For example, you can create a login sequence in which the computer checks users' names with their passwords. Similarly, a Text Entry interaction is an excellent technique to enter information that will be stored in a database. Information stored in a database can be as diverse as users' comments and opinions, demographic data, or coordinates to be entered into a simulation.

The Following Exercise Demonstrates How to Create Text Entry Interactions

The goal of this exercise is to create a question to which the user types a response and receives feedback. Different feedback is given for correct responses than for incorrect responses.

- Place an Interaction icon on the flow line. Title the interaction **MLK Question**.
- Open the Interaction icon **Properties**. Mark the Pause Before Exiting option and Show Button. Click the button labeled **Text Field**. The Presentation window will open in the background, showing the Text Entry marker and the Text Entry box along with its move and resize handles. The entry marker shows where text will appear on the screen when the user starts typing, and sets the size of the Text Entry box.

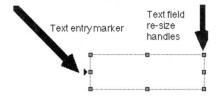

Click and drag the handles to move or resize the Text Entry marker and the size of the Text Entry field.

- When the entry marker is appropriately placed, type the following text into the Presentation window:

Whose birthday do we celebrate on January 15? Type your answer and press Return.

- Jump to the flow line.
- Select a Display icon for feedback and place it into the Interaction structure.
- At the prompt, select Text Entry for the response type.
- Type **mlk** as the anticipated response.
- Double-click to open the Feedback icon.
- Enter appropriate feedback for a correct response, and jump back to the flow line.
- Open and set the Response options:

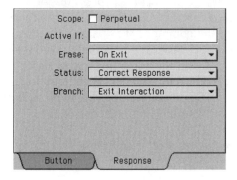

- Click OK to return to the flow line.
- Add a second Display icon to the right of the first Feedback icon.
- Select the wildcard (*) as the anticipated response.
- Enter appropriate feedback for a wrong response and jump back to the flow line.
- Open and set the Response options:

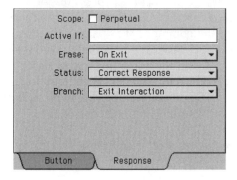

Click OK to return to the flow line.

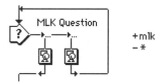

- Run and test the lesson by entering both correct and incorrect answers.

Things You Should Know about Text Entry Options

Allowing the computer to judge text entries is a powerful feature, but it is plagued with problems. From the user's perspective, it is very frustrating to type a response, only for the computer to misinterpret the entry. To facilitate the process, Authorware provides several tools that help designers to accurately judge responses.

- A feedback icon can be set to respond to any of several alternative student responses. Different correct responses are separated with the vertical bar (|).
  - Example:city|town|village|township|suburb
- Separate a comment from an anticipated response with two dashes.
  - Example:

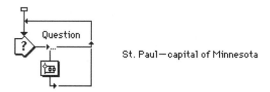

- Make a text response active only on a specific try by preceding the response with a pound sign (#) and the attempt number.
  - Example: #1Blue|#2Red
  Blue is judged correct on the first try; red, on the second try.
- The special characters used in answer judging are:
  | (Shift, Backslash key) means "or"
  Example: 8|eight
  means that either response will be accepted
  * Wildcard character accepts anything
  Example: Minneapolis|Min*
  means that Min followed by any other characters will be accepted as the correct response.
  ? accepts any single character
  Example: receive|rec??ve
  means that the characters "rec" plus any two characters, plus the characters "ve" will be accepted as the correct response
- Some Text Entry options are quite sophisticated, but rarely used. Check the Authorware manuals to examine Incremental Matching, Word Order, Extra Words, and other options.

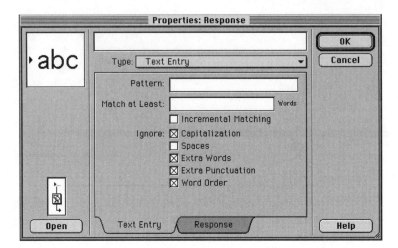

κ ⊙ Target Area

Target Area Responses

Target Area responses allow you to create questions that involve moving objects from one screen location to another. For example, you may want the user to connect words with their definitions. By linking a list of randomly ordered words to their meanings, it is possible to check a student's comprehension. Target Area responses are also particularly useful whenever users need to practice or demonstrate their understanding of the order in which a sequence of events is to be completed.

The Following Exercise Demonstrates How To Create Target Area Interactions

The goal of this exercise is to create a Target Area interaction in which the user must move a ball from one part of the screen to another. Feedback is included for correct and incorrect responses. The Snap to Center option is used for a correct response, and Put Back is used for an incorrect response.

- Place an object such as a circle into a Display icon. Title the Display icon with an appropriate name.

  Note: Filled objects are easier to move than unfilled objects.

- Place an Interaction icon on the flow line. Title the interaction **Target Area**.

Open the Interaction icon **Properties**. Mark the Pause Before Exiting option and Show Button. Click the button labeled **Open** and enter the following directions and graphics:

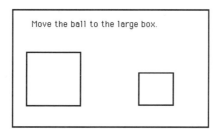

- Navigate back to the flow line. Include two Display icons for feedback—one for each anticipated response—and select Target Area as the response type.

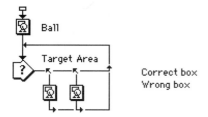

- Title the Feedback icons and enter appropriate feedback into each Display icon.
- Run the lesson. When the file comes to an undefined Target Area, the lesson will pause for you to define the areas. You will know which response you are setting by the name in the icon title field. For each Target Area response:

Select the tab labeled Target Area. The target area may be hidden behind the dialog box. If this is the case, drag the dialog box to one side, as in the figure below:

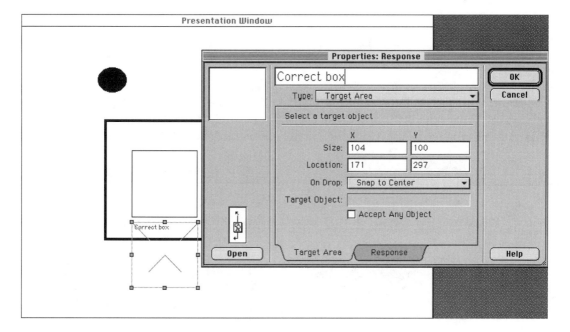

Select a target object by clicking a graphic in a Display icon with your mouse. As soon as you select an object, the target area will move to the object. After you select an object, notice that the instruction changes to "Drag object to the target position."

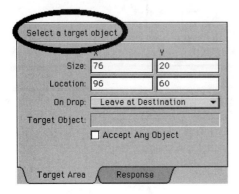 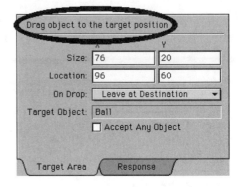

Drag the object that is to be moved (i.e., the ball) to its destination. You may need to resize the target area slightly at its destination. For the second object, you may need to rerun the lesson to move the ball if it is hidden behind the first target.

- For the correct response, set the Response options as follows:

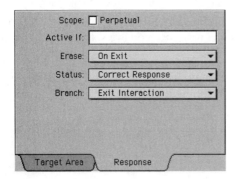 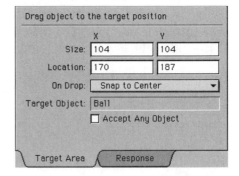

Notice that the On Drop setting is Snap to Center. Snapping an object to the center of a Target Area helps confirm that the object has been placed in the correct location.

- For the wrong response, set the Response options as follows:

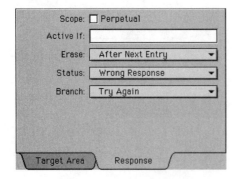 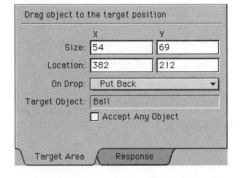

Notice that the On Drop setting is Put Back. Sending an object back to its origin provides strong visual feedback indicating that the response is wrong.

The icons should appear as follows when you are done:

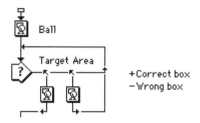

- Run the lesson and test each option.

Things to Know About Target Area Options

- Place each object to be moved in a separate Display icon that precedes the Interaction icon on the flow line.
- A separate Feedback icon is needed for each location that you anticipate for each object. If you anticipate three locations for each of four different objects, you will set twelve feedback icons.
- You must select one of the following three options for each anticipated response:

```
✓ Leave at Destination
  Put Back
  Snap to Center
```

Leave at Destination: The object remains where the user moves it.

Put Back: The object immediately returns to its original position after the user moves the object. This option is especially useful for incorrect responses.

Snap to Center: The object will snap to the center of the destination rectangle if the user moves the object within the target area. This is the normal selection for a correct answer.

▣ ◉ Pulldown Menu

Pulldown Menus

Although also used for other purposes, pulldown menus are often used for lesson navigation because they generally provide a consistent and permanent navigation source. In other words, users generally know that they will always be able to navigate from a pulldown menu. In the following example, a pulldown menu is used to move between two lesson sections, Math and English, or to quit the lesson:

As illustrated below, feedback for a pulldown menu is usually placed into a Map icon. The Map icon contains the content relevant to the path selected by the user.

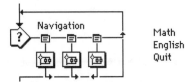

Math
English
Quit

The Following Exercise Demonstrates How to Create Pulldown Menu Interactions

- Place an Interaction icon on the flow line. Title the interaction **Navigation**. The title of the Interaction icon appears in the menu bar during the lesson.

- Open the Interaction icon and set the Erase Interaction option to After Next Entry. This is important: Without changing the Erase Interaction option, any information that is placed into the Interaction display will clutter the screen.

- Click the button titled **Open** to type instructions. For a pulldown menu response, the interaction often notifies the user to select from the pulldown menu. For example, you can type the following message into the Presentation window:

    Select an option from the pulldown menu.

- Attach two or more Feedback icons (use Map icons) to the Interaction structure. At the prompt, select pulldown menu as the response type. Name each Feedback icon with the text you want to appear under the pulldown menu (Math, English, and Quit).

- Place appropriate content into each Map icon. For this practice exercise, a single Display icon followed by a Wait icon and an Erase icon is appropriate.

- Open and set the Response options for Math and English:

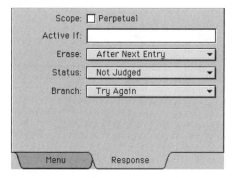

- Open and set the Response options for Quit:

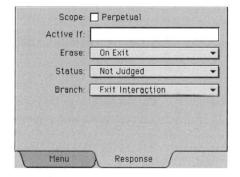

- Run the Interaction and test each option.

Things You Should Know about Pull-down Menu Options

- Options in the pulldown menu appear in the order in which the Feedback icons are positioned in the flow line.

- You can control the text style of the menu option by placing a style code at the beginning or end of the Feedback icons. The style code consists of the symbol for "less than" (<) and a letter:

<B **Bold**
<I *Italic*
<U <u>Underline</u>
<O Outline
<S Shadow

- The icon name (- causes a dotted line to appear in the pulldown menu.

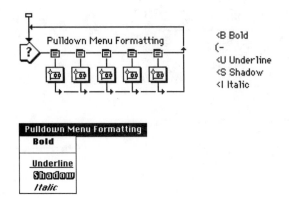

```
<B Bold
(-
<U Underline
<S Shadow
<I Italic
```

STUDY EXERCISES

1. A designer created an interaction with the following settings for a correct response:

- Branching was set to Exit Interaction
- Erasing was set to On Exit

When the question was answered correctly, feedback was erased from the screen before the user had an opportunity to read it. How could the designer have prevented feedback from being erased too quickly?

2. How do you display and move the entry marker for Text Entry interactions?

3. Total Physical Response is a foreign-language-learning technique that encourages users to learn a language by following commands. Create a brief lesson in which users must move objects to various places in a room.

To do this, you will first need to create a room with some objects in it. Remember that each object must be placed in a separate Display icon.

Use several Target Area interactions to instruct the users to move objects from one location to another. For example, you can tell users, "Move the book from the table to the chair."

Move to the next question if a correct answer is given. Move the object back to its original position and repeat the question for an incorrect response. Use appropriate feedback for correct and incorrect responses.

4. Create a navigation structure that uses pulldown menus to create a navigation structure that allows the user to switch lesson segments.

5. Create a Text Entry interaction that quizzes the user for the name of the President of the United States. Use appropriate feedback and branching for correct and incorrect responses.

6. Create a Target Area interaction in which the user must assemble three objects in a specific order. Use the Put Back option to return objects that are moved out of order.

8

The Interaction Icon: Part 3 ▣

CHAPTER OVERVIEW

This chapter presents the final four response types and introduces one of Authorware's most powerful and flexible programming techniques: perpetual interactions. The four response types we will examine are time limit, tries limit, conditional, and event. Time Limit responses allow the computer to intervene after a set period. For example, a time limit can prevent users from struggling for an unnecessarily long time on a question. Tries Limit responses are similar in operation to time limits, however; rather than reacting to the time taken, they monitor the number of attempts a user has made. For example, if a user has answered a question incorrectly three times, a Tries Limit response allows the user to exit a question. Conditional responses provide great flexibility. They allow the designer to create an interaction that matches a specified condition. As you become a sophisticated Authorware user, you will probably learn many creative ways of using Conditional responses. The final response type deals with Xtras. Xtras are like tools that add functionality to Authorware. The Event response provides a way for users to interact with Xtras and for the system to respond to different forms of interaction. Together, these four responses types provide designers with valuable tools to help identify students in need of help, or to respond to special instructional conditions.

Perpetual interactions provide design flexibility by allowing sections of a lesson to be used repeatedly. For example, the designer may wish the user to have permanent access to a series of Help buttons or a glossary. Perpetual interactions also increase programming efficiency. They often contain information that is to be accessed frequently. In other words, they operate like subroutines in traditional programming languages. Subroutines (lines of computer-programming instructions that carry out a function or computation) are used repeatedly in a program to reduce the need for duplicating programming.

CHAPTER OBJECTIVES

After completing this chapter, you will be able to expand Authorware's capabilities by using Xtras, and you will be able to create interactions using the following response types:
- Conditional
- Time limit
- Tries limit
- Event
- Perpetual interactions that allow the learner (or the designer) to access important information throughout a lesson.

KEY TERMS

Conditional responses
Time Limit responses
Tries Limit responses
Xtras
Event responses
Perpetual interactions
Return branching
Auto Match

SUPPORT MATERIALS

On the CD-ROM disk, run the file titled **Videos.a4r** and select the button labeled **Chapter 8**. **Chapter 8** includes four videos that show how to create Conditional, Time Limit, Tries Limit, and Event responses. From the SUPPORT folder on the CD, open the file titled **CHP08.a4p**. The file demonstrates Time Limit, Tries Limit, Conditional, and Perpetual interactions.

PROJECT 7: CREATING A PERPETUAL INTERACTION

Materials Needed to Complete This Project

- Your file from the previous project, **PROJ6.a4p**
- Macromedia Authorware 4.0 for Macintosh or Windows

Before You Begin

Allow approximately 15 minutes to complete this project.

Project Description

In this project, you will learn how to create a perpetual interaction that will allow you to use to the Glossary at any time during the lesson. You will also change the access point for the Glossary from the button in the Planner to a pulldown menu option at the top of the Presentation window.

Activity

Begin by opening the Authorware file from the previous project. From the File pulldown menu, choose Save As... to save a copy of the file as **PROJ7**.

Place an Interaction icon on the Level 1 flow line after the icon titled **Title text erase** and title it **Help**.

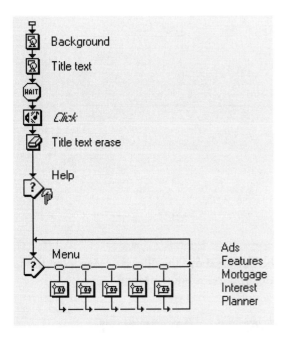

Double-click the Planner Map icon. Cut the Glossary Map icon from the Planner.

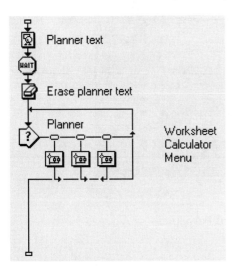

Paste the Glossary Map icon to the right of the Help Interaction icon.

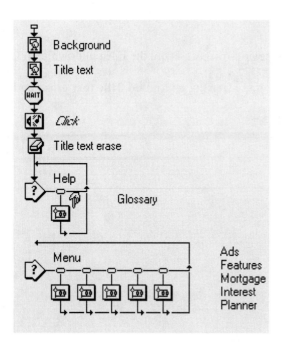

Open the Response options by double-clicking the button above the Glossary Map icon. In the Response options dialog box, change the response type to Pull-down Menu.

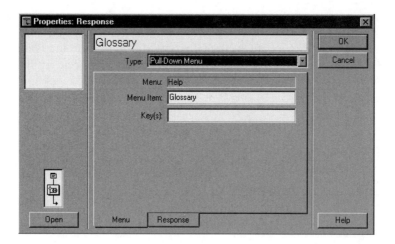

Next, select the Response tab and select the field labeled Perpetual.

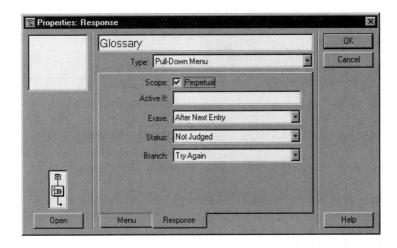

The Level 1 flow line should now appear as follows:

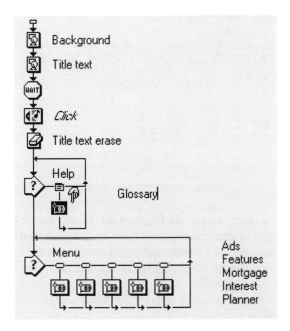

Run the file to check your work. Select the Glossary by selecting this option from the pull-down menu titled **Help**. Run through the rest of the lesson, and check for presentation and layout problems.

UNDERSTANDING THE DETAILS

Tries Limit, Time Limit, Conditional, and Event responses enable the designer to provide feedback when the following conditions exist:

- The user has attempted a question a given number of times.
- A given amount of time has elapsed.
- A condition defined by the designer has been matched. This sounds vague, but in practice it provides considerable design flexibility.
- The user has interacted with an Xtra.

\# ◉ Tries Limit

Tries Limit Responses

When Would I Use Tries Limit?

Tries Limit interactions are crucial whenever you think a user might get stuck in an Interaction. They allow the designer to give hints and help to prevent the user from entering an endless question loop. An endless loop occurs when the user cannot give a response that the computer expects, and the machine simply repeats the question. Imagine the following scenario: You are asked to name the capital city of Liechtenstein. You vainly attempt to answer the question by typing the names of European cities that come to mind. Each time you enter a response the computer delivers the same reply: Wrong try again.

```
>Hamburg
    Wrong try again.


>Belgrade
    Wrong try again.


>Berlin
    Wrong try again.
```

and so the lesson continues until you turn off the machine in frustration.

Tries limit Interactions help prevent such frustrating experiences by providing feedback after a given number of attempts. For example, you could provide clues that gradually steer the user toward the correct response.

How Do I Set Tries Limit?

The following example includes a Tries Limit that prompts the user after three incorrect responses.

- First create an interaction that includes a question and appropriate feedback and looping for correct and wrong answers.
- In the Interaction structure, insert a Display icon at the end of your set of Feedback icons. Open the Response options, set the response type to Tries Limit, and label the icon.
- Enter the maximum number of tries. This is the number of responses the users can enter before the tries limit Feedback icon is triggered.
- Set the judging option for the tries limit to Not Judged so that the system variables for correct and incorrect answers will not be updated.
- Set Branching to Exit Interaction if you want the user to exit the question after a given number of tries. Set Branching to Try Again if you want to display a hint, but do not want the user to exit the question.

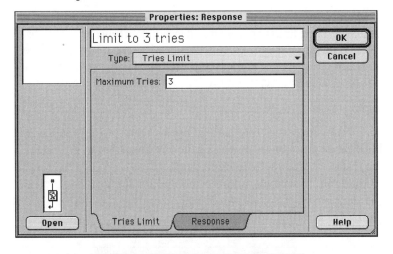

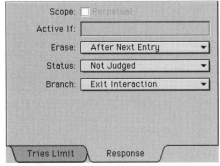

- Click **Open** to enter feedback into the Display icon for the tries limit.

- When you are done the Interaction structure should look like this:

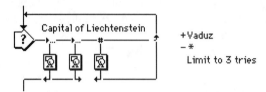

Things to Know About Tries Limit Options

Be careful where you place Tries Limit responses. Placing a Tries Limit response at the beginning of the flow line causes the tries limit to bypass any other options. However, by placing it at the end of a series of anticipated responses, Authorware can match other responses and still present the feedback associated with the tries limit.

⊕ ⦿ Time Limit

Time Limit Responses

When Would I Use a Time Limit?

Use a time limit whenever you want to branch a lesson based on the amount of time a user has spent on an interaction. Time limits operate like tries limits. However, whereas tries limits allow you to branch after some number of tries, time limits allow the designer to intervene after a set period. Time limits are often used in games to create time challenges and stimulate motivation. They also may be used to give hints when the learner is taking a long time to respond.

To Set Time Limits

- In an existing Interaction structure, add a Display icon to your Feedback icons. Insert the icon at either the beginning or the end of the Feedback icons.
- Change the response type to Time Limit.
- Enter the time limit, in seconds, and type a label for the Feedback icon.
- Decide whether you want a clock, which indicates time remaining, to be displayed. If so, click the Show Time Remaining option.

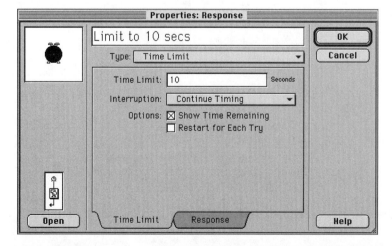

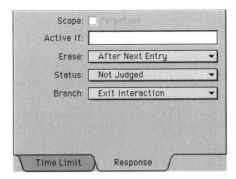

- In the Interaction structure shown below, a Feedback icon appears after 30 seconds.

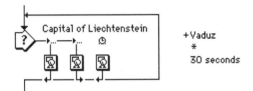

Things to Know About Tries Limit Options

- Show Time Remaining places a clock on the screen to indicate the proportions of time gone versus time left.

- Perpetual interactions (to be addressed later in this chapter) and navigation links can ruin timed responses. The Interruption dropdown menu provides options that allow you to control whether timing is reset, ignored, or repeated when the user goes to another activity or is interrupted by a Perpetual interaction.

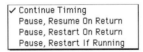

Conditional Responses

When Would I Use a Conditional Response

Watch out! This section may be confusing! Unless you understand how functions and variables work in Authorware, Conditional responses will not make much sense. Functions and variables will be introduced in Chapters 11 and 12.

In general, Conditional responses are activated when Authorware notices that some condition has been met. For example, imagine that a lesson includes a quiz to allow the user to self-evaluate. The designer wants Help to be turned off during the quiz to ensure that answers come from the user, not the computer. In this case, the designer can use a Conditional response to create a rule that turns off Help when the quiz begins. Alternatively, Authorware can keep track of the time spent exploring a game, and use this information to determine when to release more clues to help the player. The most important point to understand is that Authorware executes a Feedback icon associated with the Conditional response when some condition is matched. The content stored in that Feedback icon is limited only by the designer's creativity.

The Following Exercise Demonstrates How to Create a
Conditional Interaction

In the following scenario, you will need to use a little imagination. Imagine that you are designing a system that allows a user to enter a database to access information, but must restrict access at certain times as a security precaution. The restriction must be set to prevent users from accessing the database between the hours of 10 P.M. and 2 A.M., since automatic backup occurs at this time and using the database may conflict with the backup process. To restrict access, you will use a Conditional response to prevent users from accessing the database at forbidden times.

- Place an Interaction icon on the flow line. Title the interaction **Database protection**.
- Open the Interaction icon. Mark the Pause before exiting option.
- Add a Display icon to the Interaction icon for feedback.
- Select Conditional for the response type.
- Open the Conditional Response options icon, and type:

Hour>22|Hour<2

- Select the Conditional tab and set the Automatic option to When True.

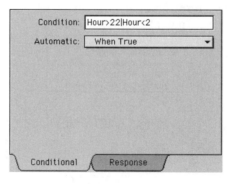

- Select the Response Tab:
  - Set Branching to Exit interaction
  - Set Erasing to On Exit

- Add a Map icon to the right of the first Feedback icon. Open the Response options and type the following conditional statement into the icon:

Hour≤22&Hour≥2

Note: To enter ≦ into a field, type <=. Authorware will recognize the entry and replace it with the "less than or equal to" symbol. The reverse is true for "greater than or equal to."

- Select the Conditional tab and set the Automatic option to When True.

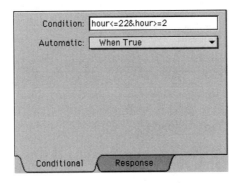

- Select the Response tab:
  Set Branching to After Next Entry
  Set Erasing to Try Again

The icons should appear as follows.

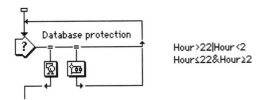

Hour>22|Hour<2
Hour≤22&Hour≥2

- Open the Map icon and place a Display icon titled **Proceed** and an Interaction structure titled **Password check** onto the flow line, as illustrated below. The password check will not be completed at this time; it's there simply to show what might come next in the sequence and to pause the file.

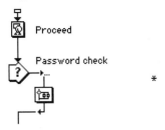

- Enter feedback into the Display icons attached to each anticipated Conditional response. The illustrations below show the text in the Display icons.

```
                              ┌──────────────────────────────┐
                              │  Access to database denied.   │
                              │                               │
                              │  You may not login to the system
                              │  between 10 p.m. and 2 a.m.   │
a. Hour > 22 │ < 2            └──────────────────────────────┘
```

```
                       ┌──────────────────────────────┐
                       │  Access to database approved. │
                       │                               │
                       │  Please enter your password to│
                       │  continue.                    │
b. Proceed             └──────────────────────────────┘
```

- Run the file and observe the results.

Things to Know about Conditional Options

The Automatic option is a powerful feature. The default value is Off. When Auto Match is off, Authorware waits for the user to enter information into the computer at an Interaction icon before checking to see whether a condition has been met.

```
          ┌──────────────────────┐
          │   Off                │
          │ ✓ When True          │
          │   On False to True   │
          └──────────────────────┘
```

However, instead of waiting for the user to make an overt response before checking for a match, Authorware automatically matches a response when a condition exists if When True is selected. This is a powerful tool because it allows the lesson to take a particular path even though the user has not made a response. In a sense, this option works like the Perpetual option that will be examined later in this chapter.

Xtras

As you become a sophisticated Authorware user, you will probably encounter specialized problems that cannot be solved easily within Authorware. For example, I once worked on a project where it was important to know the name of the floppy diskette that was in the disk drive on a Macintosh. This problem could not be solved within Authorware, so it became necessary to write a small program in another programming language that would perform the task. This program was then be imported into Authorware to solve the problem.

You can use Xtras to add capability to Authorware. There are two classes of Xtras: Transitions and Sprites. Transition Xtras allow you to add new transitions that extend the range of display and erase capabilities. Sprites allow you to add functionality to Authorware. To use a tool metaphor, if Authorware is a socket set, Xtras are special-purpose sockets that you purchase from the hardware store. For example, you might buy a socket that is specifically designed to remove spark plugs, or an extension that allows you to use sockets in awkward locations. The point to stress is that the socket set is expandable and additional functionality can be made or purchased.

The task of creating such tools has become a small industry. The tools used to be called XCMDs or DLLs, and were somewhat difficult to manage. However, the process has now been streamlined through the development of cross-platform Xtras.

To use an Xtra, you must first make sure that the Xtra is loaded properly in Authorware. To load an Xtra:

- Quit Authorware.
- Locate the Xtras folder. This should be found inside the folder where Authorware is stored.

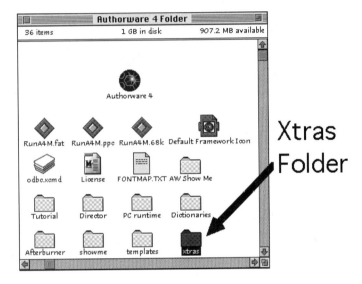

- Make sure that the Xtra labeled OvalSpriteFat is inside the Xtras folder.

- Start Authorware and open a new file.
- Click the flow line with the mouse.
- From the Insert pulldown menu, select Sprite Examples > Wacky Oval to insert a Sprite icon onto the flow line.

- Although you don't need to do so at this time, you can open the Sprite icon **Properties** by double-clicking its icon.

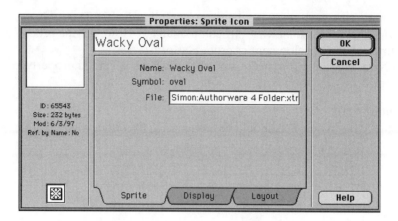

- Running the file will reveal the Xtra titled Wacky Oval. This Xtra places a pulsating circle on the screen. (When clicked with the mouse, the circle transforms into a cross. Click the cross to restart the pulsating circle.)

Event Interactions

Some Xtras require the learner to interact with them to make them work. The Event response type is designed specifically to help you interact with Sprite Xtras.

- To interact with a Sprite Xtra, place an Interaction icon on the flow line, below a Sprite icon.
- Add a Feedback icon and choose Event for the response type.

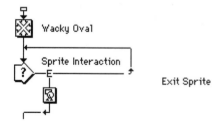

- Opening the Response options reveals a list of all the Sprite Xtras available in the current file. In effect, these are the Sprite Xtras that have been preloaded into the Xtras folder.

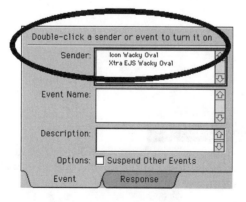

- To link a Sprite with an Event response, select a Sprite from the Sender field. Clicking once highlights that item and places an entry in the Event Name field. Clicking twice selects the item and marks it with a check mark to indicate that the item has been turned on.
- The field titled Event Name indicates the action that will trigger the Event response. In the illustration below, the action of clicking the Sprite Xtra with the mouse (i.e., mouse-Down) activates the Event. Double-click the Event Name to activate that item and open a description in the Description field.

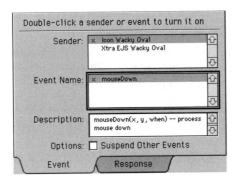

- Create feedback for the Event in the same way you would for any other response type.
- Finally, run the file and test the result.

Perpetual Interactions

Perpetual interactions are one of the most flexible and important design techniques available in Authorware. Once a student has completed an Interaction icon, that icon is essentially "dead." That is, the icon cannot be easily reused. Very often, however, the designer would like the user to access an interaction throughout a lesson. Perpetual interactions provide this capability by keeping interaction structures "alive" during lessons. Perpetual interactions contain information that is to be used repeatedly.

Perpetual interactions considerably increase programming efficiency. Because they contain information that is accessed often (i.e., they function like subroutines), there is no pressure on the designer to duplicate icons on the flow line.

When Would I Use a Perpetual Response?

- Use Perpetual interactions whenever you need permanent access to some section of a lesson.

Example

Imagine that you want to create a Help option. If you employ the "normal" linear lesson structure, the Help option will not be available to the student after it has been used once. How can you make the option permanently available, or turn the option off and on as needed?

*The Following Exercise Demonstrates How To Create a Perpetual
Interaction.*

- Place an Interaction icon on the flow line. Title the interaction **Perpetual help button**.

    Note: Perpetual interactions are often placed at the start of a lesson, before lesson sections that might use the interaction. This is important because Authorware must store Perpetual interactions in memory before they can be used.

- Select a Map icon for feedback and place it in the Interaction structure.
- At the prompt, select Button for the response type.
- Type Help for the title of the Feedback icon. Open the Map icon and place a Display icon, a Wait icon and an Erase icon onto the flow line.
- Open the Feedback icon and enter some appropriate content for a Help screen.
- Open the Response options. Select the Perpetual check box.

    Scope: ☒ Perpetual

- Controlling Erasing: You must control when information is erased from the icon being used in the Perpetual interaction, as well as from the screen from which you came. You may want to erase the screen from which you came, or leave the information showing when you use a Perpetual interaction. The screen will be erased if the branching for the Perpetual response is set to Exit interaction. However, if the branching is set to Return, then no erasing will take place. In the second case, it may be necessary to use "masking" to temporarily hide a screen. Masking is achieved by covering a display with a (borderless) box filled with paint (usually the background color).

    It is often easiest to control the erasing of information in the Perpetual interaction by using Erase icons rather than the Erase Feedback response options. This is why you used a Map as the Feedback icon. By using Display icons followed by Wait and Erase icons, you can ensure that information is erased when the user exits the Perpetual interaction.

- Do not judge the interaction.
- Choose Return for branching. "Return" branching sends the user back to the icon that calls the Perpetual response.

```
Try Again
Continue
Exit Interaction
✓ Return
```

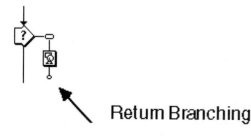

Return Branching

- Add a Display icon to the flow line and enter some text. Run the lesson to test the Perpetual interaction. Notice that the Help button is available. Selecting Help places the content of the Perpetual interaction onto the screen, together with a Wait button. Resize and place the Wait button on top of the Help button so only one button shows at a time.

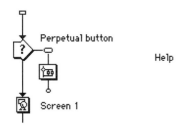

- To use a Perpetual response, first create the Perpetual interaction, and then "call" the interaction whenever it is needed. The method used to call a Perpetual interaction varies according to the response type. For a Button response, simply clicking the button on the screen activates the interaction.

Things to Know about Perpetual Interactions

- To remember which response types support Perpetual interactions, notice that, with the exception of Conditional responses and Event responses, the response types require the use of the mouse to interact.

STUDY EXERCISES

1. Create an interaction in which the user is given a prompt after two incorrect answers, and is given the correct answer after three incorrect answers. Set branching to Try Again after two incorrect answers and Exit after three incorrect answers.
2. Create an interaction in which the user is given a prompt after 20 seconds (if the correct answer has not been given), and the correct answer after 60 seconds. Set branching to Try Again after 20 seconds, and Exit after 60 seconds.
3. A pulldown menu cannot be reused after it has been passed on the flow line. This can be a problem if you want the options in a pulldown menu to be available throughout a lesson. One solution to this problem involves using the Perpetual option in the pulldown menu. Use this approach to create a perpetual Help button that the user can access at any time during the lesson.

   Note: The following questions involve the use of variables. You may want to complete Chapter 11 before attempting these questions:

4. Create a Keypress interaction in which you ask the user to identify the names of the last three presidents of the United States from a list of six presidents. Use a Conditional response and the system variable TotalCorrect to match the third correct response. Provide appropriate feedback after each correct or incorrect response.
5. Did you notice in Exercise 4 that the user could select the same correct answer three times? How can you make a response inactive once it has been selected?
6. Create an electronic notepad for the user to write notes or comments during the lesson. Use a Perpetual interaction with a Button response to activate the notepad, which should be available throughout the lesson.

9

Libraries and Models

CHAPTER OVERVIEW

In this chapter, we will examine two development tools that multimedia designers use to improve design productivity and lesson execution: Libraries and Models. Libraries accelerate design by providing easy access to commonly used icons. Models play a similar role; however, rather than providing access to individual icons, Models provide access to sets of icons that perform tasks.

Libraries are very important. In addition to allowing icons to be used repeatedly without increasing file size, a single Library can be shared by more than one Authorware file, and multiple icons can easily be edited by altering a single Library icon. Thus, multiple files can be edited by modifying a Library. Models contain sets of icons that are used frequently. By storing icons in a Model, developers can quickly reproduce lesson logic that might otherwise take hours to re-create.

CHAPTER OBJECTIVES

By the end of this chapter, you will be able to:

- Create Libraries to store and reuse icons.
- Create Models to store and reuse lesson logic.

KEY TERMS

Libraries
Library links
Broken links
Models

SUPPORT MATERIALS

On the CD-ROM disk, run the file titled **Videos.a4r**. Select the button labeled **Chapter 9**, and watch the video to see how Libraries and Models are created.

UNDERSTANDING THE DETAILS

What Is a Library?

We used a Library in Chapter 4 to store a sound file. Libraries store icons that are used repeatedly in a lesson, or even in several lessons. Libraries improve productivity and reduce file size. By reusing icons, Libraries allow you to reproduce lesson content or ideas that you developed elsewhere. Reproducing icons is faster than creating original icons. Moreover, you can make changes to icons copied from the Library simply by changing the Library icon. Although the following example again uses a Library to store a sound file, it is important to understand that other types of icons can also be used in Libraries: Display, Interaction, Sound, Movie, and Calculation icons can all be stored in a Library file.

Imagine a lesson that uses sound files to deliver spoken feedback. In the example below, a sound file "tells" the user whether an answer is correct or wrong.

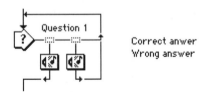

Repeatedly using Sound icons to deliver feedback causes two problems. First, it is labor intensive. Each time you use a Sound icon, you must identify a sound file. Second, using the same sound file repeatedly increases file size. A small sound file recorded at a low sampling rate often increases lesson size by 50 K. Using two sound files ten times in a lesson could increase the file size by at least 1000 K. In other words, the lesson could be 1 MB larger to include simple spoken feedback!

A solution to both problems involves using a Library. By placing the original Sound icon into a Library, the designer can select copies of the Sound icons by dragging icons from the Library onto the flow line. Better still, each copy is not a real copy! Libraries use aliases to point from the copy on the flow line to the original icon stored in the Library. The following illustration shows the Sound icon after it has been reproduced from the Library. Notice that the Sound icons' labels are italicized, indicating that the icons come from a Library file.

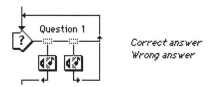

In addition to improving development efficiency and reducing file size, Libraries also can enhance file editing. When an icon is used several times in a lesson, minor edits must be made by modifying each affected icon on the flow line. However, when an icon is stored in a Library, changes to aliases on the flow line can be made simply by modifying the icon stored in the Library.

How Do I Create a Library?

To create a new Library, select New > Library from the File pulldown menu.

It is important to remember that the Library is a separate file and that the information in the file must be saved. To save a Library, you must first make sure that the Library window is active (as opposed to the Lesson File window). To do so, position the cursor of the mouse on the Library window and click the mouse buttom to select it. Now select Save from the File pulldown menu, and Authorware will know that you want to save the Library file, not the Design file.

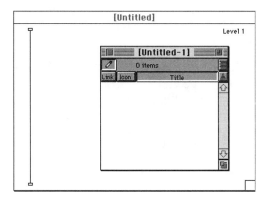

When saving a Library, Authorware will automatically add the suffix .a4l. For example, the following illustration shows a Library file that was originally saved as **library**, but Authorware added a suffix and renamed the file **library.a4l**:

Once opened and saved, the Library window will appear as in the following illustration:

At first the Library is empty. To add items to the Library, drag an icon from the icon palette or from the flow line and drop the icon in the main Library window. When you add an icon from the flow line to the Library window, a copy of the Library icon automatically replaces the old icon on the flow line. To place copies of Library icons into lessons, simply drag the icons from the Library window rather than from the icon palette.

The Library file listed below shows four icons, although others are available if you scroll down with the scroll bar. In addition to being named, each Library icon can be labeled to remind the designer of the icon's contents at a later date.

Notice that the title of the Sound file on the flow line that follows appears in italics to indicate that it is an alias:

Remember that icons from the Library create links from the Library to the flow line. You can edit the contents of a Library icon and instruct Authorware to apply the changes to all the icons in a file, or to just a subset of icons. First open and edit an icon in the Library. Next, highlight the icon and select Library Links... from the Xtras pulldown menu.

At the dialog box, select the icons you want to update using standard shift-clicking techniques to choose multiple items from the list. Click Update when you are ready to apply the edits to the selected icons.

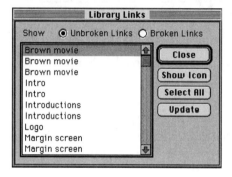

As mentioned previously, not all icons can be added to a Library. Notice that some icons produce the following error message if you attempt to drag them to a Library:

When a lesson file is finally packaged (see Chapter 16), it is very important to include any Library files with the finished product. However, Authorware is smart enough to include only those Library files that are critical to smooth lesson performance. Consequently, Authorware designers can develop extensive Library files containing icons that may be used frequently in several different files without being concerned that the entire Library content must accompany every lesson.

What Is a Model?

A Model is a set of icons that you can save and reuse. Designers often spend many hours creating sets of icons to perform complex tasks. When the same logic is required in another file, it makes sense to reuse the icons. To do so (without using Models) requires copying and pasting icons from the original into the new lesson file. This process can be time consuming. However, by saving lesson logic into a Model, designers have immediate access to the desired icons without having to leave the lesson.

Many computer programmers will be familiar with the concept of a Model, although they often use different terminology. Programmers often develop subroutine libraries containing frequently used sections of programming code. A Model is Authorware's version of a subroutine library. Once a Model has been saved, it becomes a permanent part of the Authorware application (although it can be removed), and can easily be pasted into another lesson.

At first it is easy to confuse Libraries with Authorware Models. The difference between a Library and a Model is that a Library contains many different icons without any accompanying lesson logic, whereas a Model contains icons that have been carefully arranged in a predetermined logical sequence.

Models are important productivity tools. Many lessons contain identical lesson sequences. For example, the introductory screens for a series of lessons may include identical elements. Rather than re-creating the icon sequence in every lesson or copying and pasting icons from one file to another, Models allow icons to be available immediately. Some models contain important logic, but little or no lesson content. Saving sets of icons as a model allows the template to be reused simply by pasting the model onto the flow line.

How Do I Create a Model?

The Create Model option cannot be used until one or more icons have been highlighted. To highlight icons, click one or more icons while pressing the Shift key. Alternatively, drag the cursor of the mouse across several icons.

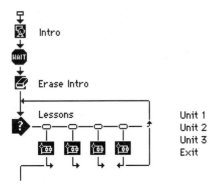

Once icons are highlighted, select Create Model from the Insert pulldown menu.

A dialog box titled Model Description must be completed, and you will be asked to save the Model to a disk.

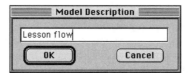

To reuse the Model, select the Load Model... option from the Insert pulldown menu, and choose a Model from the list. The icons that form the Model will immediately be pasted onto the flow line.

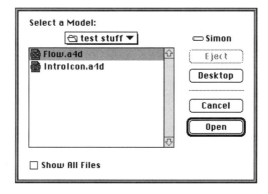

In addition to the Models you create, Models created by other designers can be imported into Authorware. Imagine, for example, that you found a sophisticated adaptive testing module that drills students on important lesson content and uses increasing ratio review to retest students on items they answer incorrectly. Such a template can be useful in many different designs, but is difficult and expensive to create. Fortunately, such a Model can be distributed on disk and loaded into Authorware using the Load Model... command.

STUDY EXERCISES

As an Authorware designer, you should attempt to create a Library containing frequently used icons and Models. A Library will greatly stimulate your productivity by speeding the development process. The following exercises are designed to stimulate such development:

1. Create a Library containing information that you believe you will use regularly. For example, you might include the following:
   - A Display icon containing a company or institutional logo.
   - A Display icon containing a frequently used background design.

- Display icons that contain a variety of buttons, navigation arrows, and other frequently used graphics. You may want to create these graphics in a drawing or painting program.
- A Sound icon containing the sound used to make a button "click."
- A Calculation icon containing several lines of instructions necessary to complete a complex task. For example, this task could involve collecting and writing lesson data to a file that is stored in a lesson folder.

2. Create a Keypress multiple-choice question with one correct answer and three distracters (incorrect answers). In place or real content, create a template indicating where the user should place the question, answers, and feedback for right and wrong answers. Save the interaction as a Model.

3. Create a model consisting of a Framework icon (see Chapters 13 and 14 on Framework and Navigate icons, respectively) that performs customized navigation.

The Decision Icon

CHAPTER OVERVIEW

In this chapter, you will learn about the Decision icon. The Decision icon is used to control the lesson flow. Attached to the Decision icon are paths that contain different content. Designers use the Decision icon whenever they wish to select one or more paths from the set of paths.

In programming terms, the Decision icon replaces the If-Then–Do-Next function. The Decision icon remembers the number of times paths have been selected and determines which subsequent paths to select.

CHAPTER OBJECTIVES

After completing this chapter, you will be able to:

- Use the Decision icon to control lesson sequencing.

KEY TERMS

Decision icon
Path

Random to Any Path
Random Without Repetition

SUPPORT MATERIALS

On the CD-ROM disk, run the file titled **Videos.a4r** and select the button labeled **Chapter 10** to see how the Decision icon can be used to control lesson logic. From the SUPPORT folder on the CD, open the file titled **CHP10.a4p**. The file demonstrates how each of four different branching options is created.

PROJECT 8: THE DECISION ICON

Materials Needed to Complete This Project

- Your file from the previous project, **PROJ7.a4p**
- Macromedia Authorware 4.0 for Macintosh or Windows

Before You Begin

Allow approximately 15 minutes to complete this module.

Project Description

In this project, you create another shell. This task will involve placing and naming icons on the flow line. You will fill in these icons in the next two projects.

Activity

Begin by opening the Authorware file from the previous project. From the File pulldown menu, choose Save As… to rename the file **PROJ8**.

This project and the next two projects will explore the Decision icon, variables, and functions. All three components work together to provide powerful interactive features. You will be able to calculate your approximate monthly mortgage payment. Also, you will be able to use the system to help you determine whether your income, less your estimated mortgage payment added to your other fixed payments, is enough to qualify for a mortgage. The full functionality of the components will not be realized until you have completed all three projects.

Place a Map icon on the Level 1 flow line beneath the **Menu** Interaction icon, and title it **Functions**.

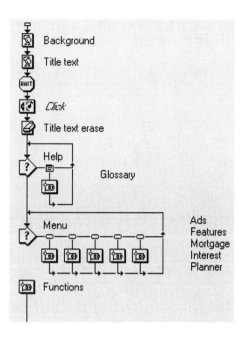

Next, place an Interaction icon on the Level 1 flow line, and title it **Can I afford a mortgage?**

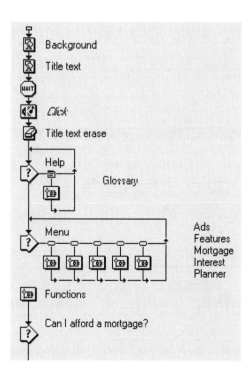

Place a Map icon on the flow line next to the Interaction icon titled **Can I afford a mortgage?** and title it **Can I afford a mortgage?** Select Button for the response type.

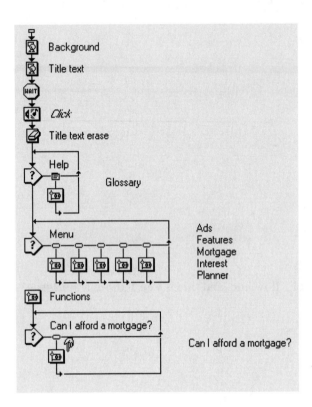

Open the Map icon titled **Can I afford a mortgage?** Place two Map icons on the Level 2 flow line, and title them as follows:

Open the Map icon titled **Decision icon**. Place a Decision icon on the Level 3 flow line, and title it **Expert advisor**. The paths attached to this Decision icon will eventually be used to help the user decide whether he or she can afford a mortgage.

Place a Display icon next to the Decision icon titled **Expert advisor**. Title it **Path 1**.

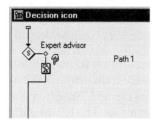

Double-click on the Display icon titled **Path 1**. Type the following:

Looks good!

Double-click on the small diamond above the Display icon titled **Path 1** to open the Decision icon properties dialog box. Set Erase Contents to Before Next Selection and check Pause Before Branching.

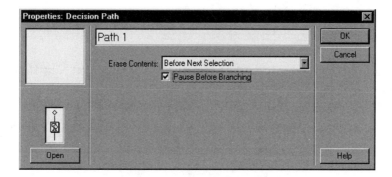

Copy the **Path 1** Display icon, and paste a copy to the right of the **Path 1** Display icon. Retitle it **Path 2**, and change the text to the following:

Looks bad!

The flow line should now look like this:

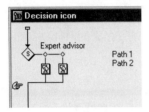

Next, you will control a Decision icon with a variable. In this case, you can think of a variable as a switch that allows you to select from one of many settings. We won't select a setting yet, but Authorware asks you to initialize (i.e., define) the variable as soon as it is created. Variables will be presented in detail in Chapter 11.

Open the Decision icon titled **Expert advisor**. In the dropdown menu titled Repeat, select **Don't Repeat**, set Branch to **Calculated Path**, and type the word "Advisor" in the empty field, as illustrated below. "Advisor" is the name given to the variable that is being created. Note that you will not give a value to the variable until you perform the project in Chapter 11. The information stored in the variable will be used to decide whether the computer takes Path 1 or Path 2.

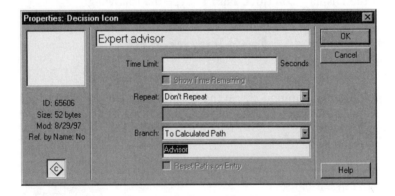

When you click OK to close the dialog box, another dialog box titled New Variable will open. This box is where you initialize the variable. It is important to write a brief description for each new variable you create. Notice the description for the new variable in the dialog box below.

Your Level 3 flow line should now look like this:

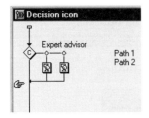

UNDERSTANDING THE DETAILS

When Do I Use a Decision Icon?

Decision icons are used to control lesson logic. For example, a Decision icon can be used to manipulate or alter the lesson flow. Consider, for example, a case in which the designer wishes to select a series of test questions from an item pool. The Decision icon allows the designer to select a given number of questions and to do so sequentially, randomly, or according to some specified criterion.

The Decision icon is also an invaluable development tool. Creative use of Decision icons can result in the solution of many awkward programming problems.

How Does the Decision Icon Work?

A Decision structure is made up of two parts: a Decision icon and one or more icons attached to the Decision icon that are called Paths. The Decision icon manages the logic of the Decision structure and controls branching and repeating. Branching refers to the path that is selected; repeating refers to the number of times the Decision structure is used.

A path is an icon attached to the Decision structure. A path may be any icon except an interaction, another Decision icon, or a Framework icon. However, because a Map icon can be used as a path, in effect, any icon can be used as a path by embedding icons within maps.

Many people routinely use maps to make Paths in Decision structures. In the same way in which they are useful in Interaction structures, Map icons are convenient because they can hold many additional icons. In the illustration below, the Decision structure includes a Decision icon and three Map icons as paths. Each icon attached to the Decision structure represents a new path. Each path is numbered. The leftmost icon is the first path in the Decision structure, the next icon is the second path, etc.

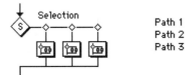

Opening Decision Icons

Two principal decisions must be made concerning the Decision icon:

- The order in which the paths will be accessed—known as branching options.
- The number of times the Decision icon will be employed—known as repeat options.

Double-click the Decision icon to access the branching and repeating options.

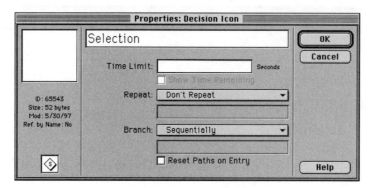

The order in which the paths are chosen is determined by using branching options:

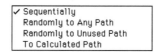

- *Sequentially* selects the paths, beginning with the leftmost path (Path 1) and continuing in order from left to right with the other icons attached to the Decision icon (e.g., Path 1, Path 2, Path 3,…).
- *Randomly to Any Path* selects a path at random from the paths attached to the Decision icon. Furthermore, the selected path is replaced in the pool and may be reselected (e.g., Path 2, Path 4, Path 2, Path 1,…)
- *Randomly to Unused Path* selects a path at random from the paths attached to the Decision icon. Once it is selected, the path will not be chosen again unless the entire Decision structure is reused (e.g., Path 3, Path 4, Path 1, Path 2).
- *To Calculated Path* uses a variable to select a path. This option is the most difficult to understand because it uses variables, and variables are still unfamiliar to many readers. To Calculated Path selects the path number equal to the value stored in a variable. Suppose, for example, that a user variable titled Choice is placed into the *n*th path slot.

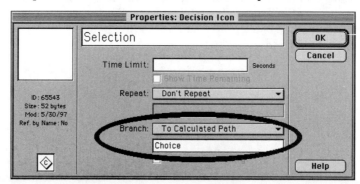

If Choice = 3, then the third path attached to a Decision icon would be chosen. It is important to realize that the Calculated Path option cannot be properly implemented until the concept of variables is understood.

Repeating controls the number of times a user must follow a path. Returning to the previous example, where each path of a Decision icon represents a test item, if the designer wants to end the test after the student answers five questions, the designer would repeat the Decision icon five times.

```
┌─────────────────────────────┐
│  Fixed Number of Times      │
│  Until All Paths Used       │
│  Until Click/Keypress       │
│  Until True                 │
│  ✓ Don't Repeat             │
└─────────────────────────────┘
```

However, if the designer wants the student to continue until five questions are answered correctly without errors, the designer might enter the following statement into the Until True box:

$$FirstTryCorrect = 5.$$

In this case, the designer would be using a variable to control how many times the Decision icon repeats.

Examples

1. The uppercase S in the Decision icon below indicates that Authorware will select paths sequentially—that is, Path 1, Path 2, Path 3 etc. However, we can discover how many paths will be selected only by opening the Decision icon.

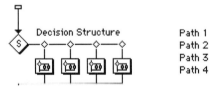

Decision Structure   Path 1
                                  Path 2
                                  Path 3
                                  Path 4

2. In the case below, Authorware will select a path at random. No item will be selected twice. Authorware will repeat the Decision icon until all the paths have been selected.

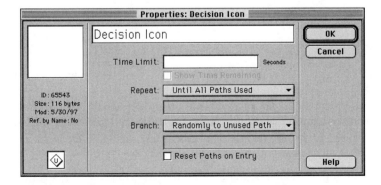

3. In the case shown below, the path chosen is dependent upon a user-defined variable titled Lesson.

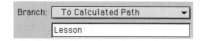

How Can I Use a Decision Icon as a Programming Tool?

It must be emphasized that the next example will make sense only to those who have at least a working knowledge of variables. Other readers may want to skip this section until after completing Chapter 11.

One common development problem occurs when the designer wants to vary the lesson sequence for different users. For example, a designer may want the lesson to follow a given path only if the user has already completed some part of the lesson. In such cases, the path can be attached to a Decision icon and controlled with a variable.

The illustration below describes such a case. Here, one path is attached to a Decision icon. On the surface, it may appear that the path (titled Glossary Help) is available to all users. However, inspection of the Decision icon reveals that the path is controlled by the user variable titled Event. The paths in the Decision icon are numbered, with the leftmost path starting at 1. In other words, no path will be selected.

In this case, Glossary Help will be available only if the current value of the variable $= 1$. If the variable $= 0$, then Path 0 will be selected.

To provide access to the information stored in Path 1, the designer must include the calculation

$$Event = 1$$

at some point in the lesson and prior to the Decision icon. This task can be done, for example, at the end of an icon sequence presented earlier in the lesson:

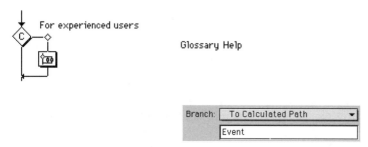

STUDY EXERCISES

1. Construct a five-item quiz that ends when the student has completed four items. Present items in random order, but present each item only once.

2. • Use the Decision icon to simulate the rolling of a single die, and display the result in a Display icon.
   • Use the Decision icon to simulate the rolling of two dice, and display the results in a Display icon.

3. The following questions require the use of a variable and should not be attempted until after completing Chapter 11 on variables.

Create three branches for a tutorial, and store each branch as a Decision icon path. Place an Interaction icon immediately before the Decision icon to ask the user to type 1, 2, or 3 to indicate the branch he or she wishes to select (e.g., type "1" to choose math, "2" to choose science, etc.). Use a Calculated path in the Decision icon to select Branch 1 if the student types 1, Branch 2 if the student types 2, and Branch 3 if the student types 3.

4. Create a file that randomly selects playing cards from a deck of cards. Each time the user presses a button, a randomly selected card should appear on the screen. The user should be able to select cards until every card has been chosen.

There are several ways to create such a file. You might use Decision icons to:

- Determine a card number between 1 and 13.
- Select one of four suits.

You must also keep track of cards that have already been selected (i.e., make sure that cards are not returned to the deck).

11

Calculation Icons: Variables $\boxed{=}$

CHAPTER OVERVIEW

Before the advent of the desktop computer, many people shied away from computers because they were so difficult to use. Operators were required to use awkward sets of instructions to make their machines work, and even tiny errors were sufficient to generate lengthy error reports. Recently, computers have become much easier to operate. Thanks to the creation of the mouse and the development of new computer interfaces, most people learn to use computers quite easily.

Despite the improvements in software interfaces, many new users soon look for shortcuts to operate their computers and begin to use sets of keystrokes that resemble those used by their predecessors. For example, you are probably used to running an Authorware file by pressing Command-R (or Control-R, on a PC) instead of using the pulldown menu or the Run button. In effect, one's need for a graphic interface—once critical to effective computer use—diminishes.

The manner in which users operate their computers has a parallel in the use of variables and functions within Authorware. The icons you have examined to date are actually graphic interfaces for various operations. These interfaces are generally easy to use because they include many prompts and instructions, in addition to providing fields and menus that are often intuitive.

As your confidence with Authorware expands, your dependence on the interface will decrease, and your willingness to work abstractly will increase. When this occurs, you are ready to begin to work with variables and functions. Authorware's potential cannot be unleashed until functions and variables are understood. They make design flexible, and their creative use can bypass many development problems.

Many designers will find this chapter and Chapter 12 difficult to comprehend at first. The difficulty tends to be greatest for those who have never used a computer-programming language. However, with practice, most people prevail and become much more effective designers.

Chapters 11 and 12 introduce functions and variables. Mastering their use involves many months, or even years, of practice. Most people become adept at using them when they become involved with a real-life development task that requires designers to seek out tools that will resolve specific needs.

CHAPTER OBJECTIVES

After completing this chapter, you will be able to:
- Open the Calculation icon to use variables and leave written comments.
- Understand differences between numeric, character, and logical variables.
- Create your own variables.
- Type variables into Display icons to display their contents.
- Type variables into fields within dialog boxes to control icons.

KEY TERMS

Calculation icon
Variables
System variables
User variables
Ornaments
Leaving comments
Variables

SUPPORT MATERIALS

On the CD-ROM disk, run the file titled **Videos.a4r** and select the button labeled **Chapter 11**. **Chapter 11** includes three videos that examine three types of tasks that can be performed with variables. From the SUPPORT folder on the CD, open the file titled **CHP11.a4p**. Run the file and examine how variables can be used to control page numbering and other valuable lesson information. Use the Text tool to examine each of the variables on the screen.

PROJECT 9: VARIABLES

Materials Needed to Complete This Project

- Your file from the previous project, **PROJ8.a4p**
- Macromedia Authorware 4.0 for Macintosh or Windows

Before You Begin

Allow approximately 30 minutes to complete this project.

Project Description

In this project, you will add functionality to the shell you created in Project 8. You will collect data from the end user and store this information in variables. These variables will be used in the following project to guide the user to a decision about his or her ability to afford a mortgage.

Activity

Begin by opening the Authorware file from the previous project. From the File pulldown menu, choose Save As ... and name the file **PROJ9**. Open the Map icon titled **Can I afford a mortgage?** Open the Map icon titled **Variables**. Place an Interaction icon on the Level 3 flow line and title it **Mortgage wanted**.

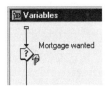

Place a Map icon into the Interaction structure. Select Text Entry as the response type, and title it * (i.e., an asterisk for a wildcard). See Chapter 5 for a summary of wildcards.

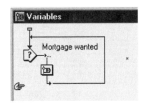

Select the wildcard Map icon. From the Modify pulldown menu, select Icon > Calculation ... and type the following text:

$$Mortgage:=EntryText$$

EntryText is a variable that records whatever information the user types into a text-entry interaction. The Calculation we are entering here will transfer the contents of EntryText into a new variable titled Mortgage. If we don't transfer the information into another variable, the contents of EntryText will change at the next text-entry interaction.

When you close the window, a dialog box will appear. Click on Yes to save your changes to the Calculation.

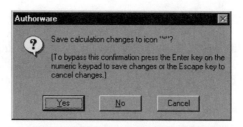

Another dialog box will wait for you to initialize the variable you have just created (i.e., Mortgage). Type the following description of the variable, and then click OK:

Open the Interaction icon titled **Mortgage wanted** and type the following text:

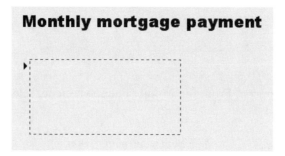

Open the Response options for the wildcard response either by selecting the wildcard Map icon with the mouse and choosing Icon > Response ... from the Modify pulldown menu or by double-clicking the Response options button located just above the wildcard Feedback icon.

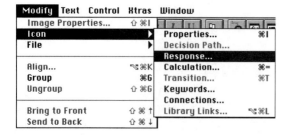

Set the following options for Erasing, Judging, and Branching.

Now you will create four more Interaction structures to collect more data from the user. Specifically, the user will enter his or her monthly gross income, credit-card debt, car payment, and other financial obligations. To save time and to ensure consistent text placement, copy the Interaction structure you just created and paste four copies onto the flow line.

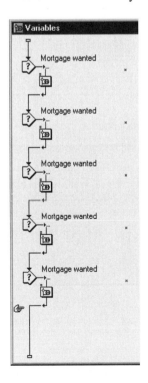

Rename the second Interaction icon **Gross income**. Open the attached ornament (the small equals sign in the top left corner of the Map icon) either by highlighting the Map icon and selecting Icon > Calculation … from the Modify pulldown menu or by double-clicking on the equals sign.

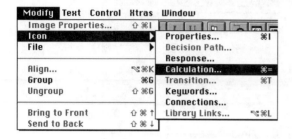

Replace the current contents with the following:

GrossIncome:=EntryText

Close the window. In the New Variable dialog box, enter the following description for the variable titled **GrossIncome**, and then click OK:

Open the Interaction icon titled **Gross income** and type the following text:

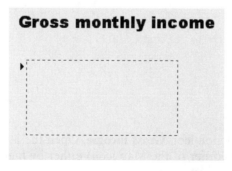

Rename the third Interaction icon **Credit cards**. Open the attached ornament, delete the current contents, and type the following:

CreditCards:=EntryText

Close the window and save the contents. In the New Variable dialog box, enter the following description, and then click OK:

Open the Interaction icon titled **Credit cards** and type the following text:

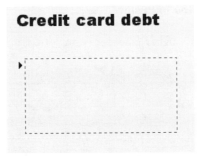

Rename the fourth Interaction icon **Cars**. Open the attached ornament, delete the current contents, and type the following:

Cars:=EntryText

Close the window and save the contents. In the New Variable dialog box, enter the following description, and then click OK:

Open the Interaction icon titled **Cars** and type the following text:

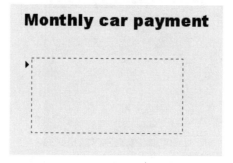

Rename the fifth Interaction icon **Other commitments**. Open the attached ornament, delete the current contents, and type the following:

OtherExpenses:=EntryText

Close the window and save the contents. In the New Variable dialog box, enter the following description, and then click OK:

Open the Interaction icon titled **Other commitments** and type the following text:

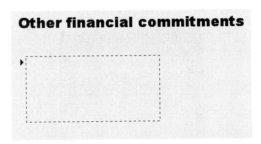

Now place two more Calculation icons on the flow line and title them **Total liabilities** and **Expert advisor**. Two operations will be performed in these icons to sum the user's personal debt and to determine whether his or her personal debt falls within acceptable loan limits.

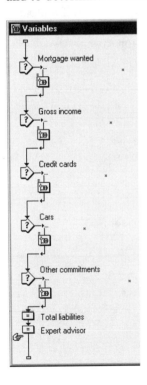

The next variable is used to store the sum of the user's debts. Open the Calculation icon titled **Total liabilities** and type the following:

Debts:=CreditCards+Cars+OtherExpenses

Close the window and save the contents. In the New Variable dialog box, enter the following description, and then click OK:

The following function subtracts debts from income, multiplies the result by 28%, and compares the result to the requested mortgage amount (this statistic is often used by banks and other lenders to decide whether to extend a loan). In plain English, the function says:

1. Subtract total monthly debts from total monthly income.
2. Multiply the result of Step 1 by .28.
3. Determine whether the result of Step 2 is greater than the amount stored in the variable titled Mortgage to assign the value True or False.
4. If Step 3 is True, then place the value 1 into the variable titled Advisor.
5. If Step 3 is False, then place the value 2 into the variable titled Advisor.

Open the Calculation icon titled **Expert advisor** and type the following:

```
Test((GrossIncome-Debts)*.28>Mortgage,Advisor:=1,Advisor:=2)
```

Close the window and save your work.

UNDERSTANDING THE DETAILS

How Do I Enter Information into a Calculation Icon?

There are two ways to enter information into a Calculation:

1. By opening a Calculation icon on the Course flow line.
2. By embedding a Calculation into another icon.

To open a Calculation icon, drag the icon onto the Course flow line and double-click the icon.

Now, type your entry and save before closing the Calculation icon window. If you close the icon window before saving, you will be asked to save your entry. If you fail to do so, you will lose any changes you may have made.

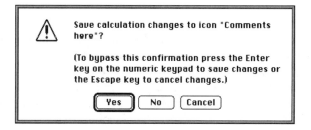

Can Other Icons Perform Calculations?

You can also embed a calculation into any other icon. This approach is useful when you want to ensure that an icon and a calculation are directly connected. Embedding a calculation into an icon is like merging two icons into one.

Embedding calculations into other icons also helps ensure that commands are executed in the correct sequence. Whenever an icon includes an embedded calculation, the commands in the Calculation icon are performed before the icon is executed.

You can tell whether an icon has an attached calculation simply by looking at the icon. Icons with attached calculations have an equals sign attached to them. This marker is referred to as an ornament. For example:

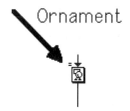

The ornament in the above illustration indicates that the Display icon includes an embedded calculation. The Display icon in the next picture does not.

To create an ornament (i.e., embed a calculation in an icon) or to read the contents of an ornament, highlight the icon and select Icon > Calculation... from the Modify pulldown menu. Enter text into the Calculation window that opens.

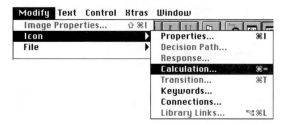

Leaving Comments

A Calculation icon can be used as a notepad. You can leave comments to yourself or other designers by typing two dashes (i.e., --) followed by the comment.

Comments are generally used in two ways. First, they are used to document complex processes that may be easily forgotten. Sometimes designers use several variables and functions in a single Calculation icon to resolve a problem. Comments help you retrace your steps, especially when you have not worked on a file recently. Second, comments help designers communicate lesson details to each other.

What Is a Variable?

Variables are like containers. However, whereas containers usually hold different types of objects—such as fuses, nails, or spaghetti—variables contain information that may be useful in a lesson. For example, variables may contain students' names, dates on which lessons were completed, students' achievement levels, and other information that may guide the design process.

Where Do I Use Variables?

Variables may be used in three locations:

- In Display icons

- In Calculation icons
- In fields within dialog boxes

How Do I Use a Variable?

To use a variable, either type the variable's name where you want it to appear (for example, in a Display icon or a field in a Dialog box) or place the cursor where you want the variable to be and select Paste from the Variables dialog box in the Window pulldown menu.

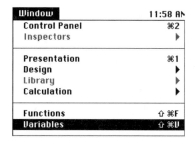

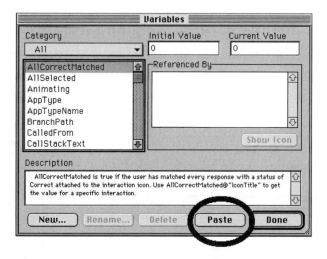

When Do I Use Variables?

Variables are used to perform three types of tasks: to present information in Display icons; to trigger events; and to track information.

To Display Information on the Screen

The contents of a variable may be displayed on a screen by typing the variable name within curly braces in a Display.

Note: You **must** use { }, not [ ].

Example: Type the following text into a Display icon. When you are done, choose the Selection tool with your mouse.

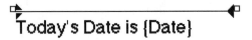

Today's Date is {Date}

This input produces the following display when the selection tool is chosen:

Today's Date is 9/3/97

To Trigger Events

You may have noticed that some icons include a field titled Active If.

In the field, you may compare a variable to a condition. If the condition is true, the event is triggered.

> *Example*: Imagine that you want a Help button to become active only when students have scored below 70%. If you type into the Active If True field

```
PercentCorrect<70
```

the option will be activated only when the value of the variable PercentCorrect falls below 70.

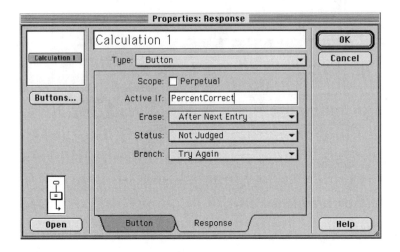

To Track Information

Variables can be used as counters. Each time an event occurs, a counter can be used to "keep score."

> *Example*: To increment a student's score following a correct response, you can enter the following statement into a Calculation icon:

```
TotalCorrect:=TotalCorrect+1
```

This statement adds 1 to the old value of the system variable TotalCorrect. So, if the student had previously answered six questions correctly, the total is updated to seven following another correct response.

Types of Variables

Although recent versions of Authorware do not explicitly refer to different classes of variables, it is important that you understand that different classes do exist, that each class stores different types of information, and that Authorware expects information to be entered in different ways.

Authorware uses three types of variables: numerical, character, and logical. Numerical variables contain numbers; for example, the mathematical constant Pi contains the value 3.1415926536. Character variables contain text; for example, the words "Happy birthday!" can be stored in a character variable. Logical variables contain the truth of a variable; that is, either true or false. For example, the truth of the statement "Today is Tuesday" can be stored in a logical variable.

The difference between numerical and character variables is especially important. Numerical variables can be manipulated with mathematical functions. However, character variables contain only text and, therefore, cannot be manipulated mathematically. For example, if two numeric variables named First and Last contain the values 1 and 5, respectively, then

```
First + Last = 6
```

However, if First and Last were character variables containing the words "Happy" and "Sad", we could *not* add the variables! Luckily, Authorware is rather forgiving and "senses" whether you are working with numeric or character variables. In general, Authorware recognizes character variables by noting quotation marks around the contents of variables. In the example below, the variable BestFriend is a character variable because the information stored in the variable is presented in quotation marks.

```
BestFriend:="Bill"
```

However, the statement

```
BestFriend:=21
```

is just as valid. In this case, however, BestFriend contains numeric data.

Note: The values 0, False, and Off are equivalent. Likewise, the values 1, True, and On are interchangeable.

System Variables

One of Authorware's strengths is that numerous system variables have been created for you. System variables can be accessed through the Window pulldown menu.

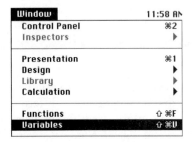

System variables are programmed to contain information that may be useful during a lesson. For example, the system variable PercentCorrect contains an up-to-the-minute record of the student's performance during a lesson. System variables save the designer considerable development time that otherwise would be needed to collect such information. However, if a variable fails to perform a given task, the designer may need to create his or her own variables. These variables are known as user variables.

The Variables window displays a list of system variables. Click a variable to learn information relevant to that specific variable. The illustration below shows the variable titled CursorX. CursorX has an initial value of zero and a current value of 96. Based upon information listed in the Description window, it is evident that the mouse on my computer is 96 pixels from the left edge of the monitor.

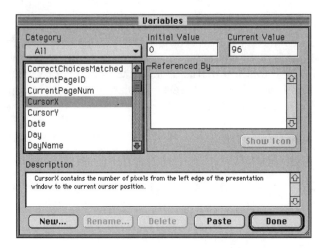

System Variable Categories

Learning to use variables productively takes months, or even years, of practice. Consequently, it is beyond the scope of this text to study variables in depth. Instead, I will outline some of the more commonly used and important variables. Hopefully, this brief examination of variables will convey the broad variety of information that is stored automatically in system variables.

System variables are organized into categories for convenience. This categorization helps prevent the need to search the entire list to find one specific variable. To see the list of categories, click-hold the pulldown window beneath the label Category. You can view an alphabetized list of all the system variables by selecting the All category.

```
✓ All
  Decision
  File
  Framework
  General
  Graphics
  Icons
  Interaction
  Time
  Video

  Variables.a3p
```

Decision Variables

Decision variables store information about decision structures. The variable AllSelected is a logical variable that reports whether all the paths attached to a Decision icon have been selected at least once.

You can use AllSelected to check whether a user has examined every path in a decision structure. Users who have not examined every path may not be permitted to continue the lesson.

File Variables

File variables store information about file sizes and the location of specific files on hard or floppy diskettes. The variable FileLocation is used to identify the location of the current lesson file. The location is important because it is common practice to store a database file containing lesson performance data in the same folder as the lesson file. FileLocation stores the path to the folder that contains the current Authorware file.

For example, if you are a Macintosh user, your hard drive is named Disk500, and your Authorware file titled LessonFile is stored in a folder named Lesson1 in a folder named Practice, then FileLocation will contain the following:

```
Disk500:Practice:Lesson1:
```

If you are a PC user and are working on the "c" drive, then FileLocation will contain the following:

```
c:\Practice\Lesson1\
```

Notice that colons (except for the last one) are used to separate the names of folders. The final colon precedes the file name. On PCs, backslashes (\) perform similar tasks.

Framework Variables

Framework variables store information about framework structures. The variable CurrentPageNum contains the page number of the page in the current framework structure. PageCount contains the total number of pages in the current framework.

Embedding the text

Page {CurrentPageNum} of {PageCount}

into a Display icon in a Framework icon entry panel maintains a page-counting mechanism on the screen.

General Variables

The category General Variables provides an organizing structure for all variables that do not have another home. As such, the types of data stored in this category tend to be quite diverse.

   The variable Dragging indicates whether an object in a Display icon is being dragged by the user. If you want to play a sound file while the user is moving an object on the screen, Dragging lets the system know whether or not the object is being moved.

Graphics Variables

Graphics variables store information that is useful for placing graphics on screens. The variable Layer contains the layer number assigned to an icon. For example, the variable Layer@"Page5" contains the layer number assigned to the display titled Page5. Remember that layers are assigned in the Effects dialog box.

Icon Variables

Icon variables contain a wealth of information about different icons. The variable ExecutingIconTitle is particularly useful in prototype testing and debugging. ExecutingIconTitle contains the title of the icon that is currently being used. Embedding this variable into a display allows the designer to enter text into a display simply by modifying the icon's title.

Interaction Variables

Interaction variables store information gathered while using Interaction icons. EntryText is probably the most commonly used interaction variable. Everything that a user types at a text-entry interaction is stored temporarily in EntryText. For example, consider the following interaction:

Please type your full name.

When the user's name is typed into the computer, the text is stored in EntryText until another text-entry interaction is answered. The variable EntryText can be embedded into a Display icon, or it can be compared to other variables.

Time Variables

Time variables contain information taken from the system clock on the user's computer or from dates that accompany files. For example, the variable Hour contains the number that relates to the current hour (i.e., 0–23). At 11 P.M. Hour contains the value 23, and at midnight Hour contains the value 0.

Designers often embed time variables into Display icons. Typing the variable SessionTime into a Display allows the user to view the amount of time invested in the present lesson.

Video Variables

Video variables help control digital movies and videodisk players. The variable VideoResponding is a logical variable that indicates whether a connection has been made between a video device and the computer. If the value stored in VideoResponding is true, a connection has been made. You can use VideoResponding to determine whether to start playing a videodisk.

User Variables

Although Authorware provides a diverse set of system variables, you will often find that no variable exists to meet your immediate needs. In such cases, it is necessary for you to create you own variables, known as user variables.

How Do I Create a User Variable?

To create a user variable:

- From the Window pulldown menu, select Variable (the Variables dialog box will appear).

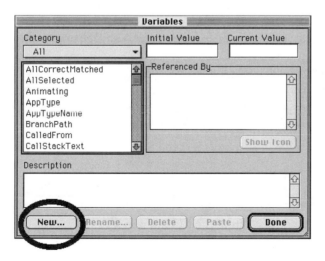

- Press the button labeled New....
- Type a name for the new variable. (Don't pick a name already assigned to a system variable!) Try to select a meaningful name rather than a set of random characters.

- State an initial value (i.e., a starting point for the variable). The initial value remains until it is changed during the lesson. Remember that values given to character variables must be entered within quotation marks. If you enter a word (as opposed to a number) and leave out the quotation marks, Authorware will assume that you are trying to enter the name of another variable.

- Document the variable in the space provided. Provide sufficient information for another designer to be able to understand the purpose of the variable.

  Note: You do not have to create a new variable before using it. Simply type the variable in a Calculation icon, a dialog box, or a display. Authorware will prompt you to define the variable and will not continue with the lesson until the variable is either defined or deleted.

What Can I Do with Variables?

The following examples demonstrate common ways that variables are used in files:

Example 1
This example illustrates how the value of a variable can be changed automatically.

- Type the variable FullTime into a Display icon and run the lesson. Notice that FullTime doesn't change its value after it has been embedded into the display, even though the time is constantly changing. However, Authorware has the capacity to update variables as soon as their values change. In other words, variables such as FullTime can change to reflect their new values.

To update the value of a variable:

- Highlight or open the Display icon containing the variable you want to update.
- Select Icon > Properties… from the Modify menu.

- Check the Update Displayed Variables box.

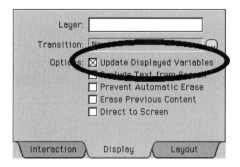

- Rerun the lesson.

What effect does this option have on the variable? Notice how the time is now constantly updated. Also, the time remains on the screen until it is removed with an Erase icon.

Example 2
This example illustrates how the contents of one variable can be transferred to another. The example illustrates how a system variable named FirstName is automatically generated from the system variable UserName. Remember that the variable EntryText stores students' responses at text-entry interactions.

- Create an interaction with a Text Entry response. Ask the user to enter his or her first and last names.
- Use a wildcard (*) to accept any entry. The text typed by the student will be stored in EntryText. The Map icon used for feedback in the following example is a "dummy" icon. It contains no information, but allows the designer to collect a response from the user.

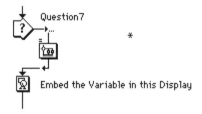

The calculation transfers the contents of EntryText into the variable UserName. The calculation contains the following:

UserName:=EntryText

- Type the variables UserName and FirstName into a Display icon.
- Run the lesson to observe the result. Notice that the system variable FirstName contains the user's first name, even though you didn't put it there! FirstName is created automatically by Authorware. It contains the first word stored in the variable UserName.

Example 3

This example illustrates how a user variable can control whether a button appears or is hidden on the screen. Hiding buttons is important when users move from one screen to another. For example, in the following illustration, the designer may want to turn off each of the navigation buttons when an option is selected in order to prevent the buttons from cluttering the following screen:

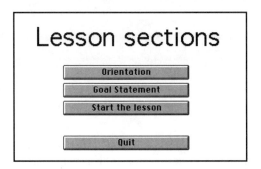

You can use a variable to hide a button. The variable can make the button inactive. The Active If: field in the illustration below contains the user variable ShowButton. The variable operates like a switch. If ShowButton is true, the button shows; otherwise it is hidden from view.

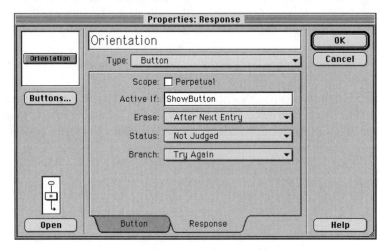

The value of the variable is entered in a calculation. You can use the following Calculation icon in the entry panel of a Framework icon to ensure that the button is off:

This technique is powerful because it allows you to make options available at different times during a lesson simply by changing the value of a variable. Be careful with calculations that turn buttons on or off. You need to be sure that you carefully plan and place calculations to ensure that buttons don't suddenly disappear when needed!

Example 4

One popular navigation technique involves marking a menu to orient the user. Together, an Animation icon and a variable can animate an object to create a navigation marker. In this example, we will animate a check mark on the navigation menu from the previous example.

First create the Menu buttons:

- Place an Interaction icon on the flow line.
- Add three Map icons to the interaction structure and select Button for the response type. Title the buttons **Orientation**, **Goal Statement**, and **Start the Lesson**. Run the icons and place the buttons to suit your taste.

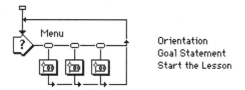

- Open the Interaction icon and type the title Lesson Sections.
- Embed calculations in each of the following Map icons:

Orientation: ButtonMarker=1

Goal Statement: ButtonMarker=2

Start the Lesson: ButtonMarker=3

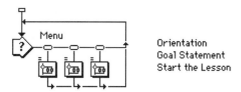

- Add another Interaction icon to the flow line. Title the Interaction icon **Animate Marker**. Add a Map icon to the interaction structure and select Conditional for the response type. Title the Map icon **ButtonMaker** $<>0$.
- Open the Response options for the Map icon and select the following options:

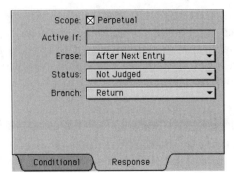

- Close the response options; then open the Map icon.

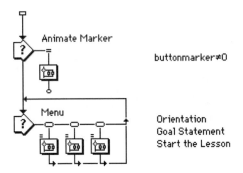

- Add Display, Animation, and Calculation icons to the Level 2 flow line. Title the icons as follows:

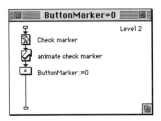

- Open the Display icon and place a check mark (or some other graphic) on the Presentation window.
- Open the Calculation icon and type the following: ButtonMarker:=0
- Run the lesson. Select an option from the menu. The file will stop when it reaches the undefined Animation icon. Select Direct to Line for the animation type and set Timing to zero, as outlined below:

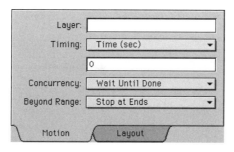

- Select the Layout tab. Click the radio button titled **Base**. Notice the instruction "Drag object to base position." Drag the check box to its starting position (i.e., the top of the list). (*Note:* You may need to move the dialog box to access the graphic.)

The instruction will change to "Select End to define end position." Select the **End** radio button; then drag the check box to the end of the list. (*Note:* Be careful not to drag the anchor at the center of the object.)

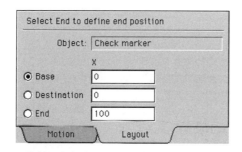

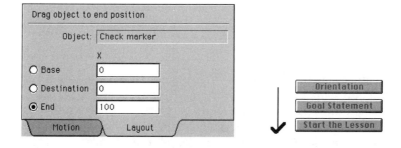

- Select the button titled **Destination** and enter the following values in the fields:

```
Drag object to destination

       Object:  Check marker

                   X
  ○ Base          1

  ⦿ Destination   ButtonMarker

  ○ End           3

         Motion          Layout
```

- Finally, test your animated navigation tool.

Special Features

The Assignment Operator

There is an important difference between the symbols = (i.e., an equals sign) and := (i.e., the assignment operator). An equals sign is usually used to test the value of a variable. For example, the calculation

$$\text{Test(Score=10,Example:=1,Example:=2)}$$

checks the value of Score.

However, the assignment operator is used to transfer information into a variable. The calculation

$$\text{Score:=10}$$

places the value 10 into the variable Score.

Authorware is often smart enough to recognize the difference between the two cases and automatically replaces the equals sign with the assignment operator when necessary. Consequently, if in doubt, leave out the colon.

Resetting System Variables

Some variables can be assigned values, but others cannot. For example, the system variable TotalCorrect can be reset to 0 (or any other number). However, most system variables are "read only." For example, the variable Day, which contains the name of the current day of the week, takes its value from the system clock and, consequently, cannot be changed.

Reusing System Variables

Variables frequently change their values during lessons. However, Authorware never forgets the values assigned to some variables. For example, the variable EntryText changes its value every time a student answers a new text-entry interaction. Luckily, although the value of EntryText changes, Authorware remembers old values of the variable. To access the value of a variable at a specific time during the lesson, use the following format: Variable@"IconName"

Example: EntryText@"question11"

This example once again illustrates the importance of using unique icon names to avoid ambiguity.

Note: Not all variables contain multiple values. Check the Authorware manual or the Variables dialog box for detailed information on each variable.

STUDY EXERCISES

1. Look up the following variables and provide a brief description of the types of information stored in each:

Variable Name	Description
ClickX	
Day	
DayName	
EntryText	
FileLocation	
FileName	
FirstName	
Hour	
MachineName	
MemoryAvailable	
PathSelected	
PercentCorrect	
Sessions	
ShiftDown	
UserName	
WordCount	

2. Type the text below into Display icons to show the contents of the variables:
- Today's date is {Date}.
- The present time {FullTime}.
- The type of computer on which I am working is a {MachineName}.
- The value of pi is {Pi}.
- I have been working on this lesson for {SessionTime} hours and minutes.

Search the list of system variables and select five more variables to embed in displays. Read the description of each variable in the Variables dialog box.

3. Authorware includes a system variable to store students' names. The variable is titled UserName, and it contains students' first and last names. When UserName is used, Authorware automatically creates a new variable that contains the user's first name. Not surprisingly, this variable is titled FirstName!
   How can you obtain the student's first name?

   - Ask the user to type his or her first and lastpbb names at a Text Entry interaction.
   - Embed the following Calculation into a Feedback icon:

   Remember to close and save the changes to the Calculation icon.

   - Now type the following two variables into a Display icon within curly brackets: {UserName} and {FirstName}.

5. User-defined variables can be used to collect information during a lesson. User variables are particularly useful when the designer wants to collect information that is not stored in system variables. The next question employs user variables to assist lesson navigation.
   One of the greatest difficulties in computer-based lessons is navigating through information screens. Navigating through a book is much easier: Just skim the pages. To compensate, many designers include page numbers and indicate the total number of pages or screens in a unit (e.g., This is Page 3 of 7 pages).
   The following exercise illustrates how to use user variables to keep track of page numbers:

   - Create a linear sequence of Display and Wait icons (approximately six screens). Title the screens Screen1–Screen6. (Although the information is not important, make sure that you include some content in each Display icon.)
   - Create a new variable titled Screencount. Set the initial value of Screencount to the number of pages in the presentation.
   - Create a new variable titled Counter. Set the initial value of Counter to 0.
   - Place a new Display icon titled **Page Counter** at the top of the flow line. Embed both Screencount and Counter into the Display icon at the border of the screen (i.e., Type the following: Page {Counter} of {Screencount}).
   - While still in the Display icon titled **Page Counter**, select Icon > Properties from the Modify menu and select Update Displayed Variables.

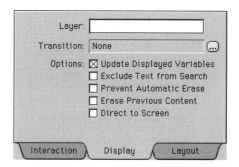

- Embed the following Calculations into Screen1, Screen2, etc.
  Counter:=1
  Counter:=2
  Counter:=3
  etc.

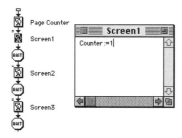

- Run the lesson and notice how the page numbers are updated.

6. Now repeat the exercise using a counter to update the value of the variable. This exercise employs the concept of incrementing variables. In this exercise, page numbers are updated by increasing the value of the variable Counter by 1 in each new display, as opposed to including a specific value for the variable.

   That is, the variable Counter is updated without the specific page number attributed to each screen frame constantly having to be entered.

   - Use the same linear sequence of Display, Wait, and Erase icons used in question 5.
   - Replace the Calculation embedded into Display1, Display2, Display3, etc. with the following:

   $$Counter:=Counter+1$$

   - Run the file and observe the result.

7. One way to make instruction more relevant involves using personal data to individualize questions. In the following question, you will use data collected during a lesson to personalize instruction.

   Create a series of text-entry responses in which you ask the user to input personal information. For example, you may ask the user to name his or her favorite food, friends' names sport, hobby, etc. Remember that information typed into the computer at text-entry interactions is stored in the variable named EntryText. After collecting each entry, assign the contents of EntryText to user variables. For example: Food:=EntryText; Friend:=EntryText; etc. Now, create either a story or a series of questions that is "personalized" by including the information gained from the user.

Calculation Icons: Functions ▣

CHAPTER OVERVIEW

Consider the following scenarios:

1. You ask a user to enter his or her full name into the computer. From this information, how can you separate the user's first name and last name?

2. A user enters two numbers into a simulation to find the approximate area of a rectangle. The computer will multiply these numbers and print the result on the screen. However, you want to display only whole numbers. How can you remove any decimals from the result?

3. In a backgammon game, the user will play against the computer. How can the computer generate random numbers to determine the values for the dice?

4. You want to collect lesson information; such as the names of users who have completed a lesson, the dates lessons were completed, and lesson scores. How can variables be connected into a single variable?

5. Many lessons record students' performances and store the information in a data file. How can you record the information from the previous scenario in a text file on the computer?

6. You want to use and display the history of a student's progress. Such information is commonly stored in a data file on the user's computer. How can you read the content of a data file into an Authorware display?

7. In a concept-learning lesson, users must create concept maps that connect related ideas. How can you use Authorware to create a graphics program that will allow the user to create concept maps?

8. Designers often transfer data files into lessons. These files can be disassembled and stored in many different variables so that the information can be used in the lesson. How can you transfer records from a text file into a lesson without having to use many variables?

Creating files to achieve each of these scenarios involves understanding and using system functions. In this chapter, we will examine how functions work and illustrate their capabilities.

Functions are one of the most important and most difficult concepts to understand and use. To understand the full potential of Authorware's functions, try to become involved in a development project. Solving real-world design problems will help you understand how functions work.

CHAPTER OBJECTIVES

After completing this chapter, you will be able to:
- Understand the differences between variables and functions.
- Know how to use functions.
- Know where to find online documentation about functions.
- Apply system functions to perform a range of tasks, including:
  - Manipulating data
  - Creating data files
  - Concatenating variables
  - Collecting important lesson data

KEY TERMS

Functions
Online documentation
Concatenation

SUPPORT MATERIALS

On the CD-ROM disk, run the file titled **Videos.a4r** and select the button labeled **Chapter 12**. **Chapter 12** includes two videos that examine functions. From the SUPPORT folder on the CD, open the file titled **CHP12.a4p**. Run the file to see how functions can generate sounds or create a simple graphics application.

PROJECT 10: FUNCTIONS

Materials Needed to Complete This Project

- Your file from the previous project, **PROJ9.a4p**
- Macromedia Authorware 4.0 for Macintosh or Windows

Before You Begin

Allow approximately 60 minutes to complete this project.

Project Description

In this project, you will continue to add functionality to the shell you developed in Projects 8 and 9. You will use functions and variables to create a mortgage calculator that will be used to determine the user's mortgage payments.

Activity

Begin by opening the Authorware file from the previous project. From the File pulldown menu, choose Save As... to rename the file **PROJ10**.

Open the Map icon titled **Functions** and place an Interaction icon on the Level 2 flow line. Title the Interaction icon **Calculator**.

Place a Map icon to the right of the **Calculator** Interaction icon and select Button as the response type. Title the Map icon **Mortgage Calculator**. Open the response options and make the following selections:

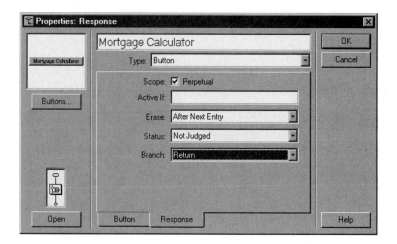

The flow line should now look like this:

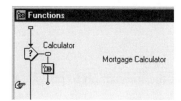

In a moment you will paste icons into the Map icon titled **Mortgage Calculator**. To access the icons you will copy and open the Map icon titled **Can I afford a mortgage?** from the Level 1 flow line; then open the Map icon titled **Variables**. Select and copy the first interaction structure.

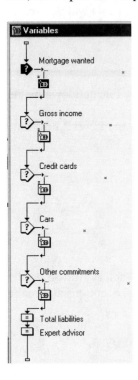

Now paste it onto the **Mortgage Calculator** Level 3 flow line. The flow line should now look like this:

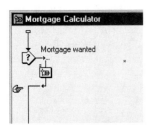

Retitle the Interaction icon **Annual interest rate (as a percentage)**. Add an ornament to this Interaction icon by selecting the icon using the mouse and choosing Icon > Calculation… from the Modify pulldown menu. Enter the following variable:

PresetEntry="%"

This variable will place a percentage sign in the text entry field in the interaction to provide a hint to the user.

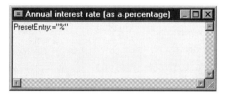

Close the window and save your changes. Open the Interaction icon titled **Annual interest rate...** and change the text to the following:

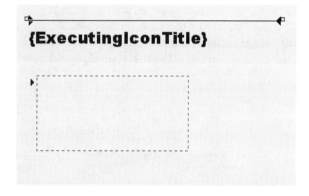

Open the ornament in the upper left corner of the Map icon titled *. Type the following:

AnnualInterestRate:=EntryText

Close the window and save your changes. In the New Variable dialog box, type the following description, and then click OK:

The flow line should now look like this:

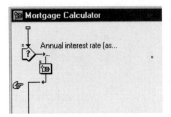

You will use each of the new interaction structures that you create as templates for more inter-action structures. Copy and paste the interaction structure, including the Interaction icon titled **Annual interest rate** and the attached Map icon, immediately beneath the first interaction structure. Retitle the Interaction icon **Principal**. Open the attached ornament and delete the PresetEntry variable. Open the ornament attached to the Map icon and replace the entry with the following:

```
Principal:=EntryText
```

Close the window and save your changes. In the New Variable dialog box, type the following description, and then click OK:

Copy and paste the interaction structure, including the Interaction icon titled **Principal** and the attached Map, onto the flow line immediately beneath the first two interaction structures. Reti-tle the Interaction icon **Years**. Open the ornament attached to the Map icon and replace the entry with the following:

```
Years:=EntryText
```

Close the window and save your changes. In the New Variable dialog box, type the following description, and then click OK:

The flow line should look like this:

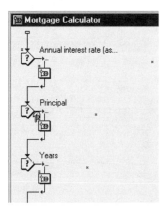

Place a Calculation icon on the flow line below the Interaction icon titled **Years** and title it **Conversions**. Open the icon and type the following (exactly as it appears):

```
MonthlyInterestRate:=AnnualInterestRate/(12*100)
TotalPayments:=Years*12
```

The first line in the Calculation icon determines the interest rate per month. The second line calculates the total number of payments over the life of the loan. Both variables are used later in a formula to compute the interest payment.

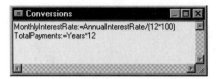

Close the window and save your changes. As you close the window, you will be asked to define the variables. In the New Variable dialog box, type the following description, and then click OK:

In the next New Variable dialog box, type the following description, and then click OK:

Place another Calculation icon on the flow line below the **Conversions** Calculation icon. Title it **Monthly payment**. Open the icon and type the following (exactly as it appears):

```
Payment:=Principal*(MonthlyInterestRate/(1-(1+MonthlyInterestRate)**-
TotalPayments))
```

This formula looks difficult, but it is not really complex. The double asterisk (i.e., **) is Authorware's command for an exponent. The formula computes the approximate monthly interest payment.

Close the window and save your changes. In the New Variable dialog box, type the following description, and then click OK:

The flow line should now look like this:

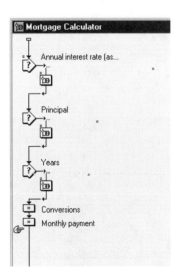

Now it is necessary to place a "mask" on the flow line to prevent text from overlapping. The type of branching selected in Mortgage Calculator (i.e., Return Branching) does not erase the screen automatically, so we need to place a graphic on the screen to cover information showing below.

Place a Display icon at the top of the flow line and title it **Mask**. Place a Display icon, a Wait icon, and an Erase icon at the end of the flow line. Title the Display icon **Mortgage results** and the Erase icon **Erase mortgage results & mask**.

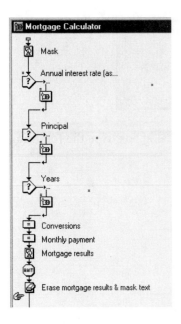

Open the Display icon titled **Mask**. Using the Rectangle tool from the toolbox, draw a large gray rectangle on the Presentation window.

Open the Display icon titled **Mortgage results**. Type the following (remember to use curly brackets to embed the variable):

Your monthly mortgage payment will be approximately =${Payment}

Place Start and Stop flags at the top and bottom of the flow line. Run the file from the flag and place the Continue button on an appropriate location, and use the Erase icon to clear the mask and text from the screen.

The following section involves moving sets of icons to their final destinations. This procedure can be confusing to follow, so try to be patient: The entire project is nearly complete. You will move the work you have completed into the main body of the lesson.

On the Level 1 flow line, open the Map icon titled **Functions**. Now select and cut (don't copy!) the interaction structure containing the **Calculator** Interaction icon and the **Mortgage Calculator** Map icon. Paste the icons onto the Level 1 flow line below the **Help** Interaction icon.

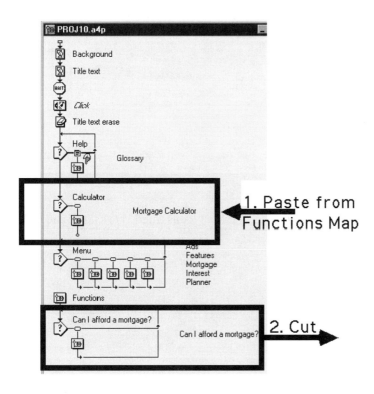

Cut and paste the interaction structure containing the Interaction icon and the Map icons titled **Can I afford a mortgage?** onto the **Planner** Map icon below the Erase icon titled **Erase planner text**.

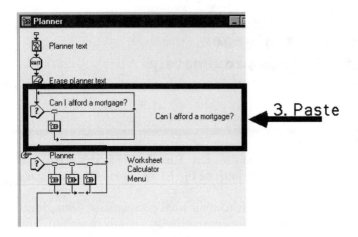

Cut (or drag) the Map icon titled **Menu** from the Planner and paste it next to the Map icon titled **Can I afford a mortgage?**.

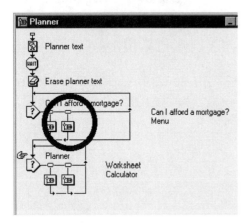

Delete the **Planner** Interaction icon and the two attached Map icons titled **Worksheet** and **Calculator**. The flow line should now look like this:

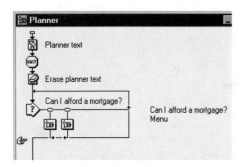

Delete the empty **Functions** Map icon from the Level 1 flow line.

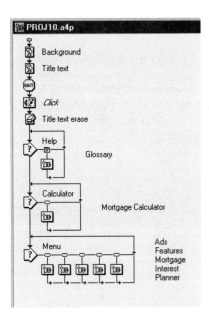

Run your file to check your work. Check that all buttons are properly customized; that text and graphics are properly aligned and erased in the proper order; and that all the navigation works. You will need to edit the buttons titled **Mortgage Calculator** and **Can I afford a mortgage?**, resize the mask to fit the screen, and modify text to make it consistent. Make adjustments as necessary.

Suggestions for Applying What You Have Learned

Obviously, it is critical to find out what is working and what is not. The process of formative evaluation is probably the single most valuable information source available to you. Formative evaluation involves observing potential end-users, who are unfamiliar with the project, as they go through the lesson.

When you conduct formative evaluation, first allow the user(s) to run through the lesson unaided. Don't give hints or explain how to use any of the features. Take notes and ask users to explain where they have difficulty using the lesson. Use this information to add instructions, modify navigation options, and adjust the content.

UNDERSTANDING THE DETAILS

The following sections will:

- Describe how functions work.
- Explain how to use functions.
- Illustrate a range of tasks that functions can perform.

What Is a Function?

Many people confuse variables and functions. However, their roles are quite different. Whereas variables simply store information, functions perform tasks.

Functions are like tools. These tools perform a variety of operations that accelerate lesson development and allow designers to perform tasks that are not normally possible. Just as a skilled carpenter carefully uses a range of tools to produce a professional product, effective Authorware designers use functions to resolve development problems.

How Do I Use a Function?

Functions, like variables, may be used in three locations:

- In Calculation icons.
- In Display icons.
- In dialog boxes.

To use a function, either type in the function's name or access the dialog box by selecting Functions from the Window pulldown menu. Functions are usually entered in Calculation icons, but they can also be used in fields in dialog boxes or in expressions entered within curly brackets in displays.

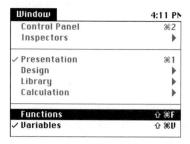

Just as variables are organized into categories, functions also are arranged into one comprehensive list containing 14 categories. To find information about a function, select a category, and then click the function name.

Clicking on the function ASIN produces the next dialog box. Notice that the field titled **Referenced By** contains a single entry, indicating that the function has been used by one icon, titled **Question2**. Double-clicking the label **Question2** leads to that icon on the flow line.

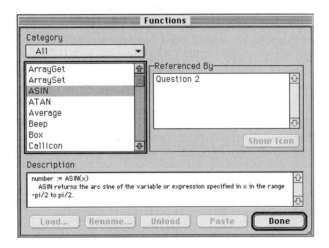

Sometimes Authorware doesn't have a function to complete a specific task. In such cases, designers can create a new function using programming languages like C and PASCAL. Once created, these functions can be loaded into Authorware, where they become a permanent part of the application.

How Can I Learn More About Functions?

Each function is described in the online documentation found in the Functions dialog box. Another approach to learning about functions is to examine the files that accompany Authorware. Examine the functions used in Calculation icons and dialog boxes in those files.

What Types of Tasks Can Functions Perform?

Functions can perform a broad range of tasks, too diverse to describe fully in this text. The following section will describe solutions to each of the problems posed at the beginning of this chapter. The problems have been chosen to illustrate functions' breadth of use and to describe some of the more common tasks performed in course development.

Manipulating Data

Scenario 1: You ask a user to enter his or her full name into the computer. From this information, how can you separate the user's first name and last name?

Solution: The following solution illustrates how functions can manipulate text. In Chapter 11, you used a system variable named EntryText to store a user's name. The system variable FirstName is automatically created by Authorware and contains the first word in UserName. You can use EntryText and the function GetWord to determine the user's last name.

- Create a text-entry interaction.

- Ask the user to type his or her first and last names into the computer.
- After the interaction, enter the following into a Calculation icon:

LastName:=GetWord(2,EntryText)

The function GetWord extracts the second word from the variable EntryText. The result of the transformation is placed into a user variable titled LastName. Remember that words in parentheses are assumed to be variables unless the words are contained within double quotation marks (i.e., " ").

Scenario 2: A user enters two numbers into a simulation to find the approximate area of a rectangle. The computer will multiply these numbers and print the result on the screen. However, you want to display only whole numbers. How can you remove any decimals from the result?

Solution: The following activity illustrates how a function can manipulate numbers:

- Create two text-entry interactions titled "Question1" and "Question2".
- At each interaction, ask the user to type a number into the computer.
- Embed the following into a Calculation icon:

Area:=EntryText@"Question1"*EntryText@"Question2"
Truncated:=INT(Area)

- Place a Display icon on the flow line and type the following text:

Your answer, truncated to the nearest whole number, is {Truncated}.

- The function INT removes any decimals from the variable Area and stores the result in the user variable Truncated. Note that Truncated and Area are user-defined variables.

Scenario 3: In a backgammon game, the user will play against the computer. How can the computer generate random numbers to determine the values for the dice?

Solution: Authorware includes a random number generator that will produce a random number between any two given values in a specified step size. For example, the function

Random(0, 1, .01)

produces random numbers between 0 and 1 in jumps of 1/100.
The product of a random number generator must be transferred into another variable. For example:

First_Die:=Random(0, 1, .01)

will transfer a single random number between 0 and 1, and measured in units of 1/100, into the user variable First_Die.

To produce numbers to use in a backgammon game, you need to generate two random numbers and transfer them into two user variables (named First_Die and Second_Die). The random numbers must be between 1 and 6 and must be whole numbers. The following calculation will produce the desired random numbers:

```
First_Die:=Random(1,6,1)
Second_Die:=Random(1,6,1)
```

Now you can embed the user variables First_Die and Second_Die into a Display icon or into a dialog box, or use them in another calculation.

Concatenation

Scenario 4: You want to collect lesson information, such as the names of users who have completed a lesson, the dates lessons were completed, and lesson scores. How can variables be connected into a single variable?

Solution: Although storing information in variables is a relatively straightforward task, connecting two or more variables into a single variable can be problematic. The technique used to combine two or more variables into a single variable is called Concatenation. The following exercises illustrate how variables can be connected through Concatenation:

Imagine that you have two user variables, one named FirstWord and the other named SecondWord. FirstWord contains the word "Happy". SecondWord contains the word "Birthday". You want to create a variable (named ConnectedText) that contains the contents of FirstWord and SecondWord, separated by a space (i.e., "Happy Birthday"). Remember that text stored in variables cannot be simply "added" together. In other words:

```
FirstWord + Space + SecondWord ≠ Happy Birthday
```

The concatenation operator essentially "glues together" character variables. It is indicated by a ^ (i.e., a carat, or Shift-6) between the variables. Consequently, the solution to the question is:

```
ConnectedText:=FirstWord^" "^SecondWord^"!"
```

Note that a space has been entered to separate the two variables and an exclamation point has been added. Typing the variable ConnectedText into a Display icon will produce the desired result.

Returning to the original scenario, collecting lesson data into a variable is achieved by concatenating several variables. One solution is:

```
StudentData:=LastName^TAB^FirstName^TAB^FullDate^TAB^TotalCorrect^Return
```

Note: Tabs and carriage returns have been used as separators. Tabs and carriage returns have important meaning in most database programs. A tab enters data into a new field, and a carriage return creates a new record.

Writing Data Files

Scenario 5: How can you record the information from the previous scenario in a text file on the computer?

Solution: The following activity creates a file on a hard disk or floppy disk. Before attempting this exercise, make sure that your current Authorware file has been saved onto a hard drive or a floppy diskette: The activity uses the name of the diskette and the folder where the lesson file is stored.

In the previous scenario, you stored lesson information into a variable named StudentData. You will now store this information in a text (ASCII) file using the function AppendExtFile. This function creates a text file in the specified location on the computer. If it already exists, the file is updated. In other words, the new information is added to the existing file.

The function AppendExtFile uses the following syntax:

```
AppendExtFile("filename", string)
```

To use the function, you must provide Authorware with two pieces of information:

filename contains the location and name of the file that you will create or update.
string contains the information that is to be stored inside the data file.

The filename includes the route to the folder where the file is stored and the name of the data file. Remember that the variable FileLocation contains the path to the folder where your lesson file is saved. For convenience, this is the same location where we will store the data file. The string is usually a variable containing organized lesson information.

In the following example, the variable FileLocation and the filename (datafile.txt) have been concatenated using the concatenation operator (i.e., ^). The variable containing data is titled LessonData.

Type the following into a Calculation icon **exactly** as it appears below, without additional characters or spaces:

```
LessonData:="lots of good stuff"
AppendExtFile(FileLocation^"datafile.txt",LessonData)
```

Close the Calculation icon and run the file. After running the file, look inside the folder on your computer that contains your saved Authorware file (note that you must save your file before completing this operation to ensure that Authorware knows where to place the text file). Notice that a new file titled **Datafile.txt** now exists. This file can be opened in a word processor. Open the file and look at its contents. The file should contain the words "lots of good stuff".

To solve the problem presented in the scenario, type the following into a calculation (assuming that the variable StudentData contains some information):

```
AppendExtFile(FileLocation^"datafile.txt",StudentData)
```

Each time Authorware encounters this statement, another entry is added to the file **datafile.txt**. In this way, a database of student performance can be established. The file can be opened in a word processor, database, or spreadsheet program.

Reading an External Data File

Scenario 6: You want to use and display the history of a student's progress. Such information is commonly stored in a data file on the user's computer. How can you read the content of a data file into an Authorware display?

Solution: The following activity will read data from an external text file into Authorware:

- First, use a word processor to create a text file named **Data** that contains a message. Remember to save the file in Text Only format. Place this file on your hard drive in a folder titled Information.
- In Authorware, create a user variable titled Message.
- Use the ReadExtFile function to read the contents of the file titled **Data**.

Type the following into a Calculation icon:

On a Mac

```
Message:=ReadExtFile("your hard drive's name:Information:Data")
```

On a PC

```
Message:=ReadExtFile("c:\Information\Data")
```

- Now embed Message into a Display icon as follows:

```
The content of the data file is {Message}.
```

- Run the file. The text that you typed into the word processor now appears on the computer screen. If it does not appear, place the data file into the folder on your computer where your current Authorware file is stored, and replace the function in the Calculation icon with

```
Message:=ReadExtFile(FileLocation^"Data")
```

Generating Graphics

Scenario 7: How can you use Authorware to create a graphics program that will allow the user to create concept maps?

Solution: Authorware functions allow you to create graphics. You can combine hot-spot interactions with functions to create a graphics palette that can be used to create concept maps that outline relationships between important lesson ideas. Users can draw ovals around related ideas or identify connections with straight lines.

The illustration below describes how to set up graphics tools for users. The interaction creates a hot spot on the screen. The function DrawLine(1) is responsible for creating a drawing tool. The user draws a line by clicking and dragging the mouse anywhere within the hot spot. Remember to resize the hot spot in the interaction display to provide the user with enough space to draw the shape.

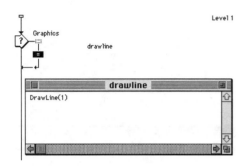

You can create a tool palette by combining multiple drawing functions and an interface that switches on the drawing tools. In the illustration below, the Interaction icon titled **Interface** allows the user to select from three drawing tools—a line, a circle, and a box. Each tool is controlled by using appropriately named user variables in the Active If True box in the hot-spot response options. For example, the options for the hot spot titled Line=true are set as follows:

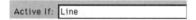

Each hot spot in the interface also switches on the tool to be used. The tool is switched on with a variable. For example, the hot spot titled Line=true contains the calculation:

$$Line=true$$

Switching on the tool allows the user to draw the shape in the drawing area. After using the tool, a user variable switches off the tool, as illustrated below.

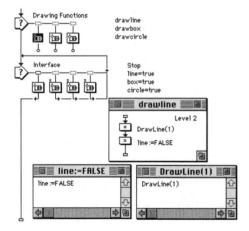

Data Transfer

Scenario 8: How can you transfer records from a text file into a lesson without having to use many variables?

Solution: An array is an organized framework for storing indexed data. The array contains 2,501 cells numbered 0–2,500. Each cell can hold a virtually unlimited supply of information. Importantly, because each cell is numbered, it is possible to systematically store and retrieve information from the array.

Functions are used to place information into or to retrieve information from a cell. The function ArraySet places information into the array. The function ArrayGet retrieves information from the array. For example:

$$ArraySet(251,StudentData)$$

places the contents of the user variable StudentData into cell 251 in the array.

$$ArraySet(777, \text{``Completed''})$$

places the word "Completed" into cell 777.

$$Question1:=ArrayGet(1234)$$

places the contents of cell 1234 into the variable Question1.

To read several records from a text file into an array

Before beginning this exercise, place a text file titled **datafile.txt** into the folder containing your current Authorware file. The text file should contain at least 10 lines of text.

1. Type the following into a Calculation icon titled **Calculation1**:

```
Data:=ReadExtFile(FileLocation^"datafile.txt")
Records:=LineCount(Data)
```

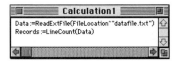

- The function ReadExtFile transfers the contents of the data file into a user variable titled **Data**.
- The number of records (or lines) in the variable Data is counted by the function LineCount and the result stored in the user variable Records.

2. Type the following into a Calculation icon titled **Calculation2**:

```
ReadData:=GetLine(Data,1)
ArraySet(Line,ReadData)
Line:=Line+1
Data:= DeleteLine(Data,1)
```

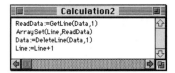

- •The function GetLine transfers the first line of text from Data into the user variable ReadData.
- •The function ArraySet transfers the contents of the variable ReadData into the first cell (cell 0) of the array. (Line is a user variable created with an initial value of 0.)
- •The statement Line:=Line+1 increments the value of the variable Line to move to the next line in the array.
- •The statement Data:=DeleteLine(Data,1) cuts the first line from the variable ReadData.
3. Place a Decision icon on the flow line. Select paths sequentially, and repeat the Decision icon "Records" times.

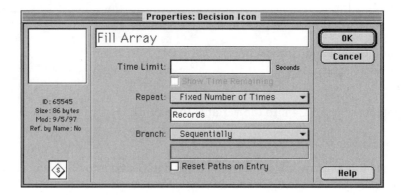

4. Attach **Calculation2** to the Decision framework.
5. Running the file will place the contents of the text file into the array. To see the contents of the array, it is necessary to use the ArrayGet function to transfer the contents of the cells from the array into variables. The following calculation transfers the content of the array into user variables: Cell1, Cell2, Cell3, etc.

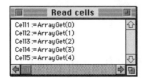

Finally, the variables must be embedded into a display to show their contents.

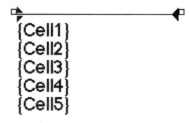

The flow line should appear as follows:

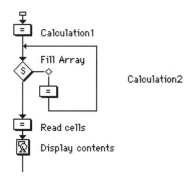

Arrays are very important in advanced courseware design. They are often used to store data sets in what is sometimes called "data-driven design." Data-driven design involves creating templates that use variables to display lesson content in Display icons, instead of typing content directly into Display icons.

Data are transferred from a data file into cells in the array. Functions are used to transfer information from the array into the variables. This technique can greatly improve design efficiency because a single template can be used to create multiple lessons. When using a data-driven design approach, changing lesson content involves creating a new data file or editing an existing file in a word processor, as opposed to developing an entirely new lesson file in Authorware.

STUDY EXERCISES

1. Create a new file and embed the following functions into separate Calculation icons. Examine each function separately.

   - Beep()

   - Box(3,50,50,100,100)

   - Place two Calculation icons on the flow line and place a Wait icon between them.

   In the first Calculation icon, type: ShowTitleBar(Off)

   In the second Calculation icon, type: ShowTitleBar(On)

   Now run the file. What do you notice happening?

2. Create a lesson that asks the user for his or her last name. At the end of the lesson, create a data file, using the given name to title the file. Inside the file, record the time that the student took to complete the lesson.

3. • Use the function titled Random to simulate the roll of a single die.

   • Repeat the exercise to simulate the sum obtained from rolling two dice.

4. Create a generic bank of feedback items that includes statements such as "Great," "Well done," "That's right," etc. Create a mini-lesson and randomly generate such feedback. Try to do the same for incorrect feedback.

   Note: You can also use alternate keys with Hot Spot and Button responses. These alternate keys can be used to activate perpetual responses. That is, within the perpetual response, you can accept a given keypress to act as a Hot Spot or Button response. Then you can use the function PressKey() in a Calculation icon to send a message to the computer that a given key has been pressed (e.g., PressKey ("a")).

5. Use Functions to create a tic-tac-toe game against the computer. This is the child's game where players must connect circles or crosses on a grid. Players alternate, and the winner is the first to connect three like objects in a straight line. An example of a game in progress is as follows:

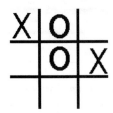

6. Use functions to create a simple game, such as "hangman" or a crossword puzzle.

7. Use functions to create your own graphics application. The application should allow the user to select from three different tools—a rectangle, an oval, or a line. Also, the user should be able to select different line thicknesses for the tools, different colors for the outlines of each tools, and a range of colors for the fills.

   To complete this activity, you will need to use the following functions:

   - DrawLine

   - DrawCircle

   - DrawBox

   - RGB

   - SetFill

   - SetFrame

   - SetLine

Framework Icons

CHAPTER OVERVIEW

The Framework icon allows you to design an entirely new set of features that are otherwise difficult or impossible to create. As such, the Framework icon may change the way you think about lesson design. Perhaps the most important change that results from using frameworks is that files are no longer linear. With Framework and Navigate icons (covered in Chapter 14), you can jump forward or backward to icons anywhere in the file. Framework icons also accelerate the development process. They can be used to navigate easily though lesson information without using Wait and Erase icons.

This chapter and Chapter 14 should be studied together because their ideas are so closely connected. The Framework icon uses Navigate icons to create navigation links. Navigate icons connect pages attached to Framework icons. In practice, Framework and Navigate icons are completely interdependent.

CHAPTER OBJECTIVES

After completing this chapter, you will be able to:

- Use the Framework icon to create navigation structures.
- Edit Framework structures to customize navigation.
- Create hypertext.

KEY TERMS

Framework icon
Entry pane
Exit pane
Navigate icon
Pages
Hypertext
Framework window
Destinations
Jump to Page
Call and Return

SUPPORT MATERIALS

On the CD-ROM disk, run the file titled **Videos.a4r** and select the button labeled **Chapter 13** to learn how to use the Framework icon. From the SUPPORT folder on the CD, open the file titled **CHP13.a4p**. Run the file and use each of the navigation buttons to help you understand how each button works. Add Display icons to a framework structure to create new pages. Use the mouse to select colored hypertext links to the glossary. To help you understand how to create hypertext, examine the text style named Hypertext and explore the navigation associated with each hyperlink.

PROJECT 11: FRAMEWORK/NAVIGATION

Materials Needed to Complete This Project

- Your file from the previous project, **PROJ10.a4p**
- Macromedia Authorware 4.0 for Macintosh or Windows

Before You Begin

Allow approximately 30 minutes to complete this project.

Project Description

In this project, you will explore the use of the Framework icon by creating another section for the Help pulldown menu you created earlier. The Framework icon will embed navigation features and graphics into the new Hidden Costs section of the lesson.

Activity

Begin by opening the Authorware file from the previous project. From the File pulldown menu, choose Save As… and rename the file **PROJ11**.

Place a Map icon next to the **Glossary** Map icon on the Level 1 flow line. Title the Map icon **Hidden Costs**.

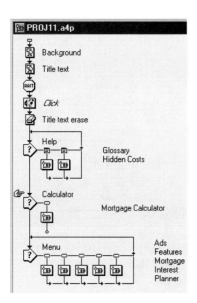

Open the Map icon titled **Hidden Costs**. Place a Framework icon on the Level 2 flow line and title it **Other costs**.

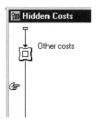

Place a Map icon to the right of the **Hidden Costs** Map icon and title it **Closing costs**.

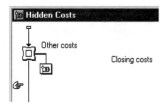

On the Level 1 flow line, open the Map icon titled **Planner**. Copy the Display icon titled **Planner Text**. Open the Map icon titled **Closing costs** and paste the icon onto the Level 3 flow line. Retitle the icon **Closing costs text**.

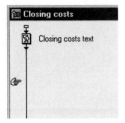

Open the Display icon titled **Closing costs text**. Change the text to the following:

Closing costs

Closing costs are some of the many hidden costs associated with purchasing a home. These fees may include points (to adjust the interest rate of the loan) and a loan origination fee (typically 1% of the total mortgage).

Be sure to budget these costs into your final home purchase price.

Copy the Map icon titled **Closing costs**. Paste three copies of the Map icon to the right of it and retitle the icons as follows:

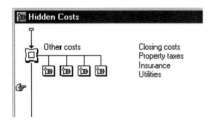

Open the Map icon titled **Property taxes**. Retitle the Display icon **Property taxes text**.

Open the Display icon titled **Property taxes text**. Change the text to the following:

Property taxes

Property taxes are another hidden cost associated with home ownership. Your home has an assessed value that you are required to pay taxes on each year.

While some homeowners prefer to pay their tax burden in one lump sum, many others have the amount spread out over the course of the year and added to their house payment. This type of pament is often referred to as a "PITI" payment, which stands for:

Principal - Interest - Taxes - Insurance

Open the Map icon titled **Insurance**. Retitle the Display icon **Insurance text**.

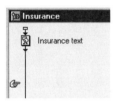

Open the Display icon titled **Insurance text**. Change the text to the following:

Insurance

As a homeowner, you are required to carry homeowner's insurance. There are a variety of agencies which provide this type of insurance. There are also many different types of coverage. Talking to your real estate agent, your mortgage loan officer, and friends and family members who own homes can help you determine the type of coverage best suited to your needs.

Depending on the region of the country, you may wish to consider special options such as flood or earthquake insurance.

Open the Map icon titled **Utilities**. Retitle the Display icon **Utilities text**.

Open the Display icon titled **Utilities text**. Change the text to the following:

Utilities

When you own a home you are responsible for
all associated utilities and services. Depending
on the area in which you live, this may include:

telephone   cable televison
natural gas   electricity
water   sewage
garbage   recycling

Find out how much the current homeowners are
paying for these items and add that sum to your
monthly budget.

Run the lesson to check your work. You can access Hidden Costs from the Help pulldown menu.

You may have to reposition the navigation buttons so that they don't obscure any text. To do
so, pause the lesson and select and drag all the buttons and graphics you want to move to their
new locations.

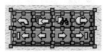

UNDERSTANDING THE DETAILS

Framework Icons

You may have noticed that, with the exception of perpetual interactions (see Chapter 8),
Authorware lessons tend to be linear. When you create a lesson, Authorware executes icons in
a vertical sequence from the top to the bottom of the Course flow line. Linear lessons can cause

problems, especially when it is important for users to review information. For example, in the Course flow line illustrated below, you cannot easily access the information on Page 1 after you have moved to Page 2.

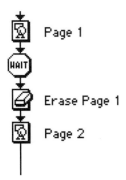

The most important role of a Framework icon is to provide a navigation system that allows the user to easily "page" back and forth between icons to review important information, to move from one lesson unit to another, or to follow a hyperlink.

A Framework icon is made up of two parts: pages and a Framework window. A page is an icon attached to the right of a Framework icon. In the following illustration, Display icons are used for three pages. The user can move between the pages by using navigation controls that are built into the Framework window.

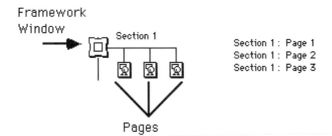

Pages are not limited to presenting information in Display icons. You can attach any of the following icons to a framework: Motion; Erase; Wait; Navigate; Calculation; Map; Movie; Sound; and Video. You can also use the Map icon to store other icons. Map icons often include Display, Wait, and Erase icons to systematically build screens.

The Framework window contains the navigation controls. These controls determine the order in which pages are accessed and can be altered to modify navigation. For example, a button in the Framework window might be used to link to a page in another framework. To open the Framework window, place a Framework icon onto the Course flow line and double-click the icon.

The Framework window includes Entry and Exit panes. These panes contain icons that are executed every time the user enters (Entry pane) or exits (Exit pane) the framework. The default Framework icon (shown below) contains a Display icon titled **Gray Navigation Panel** and eight Perpetual buttons that control navigation.

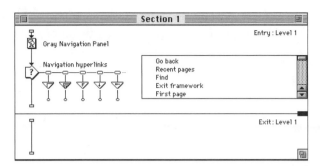

Understanding how navigation is controlled in the Framework window can be difficult at first. The following exercises are designed to help you to learn how navigation works:

Exercise 1 : Using a Framework Icon
This exercise shows the basic operation of a Framework icon. You will create a simple navigation structure using a Framework icon and some Display icons as pages.

- Place a Framework icon on the Course flow line. Title the icon Framework 1.
- Add three Display icons as pages of the framework structure (as shown below). Label the Display icons Page 1, Page 2, and Page 3.

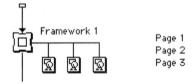

- Open each of the Display icons and type the title of each icon into its Presentation window.
- Run the file. The following (or a similar) screen will result:

- Experiment with each of the buttons and try to determine how each button works. The exact operation of each option will be addressed later in this chapter.

   Tip: Try this timesaver: Paste the variable titled ExecutingIconTitle into a Display icon. Duplicate the icon onto the flow line. Label each duplicated icon with a unique name.

To use the variable, first open a Display on the flow line. Select Variables from the Window pulldown menu, select the category titled All, and scroll down to the desired variable. Click the variable's name and press the button titled Paste to place the variable into the display.

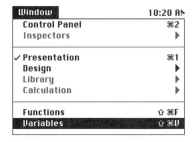

Exercise 2 : Understanding the Navigation Buttons
This exercise examines four navigation buttons in the Entry Pane. We will "disable" the other four navigation options to prevent you from becoming swamped with new information.

- Place a Framework icon on the Course flow line. Title the icon Framework 2.

Next, deactivate some of the default navigation buttons that are built into the Framework icon.

- Double-click the Framework icon. The following window will appear:

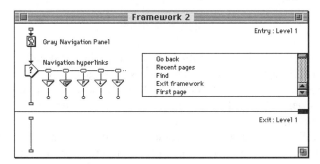

Select and cut the first four buttons from the interaction structure titled "Navigation hyperlinks." These four buttons are titled Go back, Recent pages, Find, and Exit framework. When you are done, the following buttons will remain: First page; Previous page; Next page; and Last page.

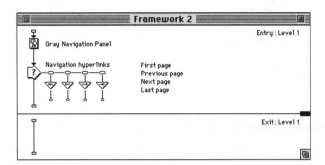

- Next, close the window titled Framework 2 to return to the main Course flow line. Attach four Display icons to the framework structure. Each of the icons attached to a Framework icon is a page. Label the pages "first," "second," "third," and "fourth."

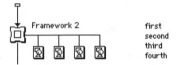

- Open each of the Display icons and type the title of each icon into its Presentation window (or embed the variable titled ExecutingIconTitle, as described earlier).

- Run the lesson. Notice that a navigation panel opens in the top right corner of the Presentation window and that four of the buttons are missing. These are the buttons we deleted earlier. Removing buttons simplifies the learning task.

- Now experiment with each of the four buttons. You should notice the following:
  - The two central buttons (Previous Page and Next Page) allow you to move backward or forward a page at a time. The other two buttons (First Page and Last Page) jump to the first or the last page attached to the Framework icon. Notice that no Wait or Erase icons are needed to control the information flow.
  - Try adding additional pages to the Framework structure and experiment with the buttons. You will find that the navigation controls are automatically applied to all the pages attached to the Framework structure.

Exercise 3 : Understanding the Remaining Navigation Buttons
You will now focus on the other four navigation buttons that make up the default Framework icon.

- Place a Framework icon on the Course flow line. Title the icon Framework 3.
- Place four Display icons to the right of the Framework icon. Label the Display icons "first," "second," "third," and "fourth."
- Add a fifth Display icon on the Course flow line and title this icon **OUT**.

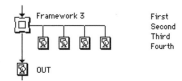

- Open each of the Display icons and type the title of each icon into its Presentation window (or embed the variable titled ExecutingIconTitle).
- *Run the lesson*: Notice that the file is identical to the one created above, with the exception that the navigation controls contain four new options. Before experimenting with these new options, take a few seconds to reuse the Page-Forward, Page-Back, Jump-Forward, and Jump-Back buttons. Do this to create a lesson history that will be revisited in a few moments.
- *Select Recent Pages*: Recent Pages lists the titles of all the pages that have been accessed recently. When you select this button, a window similar to the following window will appear. To navigate from here, simply double-click one of the page titles in the list.

- *Select Find*: Use this option to search for words or terms. The Find button searches for text in either the current framework or other frameworks and lists the names of all the pages that include the term.

To use the Find button, enter the text you want to locate and press the Return key. The names of all the pages containing the desired text will appear in a window. You can connect to these displays by clicking the icon names (as you did for the Recent Pages button).

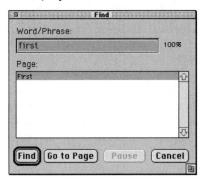

Note: If you use the variable titled ExecutingIconTitle to display icon names in Display icons, the Find button will not be able to locate pages containing the desired text. Authorware searches only for "real" text, as opposed to text stored in variables.

Select the Go Back button. The Go Back button sends the user to the previous page in the current framework. The button is somewhat different from the Previous Page button. Whereas Previous Page moves the user though a continuous loop of icons connected to a framework, Go Back retraces the history of pages that the user has visited. For example, if the user follows the path

START
First
Second
First
Second
Fourth

pressing the Previous Page button three times produces the following result:

Third
Second
First

That is, it revisits the lesson *structure*, whereas pressing the Go Back button three times produces:

Second
First
Second

That is, it revisits the lesson *history*.

Select the Exit button to move out of the current framework. In the present example, the lesson moves out of the framework titled Framework 3 and back to the Course flow line, where the next icon encountered is titled Out.

Creating Hyperlinks

Navigation links are sometimes limited to pages within a framework. However, at other times users want to jump to pages in other frameworks. For example, a user may wish to link to a glossary to look up the meaning of a word, or to connect to frameworks containing related ideas. These connections, sometimes called hyperlinks, allow users to follow their personal interests rather than a path that has been prescribed by someone else. Hyperlinks permit users to connect to pages by clicking text. Hyperlinks are often cued to the user by using coloring, underlining, or some other form of text highlighting.

Where Do Hyperlinks Come From?

Hyperlinks are created by using styled text. Text styling is a common feature in many word processors and desktop-publishing programs. It allows a combination of font types and sizes, coloring, and other formatting options, to be applied simultaneously from a styles menu. In Authorware, styled text can also link text to framework pages. If this chapter included styled text, a link could connect the underlined words <u>styled text</u> to the section in Chapter 5 on defining styles.

Creating hyperlinks is a three-step process:

Step 1 Create a destination page for a hyperlink and attach it to a Framework icon.

Step 2 Define a style sheet that formats text and leads to the destination page.

Step 3 Apply the style to create a link to the destination page.

Exercise

The words *noun*, *verb*, and *adjective* will be highlighted wherever they appear in a lesson, and clicking the words with the cursor of the mouse will lead directly to their definitions in a glossary. The glossary will contain definitions of the words. A text style will be created that contains text formatting and a hyperlink. Applying the style will highlight words and create hyperlinks.

Step 1: Create a destination page and attach it to a Framework icon.

The destination page is a Display icon titled **Glossary**. The Glossary will contain the definitions of the verbs, nouns, and adjectives.

Step 2: Define a style sheet that formats text and leads to the destination page.

Hyperlinks are often identified by formatting text to cue the user that a hyperlink exists. Style sheets can be used to format text and to create hyperlinks.

To Create a Hypertext Style Sheet

- Select Define Styles… from the Text pulldown menu.

- In the Define Styles dialog window, click the Add button and type the name of the new style (here, the style name is Hyperlink).

- Click the Modify button when you are done. The title Hyperlink will be added to the list of style sheets.

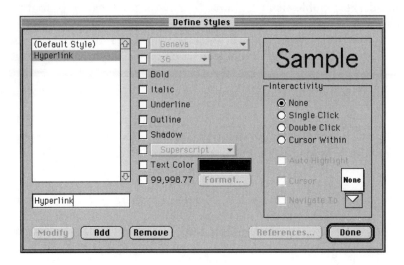

- Select the text-formatting options that you wish to apply to the hypertext. Colored and underlined text are often used to identify links. Text formatting provides users with visual clues that hyperlinks exist. In the example shown below, the hypertext is highlighted in a dark color, bolded, and italicized. Click the Modify button after making changes.

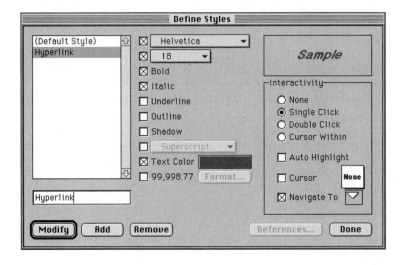

- Now you must create the hyperlink. In other words, you must identify the page where the hypertext will go. In the window labeled Interactivity, select Single Click and check the Navigate To box.
- Single-click the Navigate button ▽ to show the following window, which displays all the pages to which you can create a link:

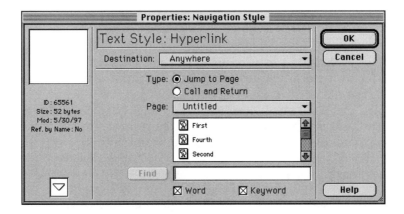

It is important to emphasize the following point: *A navigation destination must be a page attached to a Framework icon.* Navigation to a page is performed by using Navigate icons. This point may make more sense when you have completed Chapter 14, on Navigate icons.

Each destination offers different navigation options. Selecting Anywhere for the destination allows you to select either from the list of all icons in the entire file or more selectively by individual Framework icons. The illustration above shows a scrolling field containing several pages. Selecting the icon titled **First** will establish a hyperlink to this destination.

The options Jump to Page and Call and Return determine whether the link is one way or return. Jump to Page is like a one-way ticket to the specified page. Call and Return connects to a page before returning to the icon from which it came. Click OK when you have made a link and have decided on a one-way or return ticket.

Step 3: Apply the style to text to create a link to the destination page.

You can create hyperlinks by applying a style to a word or a set of words. To apply a style, highlight text in a Display icon (using the Text or Selection tools) and apply the appropriate style from the Styles list or from the Apply Styles dialog box. Clicking a word styled in Hyperlink will create a connection to the Glossary.

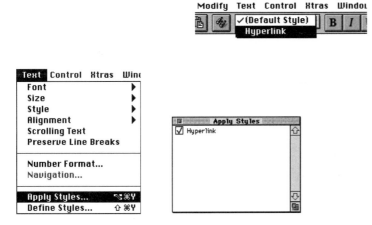

Editing Navigation

The previous example demonstrated a style sheet that created a hypertext link to one destination. All styled text landed at the same destination. Sometimes you want to connect to several different pages. For instance, in the previous example, you may want to use different pages for verbs, adjectives, and nouns.

You can create a style sheet that formats text consistently, but prompts the designer to define a destination page. The primary difference between this approach and the one described previously is that the style sheet will not specify a destination. Instead, after applying a style to text, the designer will choose a destination by selecting Edit Navigation from the Text pulldown menu. To create different navigation destinations for styled text:

- Open the Display icon from where the hyperlink will be initiated and use the Text tool to highlight the hypertext to be created.
- Select Navigation… from the Text pulldown window.

- Select the destination for the hyperlink. In the example below, the designer can choose to link to one of three pages attached to the Framework icon titled Glossary. Other destinations can be selected by changing the page organizer.

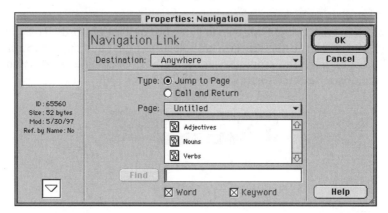

- Once a hyperlink has been created from a Display icon to a framework page, the icon containing the hypertext will be marked with a navigation marker (a small triangle), indicating that this icon initiates a link.

Note: Although the style sheet will not include the final destination for the hyperlink, the designer must select a level of interactivity in the Define Styles window. It is not sufficient to select text style alone. In the example above, Interactivity has been engaged by selecting Single Click.

Erasing

You may have noticed that when pages are attached to Framework icons, erasing occurs automatically. That is, when the user selects a navigation button to move to another page, information on the last page is removed. However, sometimes you may want information in a page to remain on the screen. For example, you may be using a framework to build a presentation in successive Display icons.

A feature exists to allow you to keep presentations on the screen and to ignore the automatic erase option. The option, titled Prevent Automatic Erase, is found in the Icon > Properties… menu under the Modify menu.

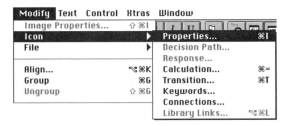

Although selecting Prevent Automatic Erase allows you to build presentations without having to re-create screen content, you should be careful in its use. Using navigation icons to backtrack through a presentation will not remove unwanted information from the screen.

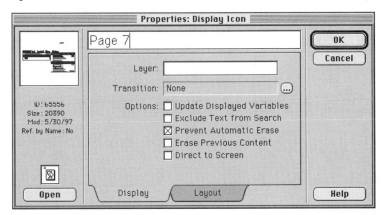

STUDY EXERCISES

1. **a.** Use a Framework icon to create a presentation of five different pages, where each page is a single Display icon. Run the lesson and experiment with each navigation button in the Presentation window.

   b. Modify the presentation by including a Map icon as one of the pages. Into the Map place a series of Display, Wait, and Erase icons that progressively build a single screen of information.

2. Experiment with the navigation buttons as outlined below:

   a. Place a Framework icon on the Course flow line and modify the navigation buttons to allow only Page Forward and Page Back navigation. Add three to four pages to the framework and try to navigate with the buttons.

   b. Place a Framework icon on the Course flow line and modify the navigation buttons to allow only Page Forward and Recent Pages navigation. Add three to four pages to the framework and try to navigate with the buttons.

   c. Place a Framework icon on the Course flow line and modify the navigation buttons to allow only Last Page, Page Back, and Recent Pages navigation. Add three to four pages to the framework and try to navigate with the buttons.

3. This exercise involves creating hypertext links. Create a Framework containing several pages that, together, make a glossary containing definitions of several terms. Place the framework at the end of the Course flow line. Create a brief lesson in which the words or terms described in the glossary appear in Display icons in the main lesson. Create hyperlinks between each of the terms and the glossary.

4. Create a Framework icon that includes custom navigation buttons.

5. As users go through lessons, they require different levels of support. What starts out being a useful Help screen often becomes useless. Framework icons are the perfect tool for creating Help screens that change during a lesson, according to the user's needs.

   Create a brief lesson that includes at least three hyperlinks to different Help screens. The Help button should not vary in appearance, but should lead to different destinations for the different types of help. The user should be able to select the Help button to bring up a Help window and to use navigation buttons in the Help window to access other help screens.

14

Navigate Icons ▼

CHAPTER OVERVIEW

This chapter examines the icon that redirects lesson flow: the Navigate icon. Navigate icons create links to pages in Framework icons. Most importantly, the Navigate icon creates nonlinear designs. Navigate icons permit forward or backward jumps within a lesson. Instead of using the Course flow line to determine lesson sequence, the lesson automatically jumps to the destination identified in the Navigate icon.

CHAPTER OBJECTIVES

After completing this chapter, you will be able to:

- Use the Navigate icon to create nonlinear lesson links.
- Customize navigation in Framework icons.

KEY TERMS

Navigate icon
Navigate To
Destinations: Recent; Nearby; Anywhere; Calculate; Search
Jump to Page
Call and Return
Navigation structures

SUPPORT MATERIALS

On the CD-ROM disk, run the file titled **Videos.a4r** and select the button labeled **Chapter 14** to learn how to use the Navigate icon to customize navigation.

UNDERSTANDING THE DETAILS

Navigate icons are one of Authorware's most important features because they allow the designer to create flexible navigation structures. Once you learn how to control Navigate icons, you can design your own lesson navigation systems. Designing navigation systems is critical if you want to customize interfaces. Most projects you develop will not be able to be completed with the standard navigation controls provided by Authorware. Instead, you will need to create navigation control that suits your specific needs. The purpose of this chapter is to help you understand how to perform such actions.

Creating Page-to-Page Navigation

All navigation links connected to Framework icons can be modified. The default Navigation buttons that accompany the Framework icon are actually a Model that is loaded into Authorware each time the program restarts. You can create your own navigation controls, modify the default Framework icon navigation controls, and save other navigation controls as Models that you can reuse.

Double-click a Framework icon to display the default navigation buttons, as shown below.

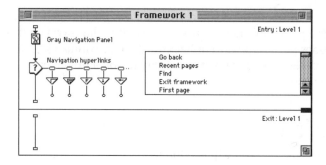

The entry panel establishes the logic that applies to all the pages attached to the framework. All icons added to the entry panel are executed when the user enters the Framework icon. The default entry panel includes a gray navigation panel that acts as a background for the navigation buttons, as well as eight navigation buttons. The figures below illustrate both the gray navigation panel graphic on which navigation icons are placed and the default navigation buttons.

  Navigation panel without buttons or icons

  Navigation panel with navigation buttons

The entry panel contains the navigation buttons. The eight navigation buttons in the default Framework window are button responses set to Perpetual. The feedback attached to each button is a Navigate icon that connects to a page.

The exit panel is used to execute events when the user leaves the Framework icon. For example, the designer may leave a message indicating that a section of a lesson is done, or an Erase icon may be used to ensure that information is cleared from the screen.

Using Navigate icons involves identifying destinations that take the user to a page. Since all pages are, by definition, attached to Framework icons, this means that Navigate icons help you to link to frameworks.

Authorware is very sophisticated in the range of destinations it will allow. To view a destination, double-click any Navigate icon.

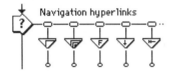

The complete set of destinations is divided into five classes: Recent; Nearby; Anywhere; Calculate; and Search. The options associated with each destination will be examined in the next sections.

Recent

The Recent class allows backtracking. In other words, it allows users to repeat pages attached to Framework icons. The designer can select from two options: Go Back or List Recent Pages. Both options are included in the default Framework icon.

Recent: Go back

Recent: List Recent Pages

Go Back sends the user back sequentially through a list of recently executed pages—in other words, the page order in which the user went. The pages may or may not be within the current Framework icon. If multiple frameworks exist, Go Back may return to pages from other frameworks. However, if only one framework exists, Go Back will eventually return to the first page in the current framework. List Recent Pages produces a navigation window that can be used to link directly to a page (see below). Double-click an icon's name to go directly to that page.

To understand how Go Back and List Recent Pages work, complete the following exercise:

- Place a Framework icon on the flow line. Label the icon **experiment**.
- Attach three Display icons to the Framework icon. Label these icons **Language**, **Math**, and **Science**.

- Type the words "Language," "Math," and "Science" into their respective Display icons.

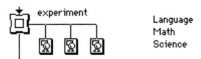

- Run the lesson. A page with the word "Language" will appear.

- Click the Go Back icon ⬅. Nothing happens because you have not yet created a history that can be reviewed.

- Click the Go Forward One Page icon ➡. A page with the word "Math" will appear. Click it again and "Science" will appear.

- Click the Go Back icon ⬅. The page containing "Math" will reappear. Click it again and the page containing "Language" will reappear. Now you are using the Go Back button to revisit recently viewed pages.

- Click the Recent Pages icon ⬅. The following Navigation window will appear:

Notice that the window lists the names of the pages you have viewed recently. You can navigate to a page by double-clicking its icon name in the window.

> *Note*: List Recent Pages uses icon names to identify the path a user has taken. Consequently, it is important to name pages meaningfully to help users navigate effectively.

Nearby

Selecting Nearby allows the designer to select from five options: Previous, Next, First, Last, or Exit Framework/Return. All five options refer to pages within the current Framework icon. Notice that the icons for each option differ slightly and provide visual clues to identify each icon's function. The icons look similar to the buttons on a VCR. All five options are included in the default navigation structure that is built into the Navigate icon.

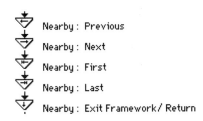

Nearby : Previous

Nearby : Next

Nearby : First

Nearby : Last

Nearby : Exit Framework/ Return

The Nearby class is used only for "local" navigation. Nearby options allow the designer only to select a page from those attached to the current Framework icon. The Previous option recycles pages in reverse order. If the user is currently on the first page, Previous selects the last page in the framework (i.e., if 26 adjacent pages were labeled A, B, C,..., X, Y, Z, then one possible outcome of selecting Previous repeatedly would be F, E, D, C, B, A, Z, Y, etc.).

The Next option presents pages in order. If the user is currently on the last page, the list continues with the first page in the framework (i.e., X, Y, Z, A, B, C, etc.).

The First option jumps back to the first page in the current framework (i.e., to icon A). The Last option jumps forward to the last page in the current framework (i.e., to icon Z).

As its name implies, Exit Framework/Return leaves the current framework and returns to the logic of the flow line or another Framework icon. This option is often critical. Without it, exiting a Framework icon may be impossible.

To understand how each of these five options works, complete the following exercise:

- Place a Framework icon on the flow line. Label the icon **experiment**.
- Attach three Display icons to the Framework icon. Label these icons **Language**, **Math**, and **Science**.
- Enter the words "Language," "Math," and "Science" into their respective Display icons.

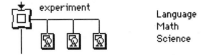

experiment

Language
Math
Science

- Run the lesson. The page with the word "Language" will appear.

- Click the Previous icon three times. Notice that "Science" appears (the item at the end of the list), followed by "Math," then "Language" again. Previous is accessing the pages of the current Framework icon in reverse order.

- Run the lesson again. The page with the word "Language" will reappear.

- Click the Next Page icon three times. The following sequence will appear: "Math," "Science," "Language." Next Page is accessing the pages of the current Framework icon in order.

- Run the lesson again. The page with the word "Language" will reappear.

- Click the First icon. Nothing will happen, because the lesson is already on the first icon. Click the Last icon. "Science" will appear. Click the First icon. "Language" will reappear.

- Click the Recent Pages icon 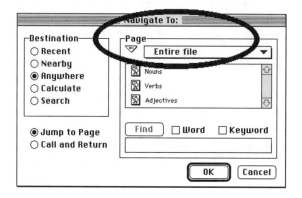. A Navigation window will appear, listing all recently visited pages. Double-click a page's title to navigate directly to that page.
- Run the lesson again. The page with the word "Language" will reappear.
- Click the Exit Framework/Return icon ⬅️. The current framework will end.

Anywhere

Remember that Navigate icons connect to pages attached to Framework structures. Whereas Nearby restricts movement to pages within the same framework, Anywhere allows the designer to create links (from icons on the flow line or pages in frameworks) to pages attached to any Framework icons in the lesson. In other words, Anywhere permits hyperlinks to be connected to a page in the current file.

Making a link using Anywhere navigation requires the designer to select a destination page from those listed in the page dropdown menu. The pages listed are grouped according to the title of the Framework icon to which they are attached. However, it is also possible to view a list of all the pages that exist in the present file. Again, remember that all pages must be attached to Framework icons.

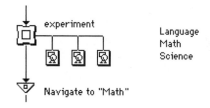

Calculate

The Calculate navigation link provides the most flexible navigation, but is the most complex to understand and use. Using Calculate requires that you understand variables.

The difference between Calculate and other navigation types is that Calculate allows the designer to create dynamic navigation. In other words, the links do not need to be predefined by the designer. Creating a navigation link usually involves using the Navigate icon to make a single connection between a Navigate icon and a given destination page. For example, in the illustration below, a link is created from the Navigation icon to the page titled Page 6. Once created, the Navigate icon cannot link to any icon other than the one to which a direct connection has been made. In effect, the Navigate icon and its destination page are glued together.

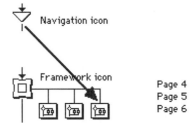

In contrast, by using Calculate to select a destination, together with an appropriately named variable, the designer can vary the destination to match the user's needs.

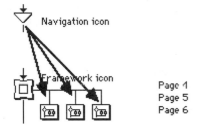

Consider the following scenario. A designer wants to create a dynamic Help option in a lesson. By clicking a word (or by using a pulldown menu), the user will connect to a Help screen that contains contextually relevant information. That is, the Help screen will be constantly updated to meet the user's ongoing needs.

One possible solution involves multiple Navigate icons. The designer could keep changing the Navigation button as the user progresses through the lesson. However, this approach is "messy" because it involves using multiple Navigate icons.

Another solution involves using Calculate navigation. Using Calculate allows the designer to choose a destination that can change during a lesson. In other words, the Navigate icon can connect to many different pages. Instead of connecting to a specific destination, Calculate connects to whatever destination is stored within a variable. For example, the value stored in the variable may point to Page 4, Page 5, or any other page connected to a framework.

Instead of connecting to a specific icon, the Calculate destination connects to an ID number stored in a variable. Every icon has a unique ID number. Consequently, icons can be identified by their names or by their ID numbers. By storing a destination in a variable and changing the value of the variable, a Navigate icon can link to multiple pages.

To find an icon's ID, highlight the icon and select Icon > Properties... from the Modify pulldown menu.

The Icon Properties dialog box contains important information about the highlighted icon, including the icon ID. For example, the illustration below shows that the Display icon titled Page 10 has the unique ID number 65555.

```
┌─────────────────────────────────────────────────────────┐
│                 Properties: Display Icon                  │
│  ┌─────────┐  ┌──────────────────────────────┐  ┌──────┐ │
│  │         │  │ Page 10                      │  │  OK  │ │
│  │         │  └──────────────────────────────┘  ├──────┤ │
│  │         │     Layer: ┌──────────────────┐    │Cancel│ │
│  │         │            └──────────────────┘    └──────┘ │
│  │         │  Transition: ┌──────────────┐ ┌──┐          │
│  ID: 65555 │              │ None         │ │..│          │
│ Size: 52 bytes            └──────────────┘ └──┘          │
│ Mod: 6/3/97 │   Options: ☐ Update Displayed Variables   │
│ Ref. by Name: No          ☐ Exclude Text from Search    │
│         │                 ☐ Prevent Automatic Erase      │
│         │                 ☐ Erase Previous Content       │
│  ┌───┐  │                 ☐ Direct to Screen            │
│  │ ▨ │  │                                                │
│  └───┘  │                                                │
│ ┌──────┐    Display  ┌─────────┐                ┌──────┐ │
│ │ Open │ ───────────┤ Layout   ├──────────────  │ Help │ │
│ └──────┘            └─────────┘                 └──────┘ │
└─────────────────────────────────────────────────────────┘
```

When you select Calculate as the destination, you enter a variable into the Icon Expression field. This variable stores the ID number for the destination page. Rather than identifying a page by name, Calculate connects to the page with the stored ID number. Most importantly, the number stored in the variable may change, thus allowing a connection to a different page. In the following illustration, Calculate connects to an ID number stored in a user-defined variable titled HelpScreen.

```
┌──────────────────────────────────────────────────────┐
│                    Navigate To:                        │
│  ┌─Destination─────┐  ┌─Icon Expression────────────┐  │
│  │ ○ Recent        │  │ HelpScreen                 │  │
│  │ ○ Nearby        │  │                            │  │
│  │ ○ Anywhere      │  │                            │  │
│  │ ⦿ Calculate     │  │                            │  │
│  │ ○ Search        │  │                            │  │
│  │                 │  │                            │  │
│  └─────────────────┘  └────────────────────────────┘  │
│  ⦿ Jump to Page                                        │
│  ○ Call and Return                                     │
│                              ┌──────┐  ┌────────┐      │
│                              │  OK  │  │ Cancel │      │
│                              └──────┘  └────────┘      │
└──────────────────────────────────────────────────────┘
```

Be careful with the Calculate destination!

The method you use to set up the Calculate destination is extremely important. As mentioned above, the Calculate destination links to a page's ID number. On the surface, it appears to make sense to identify the ID numbers of the icons to which you want to link. A single Calculate destination could link to multiple pages if the value of the variable in the Icon Expression field was changed to match the ID numbers of the destination pages.

Unfortunately, this apparent logic fails because the ID number assigned to a page may change when the lesson file is packaged. In other words, you may determine the ID number of a destination only to find that Authorware changes this number, leaving you without a clearly defined destination. If this scenario occurs, your lesson will not work properly!

Outlined below is an approach that always works. The ID number of the destination page is determined by using the variable titled IconID. IconID returns the ID number of a named destination page. Authorware never changes an icon's name. Consequently, you can use the IconID variable to find an icon's ID by naming the page to which you would like to link.

Calculations such as

HelpScreen=IconID@"Page 5"

or

HelpScreen=IconID@"Page 6"

vary the destination page. Even though Authorware changes icons' ID numbers, this approach still works, because the destination icon is identified by an icon name that will not change.

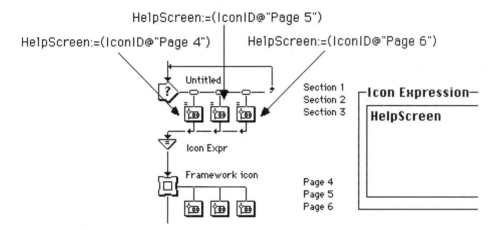

Search

Selecting Search causes a Find dialog box to appear. This box can be used by the user to hunt for pages containing specific words or phrases. Authorware searches pages for occurrences of the desired word(s) and returns a list of all matching pages. The user can use the resulting list to navigate by double-clicking on a page name.

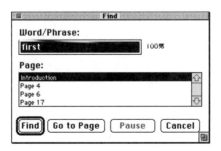

Note: The titles given to all buttons and windows for the Find dialog box can be edited.

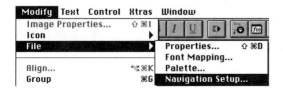

Selecting File > Navigation Setup… from the Modify pulldown menu produces the following editing window:

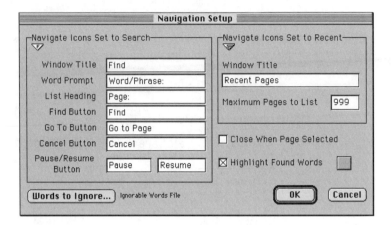

Other Types of Links

In addition to jumping between pages, Navigate icons can create links from any point on the flow line to a page. In the example below, a Navigate icon creates a link to a Help screen. This type of link is different from others we have examined because the link is not initiated from a page. However, the destination icon is still (and must always be) another page.

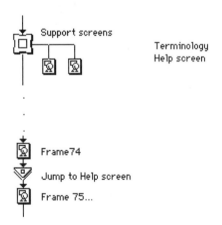

Call and Return

Sometimes you will want to link to a page in another Framework and then return to where you came from. Three destination categories (Anywhere, Calculate, and Search) include the ability to connect to pages attached to another Framework icon. Links may be one way (called Jump to Page) or round trip (called Call and Return).

Jump to Page links to a page. Once connected, navigation is controlled by the new Framework. Call and Return also links to a page, but returns to the original page (or icon on the flow line) when it encounters an Exit Framework/Return navigation link. In effect, Call and Return works like a programming call to a subroutine.

Visual clues used to identify Call and Return are outlined below.

 Outlined (link set to Call and Return)

 Not outlined (link set to Jump to Page)

Navigate icons that are "outlined" will return to the point from where they came when exiting a framework.

Erasing Pages

As you become more sophisticated as an Authorware designer, you will encounter different situations that require you to understand how Authorware erases information from the screen. Jump to Page and Call and Return use different erasing strategies when linking pages. Jumping to a page erases the contents of the current page before displaying the new page. This is convenient because you don't have to worry about erasing or hiding unwanted information. In contrast, Call and Return leaves the contents of the original page untouched. The advantage is that, on returning to the original page, the destination page is erased.

Call and Return destinations can leave unwanted information on the screen. One technique to hide unwanted text or graphics involves creating a mask. A mask is an object (such as a rectangle) filled with white paint that covers unwanted displays. Once in place, the mask can be used as a fresh background on which new information can be presented. The illustration below shows a display with a mask that partially hides the screen. The mask can be enlarged and moved to ensure that no unwanted information shows. Also, lines on the mask are usually set to "invisible" in the Line palette.

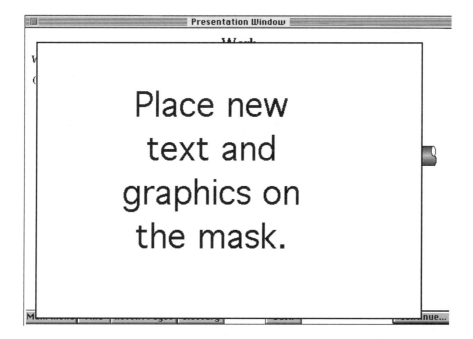

STUDY EXERCISES

1. Place a Navigate icon on the flow line and open Icon Properties either by double-clicking the icon or by selecting Icon > Properties... from the Modify pulldown menu. Explore the five options associated with the Destinations dropdown menu and state the destinations associated with each of the following navigation types:

RECENT (TWO DESTINATIONS)

> Destination 1:
> Destination 2:

NEARBY (FIVE DESTINATIONS)

> Destination 1:
> Destination 2:
> Destination 3:
> Destination 4:
> Destination 5:

2. Explain the difference between Jump to Page and Call and Return navigation.

3. Create a lesson that includes at least two Framework icons and associated pages. Establish navigation links to pages attached to the Framework icons using the Anywhere destination. Use the Jump to Page and Call and Return options to experiment with their effects.

4. This exercise is designed to help you practice customizing your own navigation structures within a lesson. For each question, add three to four pages to the Navigation structure to test the navigation buttons that you create.

   Create a Framework structure that includes the following Navigation buttons:

   a. Page Forward and Page Back

   b. Page Forward and Recent Pages

   c. Page Back and Last Page

5. Create a Framework icon that includes three different Help screens. Using a Navigate icon with the destination set to Calculate, create a Help button that links to each of the Help screens at different points during the lesson.

15

Odds and Ends 2: Erasing

CHAPTER OVERVIEW

One of the most confusing topics to understand concerns how Authorware erases information from the screen. In this chapter, we examine erasing options in Erase, Navigation, Decision, and Interaction icons and using system Functions to erase screens.

CHAPTER OBJECTIVES

After completing this chapter, you will be able to:

- Control when information is erased from the screen using Erase icons.
- Control the automatic erasing options built into Interaction, Decision, and Framework icons.
- Learn the options for erasing information when using the Perpetual option.
- Control when information is erased from the screen using Erase functions.

KEY TERMS

Prevent automatic erasing
Text-entry options
Erase interaction
- After Next Entry
- Upon Exit

- Don't Erase
Erase Feedback
- After Next Entry
- Before Next Entry
- On Exit
- Don't Erase
Backwards erasing

SUPPORT MATERIALS

On the CD-ROM disk, run the file titled **Videos.a4r** and select the button labeled **Chapter 15**. **Chapter 15** includes five movies. The movies show different ways that information can be erased from the screen using the built-in capabilities of the Erase, Interaction, Navigation, and Decision icons and two system functions.

UNDERSTANDING THE DETAILS

How Do I Erase Information from the Screen?

There are three ways to erase information from the screen:

- Using an Erase icon.
- Using Authorware's automatic erasing options.
- Using the EraseAll or EraseIcon system Functions.

Using an Erase Icon

Erase icons are used to erase text and graphics from Display and Interaction icons (although an Erase icon may also be used to erase buttons, movies, and sound).

Using Authorware's Automatic Erasing Options

There are five automatic erasing techniques to master in Authorware: erasing pages within Framework icons; erasing pages between Framework icons; erasing paths within a decision structure; erasing within an interaction structure; and backwards erasing. Each is very important and essential to an understanding of how to present and remove information from the screen in a flexible and efficient manner.

Erasing Pages Within Framework Icons

Framework pages are automatically erased as the user moves from one page to another. Consequently, you don't have to worry about erasing information as the user navigates from page to page within a framework. However, it is sometimes necessary to ensure that information is *not* erased as the user navigates. For example, you may not want to erase information when paging forward gradually adds information to a picture.

To prevent automatic erasing, first highlight the relevant Display icon from the framework structure.

Next, Select Icon > Properties... from the Modify pulldown menu and check the box titled Prevent Automatic Erase. Unfortunately, this option must be set individually for each icon in the framework structure to which the effect is to be applied.

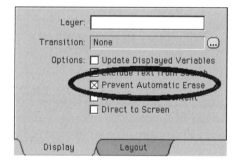

Erasing Pages Between Framework Icons

One of the most powerful features within Authorware is the ability to link to pages attached to different Framework icons. This ability is made possible by the Navigate icon. A Navigate icon creates a link from a point anywhere on the flow line to a page attached to any Framework icon.

Navigation links may be one way or return trip. One-way links automatically erase the contents of the current page(s). However, return connections do not erase pages (since their contents must be available to the user upon their return home). Consequently, it may be necessary to use masking techniques to hide information from the screen while new information is presented. Masking involves covering the screen with a white (or appropriately colored) borderless rectangle. New content can be placed on the mask without the hidden information showing through.

The following example illustrates the need for a mask. A file contains two Framework icons. Each framework has a single Display icon attached as a page. Each page contains some simple text (i.e., the icon's name). The navigation inside each Framework icons has been customized. Framework1 contains a Navigate icon that connects to the Display icon titled Page 2. The Navigate icon has been set to Call and Return. Framework2 contains a Navigate icon that simply exits the framework.

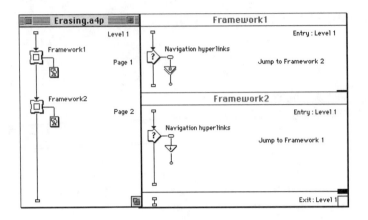

When the file runs, Framework1 displays the words "Page 1" and a button labeled "Jump to Framework 2."

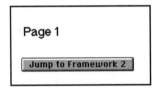

Pressing the button sends the user to Page 2; however, the contents of Page 1 are not erased, as the Call and Return option has been selected. Instead, Authorware displays the new page on top of the original page. In the illustration below, you can see that the contents of both Display icons, Page 1 and Page 2, appear.

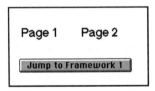

Pressing the button sends the user back to Page 1. This time, the text on Page 2 is erased. When returning to the original page, Authorware erases the destination page, revealing only the original page.

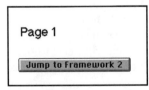

Erasing Paths Attached to a Decision Icon

In the same way that pages attached to Framework icons are automatically erased, Decision paths are automatically erased unless the designer changes the erasing option. To access the erasing options, open the Decision Path Properties dialog box by selecting an icon that is attached to a Decision icon and choosing Icon > Decision Path... from the Modify pulldown menu.

Three Decision-icon erasing options are available: Before Next Selection (the default option just described); Upon Exit, which leaves the contents of all the paths on the screen until the Decision icon is exited; and Don't Erase, which leaves the information to be erased with an Erase icon or function.

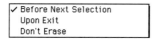

The following examples show the effects of accessing sequentially three Display icons that are attached to a Decision icon, together with the result that occurs upon exiting the decision structure. Each display contains the title of a path, each on a different line. The first example shows the effect of selecting Before Next Selection as the erasing option. Here, information is erased before proceeding to the next path.

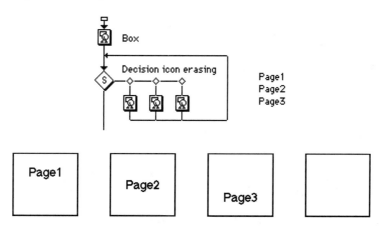

The second example uses Upon Exit as the erasing option. Here, information builds on the screen as successive paths are accessed. The information in the paths is erased automatically upon exit of the decision structure.

The third example uses Don't Erase as the erasing option. Again, information builds on the screen as successive paths are accessed. However, information remains on the screen even upon exit of the decision structure. Displays must be erased using an Erase icon or function.

Erasing Parts of Interaction Structures

Recall that an interaction structure comprises up to three different components that need to be erased: an interaction, a response by the user, and feedback. An interaction is a question or an instruction to the user that is typed into the Interaction icon's display. A response is the text typed by the user (for a text-entry response). Feedback is information that the computer gives the user following a response.

Erasing the interaction is controlled by the Erase: option inside the Interaction icon. This option can be accessed by highlighting an Interaction icon and selecting Icon > Properties… from the Modify pulldown menu. Three options are available: After Next Entry, Upon Exit, and Don't Erase.

The default option is Upon Exit. Upon Exit erases the interaction when the user exits the current Interaction icon. This setting ensures that important text and graphics remain undisturbed until an interaction has been completed.

Sometimes it is important to temporarily remove text or graphics from the screen. After Next Entry erases the interaction each time the user enters a response into the computer. Selecting this option can be important if additional room is needed to display feedback.

Don't Erase allows the designer to leave a display on screen after the user has exited the interaction. In this case, no automatic erasing occurs, and information must be removed with an Erase icon.

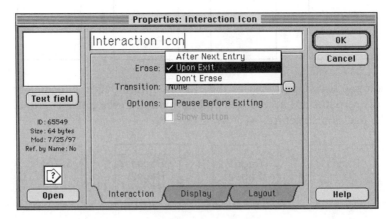

Erasing the user's typed response is controlled by the Text Entry Options from within the Inter-action icon. Check this option to ensure that the user's response doesn't remain onscreen when the interaction is complete.

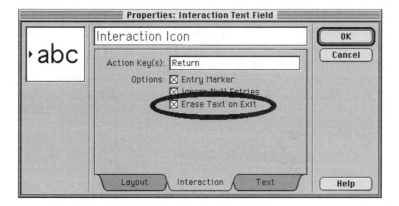

Erasing feedback is controlled by the Erase Feedback options from within the response options. Four options are available: After Next Entry, Before Next Entry, On Exit, and Don't Erase.

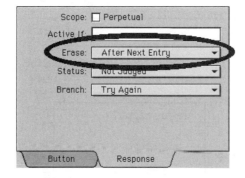

After Next Entry leaves feedback on the screen until another answer has been entered into the computer. This feature is useful because it allows the user to view feedback while attempting another response. After Next Entry is the standard option to select whenever the user answers incorrectly and must try again.

```
✓ After Next Entry
  Before Next Entry
  On Exit
  Don't Erase
```

Sometimes it is important to remove feedback from the screen before the user retries a question. In such cases, Before Next Entry erases feedback as soon as the interaction is reshown. When Before Next Entry is selected, it is often important to place Wait and Erase icons on the flow line to ensure that ugly "flashing" doesn't occur and that information is not erased before the user has had a chance to read it properly.

On Exit is the standard option for erasing feedback following a correct response, assuming that the question ends following a correct response. Don't Erase leaves feedback on the screen, to be erased later with an Erase icon. When proper erasing options are set, feedback is removed in a timely and coordinated manner.

The following examples illustrate the effects of selecting three different erasing options from the Interaction icon properties dialog. The Interaction contains an Interaction icon with two anticipated responses. Each anticipated response is a button, and each feedback icon contains a simple display.

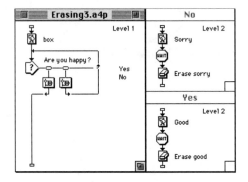

The examples illustrate four steps in the process of answering the following question:

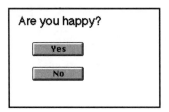

First the No button is pressed, causing the program to take the right-hand path. Next, the Continue button generated by the Wait icon is pressed. Third, the Yes button is pressed, causing the program to take the left-hand path. Finally, the Continue button is pressed again when the button generated by the Wait icon reappears.

Three erasing options are possible for the interaction. These options are listed below. The first example uses Upon Exit, the default option. As you can see, the text from the interaction (i.e., "Are you happy?"), is not erased until the interaction is complete and the user returns to the flow line.

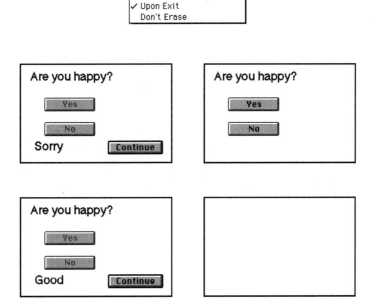

The second example uses After Next Entry. Here, the interaction text is erased temporarily from the screen as soon as the user presses either the Yes or the No button.

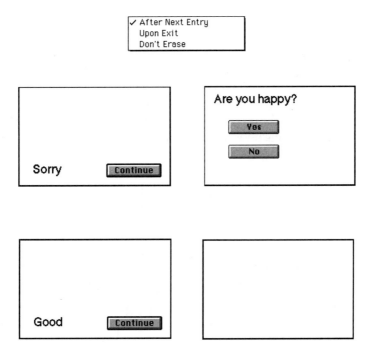

The third example uses Don't Erase. Here, the interaction text is never erased from the screen.

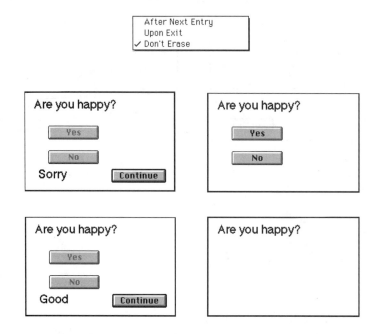

Backwards Erasing

Perpetual interactions are one of Authorware's most powerful features. They allow the user to create nonlinear links and to navigate flexibly throughout a lesson. The erasing options available for a perpetual interaction are similar to those available for Navigate icons. Remember that Navigate icons allow two erasing options: automatic page erasing for one-way links, and no-erasing when navigation is set to Call and Return. Similarly, perpetual interactions either erase screens or leave them untouched, according to how branching options have been set. Specifically, setting branching to Return has the effect of leaving feedback on the screen, whereas the other options automatically erase feedback from the screen.

Using the EraseAll and EraseIcon System Functions

If you are already comfortable with system functions, using the EraseAll and EraseIcon functions should be straightforward. EraseAll erases the entire contents of the current screen, regardless of the number of Display icons used to present the information. In effect, the EraseAll function operates in the same way as selection the Icons to Preserve option (i.e., without choosing any icons) available in the Erase Icon Properties dialog.

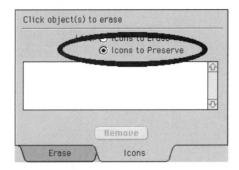

For more precise erasing, use the EraseIcon function. This capability is very powerful because it allows you to erase individual icons. This function allows you to specify the name of an individual Display icon to erase and uses the syntax

$$\texttt{EraseIcon(IconID@"IconTitle")}$$

where you must supply the name of the icon to be erased.

STUDY EXERCISES

1. Which menu controls when information is erased from an Interaction icon?
2. An electronic form is used to collect information by using several text-entry interactions in which the user must enter information (e.g., name, address, phone numbers, etc.). State two techniques you can use to leave the text typed by the user on the screen.
3. How do the four different branching options shown below affect when information is erased from the screen when using perpetual interactions?

```
✓ Try Again
  Continue
  Exit Interaction
  Return
```

16

Packaging and Distributing Files

CHAPTER OVERVIEW

The final step in the development process is converting your lesson file into a standalone application. This process is known as course packaging. In this chapter, you will examine the options that must be set, additional files that sometimes need to be distributed with packaged files, and issues that must be addressed to ensure smooth cross-platform development. Furthermore, special conditions for cross-platform development will be addressed.

CHAPTER OBJECTIVES

After completing this chapter, you will be able to:

- Transform your lesson into a standalone application.
- Understand the options that accompany file packaging.
- Distribute supplemental support files that are needed to ensure smooth lesson performance.
- Understand the issues that affect cross-platform development

KEY TERMS

Packaging a file
Packaging a Library
Including fonts

Runtime software
Support files
Cross-platform development
File conversion
Font mapping
Color palettes

SUPPORT MATERIALS

On the CD-ROM disk, run the file titled **Videos.a4r** and select the button labeled **Chapter 16**. This video examines decisions you must make when packaging and shows support files you must distribute with your finished piece.

UNDERSTANDING THE DETAILS

The files that you have created can be opened only on machines that have the Authorware application stored on the computer's hard drive. This feature causes problems when you want to distribute your lessons. Even if you could be sure that Authorware was installed on all the machines that were to be used, you wouldn't want users to change the lesson content, so you would need to find a way to prevent users from accessing the Design window. You can solve these problems by packaging your files. Packaged files will run on a computer whether or not Authorware is present. Also, packaged files are not editable and do not allow access to the Course flow line. After packaging a lesson, you will probably transfer the files to a storage medium to facilitate distribution. This usually involves transferring your lesson to a server, a CD-ROM disk, or a transportable disk such as a Syquest or Zip cartridge.

Before packaging a file, you should consider how several options in the File Properties dialog box may affect your final product. These options control how information is displayed in the finished lesson. See Chapter 6 for these options.

To package a course, select Package... from the File menu.

The following dialog box will appear:

You must decide whether to package the file with or without Runtime software. Although all Authorware files must be packaged if they are to be standalone applications, not all files need to be packaged with Runtime. Packaging with Runtime embeds special software into the packaged file. Packaging without Runtime creates a file that is no longer editable, but may not run as a standalone application on a computer.

If you package with Runtime, you must decide which version of Runtime software to select. If you are a Macintosh user, you have three options:

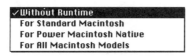

Selecting For Standard Macintosh embeds Runtime software that will work only on non-Power Macintosh computers, whereas the opposite is true for the selection titled For Power Macintosh Native. You may be tempted to select For All Macintosh Models; however, be aware that this option increases the file size by approximately 2.6 MB, almost twice the size of either of the other packaging options.

On Windows computers, similar decisions must be made. You must decide whether to package for Windows 3.1 machines or for Windows '95 and NT computers (i.e., 16-bit or 32-bit machines).

Four other options must be considered when packaging: resolving broken links; packaging libraries internally; including fonts; and using default names when packaging.

- Resolving broken links is important when using Libraries. When changes are made to Library files—for example, when an icon is cut from a Library—Authorware must reestablish connections between icons in Libraries and icons on the Course flow line to ensure that content is properly displayed. In general, select this option unless you are sure that no changes have been made to the Library file or unless a Library file is not used.

- You must decide whether to package a Library within the lesson file or as a separate file. The decision, as with deciding whether to package files with or without Runtime, depends on how many lessons reference the Library. In the same way that you can package the Runtime software within each packaged lesson file or enclose a single copy with multiple packaged Authorware files, you can embed a Library within a packaged file or place a packaged Library in the folder that contains packaged files. You can save storage space when distributing multiple lesson files by adding a single packaged Library file into the folder with the packaged lesson files. If you package Library files externally, they, too, must be included in the folder that contains the packaged lesson.

If you do not package Libraries internally, you must package each Library file. To do so, select the Library window with the mouse select Package... from the File pulldown menu, and follow the instructions.

If you have only one lesson file, then package the Library internally. However, if you have several lesson files that share a Library, include the Library as a separate file. The following illustration shows a file packaged with a separate Runtime file and a separate packaged Library file.

- Including fonts helps ensure that information will appear during the lesson just as it was designed. It is often difficult, or impossible, to ensure that users will have on their computers the same fonts and font sizes as those used by the designer to create a lesson. For example, a lesson might include instructions written in 18-point Avant Garde. If the Avant Garde font is missing from the target computer, Authorware substitutes a font in its place. This feature often results in screens looking very different from the way they were originally designed!

  Including fonts helps overcome this problem and is especially important when you are using any special characters in a lesson. Including fonts adds the fonts to the lesson file, ensuring that displays will appear as intended. However, including fonts increases the size of your final packaged file. In some cases, packaging fonts only marginally increases file size; however, in others, increases are significant.

Note: This option is not available on PCs. Furthermore, the issue of font distribution on PCs is complicated by legal issues: Most fonts are copyrighted and generally cannot be distributed freely with a finished product. See the section below on font mapping for further examination of this topic.

- Using default names when packaging: Selecting this option causes Authorware to name the packaged file with its given file name plus a suffix. For example, if your lesson file is named Tutorial, and Runtime is embedded, Authorware will name the packaged file **Tutorial.pkg**. Ignoring this option presents a dialog box for you to select another name for your packaged file.

  Authorware automatically adds a suffix, or extension, to all files. Below are the extensions for various file types:

EXTENSION	MEANING
.a4p	Unpackaged design file
.a4r	Packaged file without Runtime
.pkg	Packaged with Runtime for Macintosh only
.exe	Packaged with Runtime for Windows only
.a4l	Unpackaged Library file
.a4e	Packaged Library file
.a4d	Model file

Distributing Files

You will probably need to distribute some additional files with your packaged lesson to ensure that your application runs smoothly.

You must include additional files if any of the following cases exist:

- Files were packaged without Runtime.
- Your lesson uses QuickTime or Director movies.
- Your lesson uses a videodisk player or VCR.
- Your lesson uses imported graphic images or sounds.
- Your lesson uses transitions.

Runtime Software

You must decide whether to package files with or without Runtime. To make this decision, it is important to understand how Runtime software works. It may help to think of Runtime software as a battery. Without the battery, Authorware files are powerless to run. However, a single battery is capable of running several Authorware files. Each file may be given its own battery, or multiple files on the same computer may share a battery. Sharing saves batteries.

If your lesson includes only a single Authorware file, it is typical to add Runtime to the packaged file. However, if your project uses multiple Authorware files, including Runtime software in every file greatly increases the amount of space needed to store the files. The illustration below shows a single Authorware file packaged with Runtime. Notice that only one file exists.

The file contains the lesson and the Runtime software. Packaging with Runtime software guarantees that the packaged file will run properly.

When distributing multiple files on the same disk, the packaged file shares the Runtime software. Sharing Runtime software saves disk space. Consequently, when packaging several files that will be stored together, you should package Without Runtime. You can run a file that has been packaged without Runtime if a copy of the Runtime software is placed onto each computer. For example, when multiple packaged files are distributed on a CD-ROM or over a network, only one copy of Runtime software is needed to run all the files. The illustration below includes three files: two packaged files and one copy of the Runtime software.

> *Note*: Authorware adds the suffix .pkg to a Macintosh file and .exe to a PC file when Runtime is embedded, but uses the suffix .a4r when it is not.

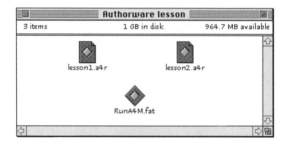

You must decide which version of the Runtime files to distribute. Macintosh users must select one of three files: **RunA4M.68k** (for a standard Macintosh); **RunA4M.ppc** (for a Power Macintosh); or **RunA4M.fat** (which will run on all models). PC users must select one of two files: **RUNA4W16.EXE** (for use with Windows 3.1) or **RUNA4W32.EXE** (for use with Windows '95 or Windows NT). The following figure illustrates two packaged lesson files and a packaged Library file, together with a separate Runtime file.

Drivers

Files known as drivers must be distributed whenever your lesson interfaces with a videodisk or tape player or a video digitizing board. Also, if you are using a PC, you must include driver files whenever you use QuickTime files in your lesson. For example, if your packaged lesson uses a Panasonic LDV-6000 videodisk player, a file titled **Pioneer LDV-6000** must be placed into the folder containing the packaged lesson file. The driver files can be found on diskettes supplied with the Authorware application. The following illustration shows a single packaged file that accesses a Pioneer videodisk:

Xtras

You must include Xtras whenever you include transitions, imported graphics (such as those created in a graphics application and stored in Photoshop, PICT, or GIF format), or sound files. The illustration below shows a folder containing three packaged files, along with several other files and folders that are needed for delivery. Xtras are placed into a folder titled "xtras." You will need to create this folder yourself and place support files into this folder. The support files can be copied from the Xtras folder that resides in the same folder as the Authorware application.

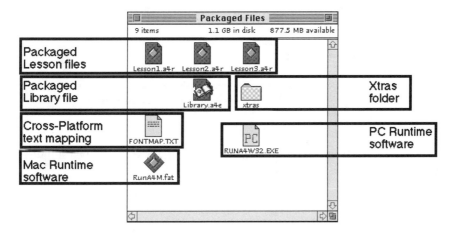

Transitions

Transitions can be customized to produce the special effects for displaying and erasing information. Although some transitions are built into Authorware, others are supplemental files that are loaded into Authorware. These supplemental transitions are placed into the Xtras folder that resides in the same folder as the Authorware application.

If you use a supplemental transition, you must place an Xtra into the Xtras folder that is distributed with your packaged files, otherwise, the transitions will not work.

However, you need not distribute the entire contents of the Xtras folder with your packaged files; you are required only to include the Xtras that create the transitions you use in your lesson. To find the name of an Xtra, select the transition with the mouse. The transition name will appear in the window beneath the Categories field.

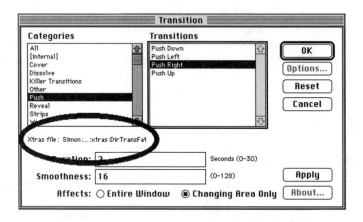

Images

If you are using any graphic images in your files (other than those created with the Authorware toolbox), you must distribute the following Xtras:

Macintosh	Windows '95 and NT	Windows 3.1
Viewer Services	VIEWSVC.X32	VIEWSVC.X16
MIX Services	MIX32.X32	MIX16.X16

You must distribute additional Xtras that correspond to the file types you use in your lessons. For example, if you use a Photoshop file, but forget to include the Photoshop Xtra, the image will not load into your packaged file. In other words, it will not appear.

Below are some Xtra files for three of the most common file formats: Photoshop, PICT, and TIFF. For a full listing, access the Macromedia Web site at:

http://www.macromedia.com

File Type	Macintosh	Windows '95 and NT	Windows 3.1
Photoshop 3.0	Photoshop 3.0 Import	PS3IMP.X32	PS3IMP.X16
	Mix Viewer	MIXVIEW.X32	MIXVIEW.X16
PICT	PICT Viewer	PICTVIEW.X32	PICTVIEW.X16
		QuickTime for	QuickTime for
		Windows	Windows
TIFF	TIFF Import Export	TIFFIMP.X32	TIFFIMP.X16
	Mix Viewer	MIXVIEW.X32	MIXVIEW.X16

The following Xtras folder contains four Xtras:

- Mix Services (required if any images are included)

- Viewer Services (required if any images are included)

- Mix Viewer (required for Photoshop images)

- Photoshop 3.0 Import (required for Photoshop images)

Sounds

If you are using any sounds in your files, you must distribute the following Xtras:

Macintosh	Windows '95 and NT	Windows 3.1
Viewer Services	VIEWSVC.X32	VIEWSVC.X16
MIX Services	MIX32.X32	MIX16.X16
Mix Viewer	MIXVIEW.X32	MIXVIEW.X16

You must distribute additional Xtras that correspond to the file types you use in your lessons. For example, if you use a WAVE sound file but forget to include the WAVE Xtra, the sound will not load into your packaged file. In other words, the sound will not play.

Below are some Xtra files for three of the most common sound-file formats. For a full listing, access the Macromedia Web site at:

http://www.macromedia.com

File Type	Macintosh	Windows '95 and NT	Windows 3.1
Authorware 3 sound	A3Snd Reader	A3SREAD.X32	A3SREAD.X16
AIFF	AIFF Reader	AIFFREAD.X32	AIFFREAD.X16
WAVE	WAV Reader	WAVREAD.X32	WAVREAD.X16

Cross-platform Development

The type of computer and operating system used to run a program is called a platform. Cross-platform development is the process of designing files that will run on more than one platform.

In the past, cross-platform development in Authorware involved an awkward and time-consuming process. First, a Design file had to be converted from one platform to another. This conversion involved owning two copies of Authorware and transferring a design file across operating systems. Second, separate packaged files had to be created for Mac and PC environments because a Macintosh couldn't recognize a packaged PC file, and vice versa.

Even worse, when a file was converted, there were few guarantees that lessons would work identically across platforms. For example, because rules for measuring font sizes differ on Macintoshes and PCs, even those fonts with the same names and sizes often failed to convert effectively, causing screen designs to be ruined. Also, because Macintosh and PC systems use different color palettes, graphics changed on different platforms.

Authorware files are now binary compatible. Binary file compatibility allows designers to create and use Design files, Libraries, Models, and packaged files (without Runtime) on both Macintosh and PC platforms. This ability has several important design implications. First, a Design file created on a Macintosh can be opened directly on a PC (and vice versa) without a file conversion. Second, a packaged file will open directly in both Mac and PC environments. In effect, binary compatibility means that a lesson can be developed on one system and used across platforms. In addition to speeding up the development process, binary file compatibility makes it possible to save space on a hybrid CD-ROM (i.e., a CD that runs both on a Macintosh and on a PC). With past versions of Authorware, cross-platform development required developers to create a full set of packaged files for both Macintosh and PC systems. When files are binary compatible, a single set of files will work on both Macintoshes and PCs. The same is true for Library files. Until recently, one Library file was needed for Macintoshes and another for PCs. Binary compatibility means that one set of Library files can be shared across the two platforms.

As will be seen in Chapter 17, the same logic applies to Shockwave delivery. Prior to the creation of Authorware 4, when files were prepared for Web delivery, separate packaged files had to be assembled and stored for both Macintosh and Windows. Binary compatibility allows one set of packaged files to be delivered via Shockwave on either system. Also, a single map file can be used to store information about the segment files for both Macintosh and Windows.

Despite the potential benefits of binary compatibility, some important rules must be followed to avoid conflicts. In particular, careful use of fonts and color palettes helps ensure smooth cross-platform program execution.

Font Mapping

When cross-platform development is being considered, one of the most important decisions that must be made early in the development process concerns which fonts will be used. The decision is important for three reasons. First, it is difficult to match fonts across platforms. For example, a font may have been created for just one platform. When a font is missing, the computer will substitute a font, with the likely result that many screen displays will be seriously compromised.

Second, even when the same fonts exist across platforms, small differences may exist in how the fonts were designed, because Macintosh and PC font-design standards follow different rules. Even small differences can result in important layout problems.

Third, developers cannot be sure that fonts will exists on users' machines. This problem can often be remedied on the Macintosh, because fonts can be packaged internally, ensuring that fonts will be available. However, selecting fonts to use on a PC is more complex, since a font-packaging feature does not exist on the PC.

The following strategies may help resolve font problems. First, developers can assume that end users have a set of common fonts. For example, all text can be created in the Arial font. Arial is a standard font that should be available on all PCs. Moreover, Arial can be packaged internally for Macintosh users. This strategy may still fail if the font is removed from a PC. System fonts are usually—but cannot be guaranteed to be—available on all machines.

Second, fonts can be distributed with packaged Authorware files. Software is available that will load Authorware files together with any necessary fonts onto users' machines. However, many fonts can only be distributed after licensing agreement have been reached. Such agreements may be difficult and costly to obtain.

Third, fonts can be created with font-generation software. For example, the application Fontographer can be used to create customized fonts. Custom fonts may be distributed free of charge.

Font Maps

A font-mapping file helps ensure that text will appear the same across platforms. The file performs two important functions. First, the file provides detailed instructions on font names and sizes that should be used when files are moved across platforms. Second, the file helps map "extended characters" across platforms. Extended characters arc symbols, such as bullet points, that use different ASCII codes on Macintosh and PC platforms.

The timing of the font conversion is somewhat confusing, yet important. Authorware carries font conversion information within a file before cross-platform conversion has occurred.

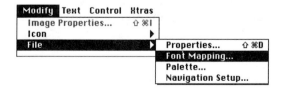

Font-conversion information may be loaded into Authorware before or after file conversion occurs. To load a font map before conversion, select Font Mapping... from the Modify pull-down menu and identify the file containing font-conversion information. If the font map is loaded before conversion, then no further use is needed for the font-map file.

Alternatively, a font-map file can be loaded after file conversion if the file titled **FONTMAP.TXT** is placed into the folder containing Runtime software and if the box titled Remap Windows Font Names has been checked.

> *Note*: To ensure smooth conversion, load the desired **FONTMAP.TXT** file into Authorware in the source platform rather than in the destination platform.

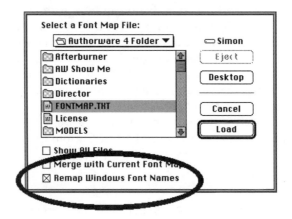

Color Palettes

As we saw in Chapter 4, the topic of color palettes is quite complex. Moreover, the topic becomes even more complicated when cross-platform color palettes are examined. It is important to understand that differences exist between how Macintoshes and PCs handle color because Macintosh and PC computers use different color palettes. The danger for developers is that graphics will not appear as they were created when transferred across platforms.

To ensure smooth color transfer, select a color palette that will be consistent across platforms.

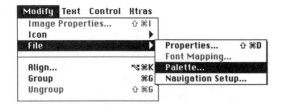

One way to do so is to check the box titled Preserve System Colors in the Palette dialog box.

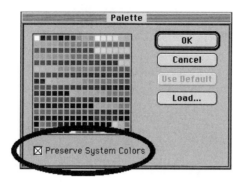

STUDY EXERCISES

1. Create a mini-lesson that you will use to experiment with packaging options.

   • Package a lesson with **RunA4M** and run the packaged file.
   • Reopen the unpackaged lesson file. Open the File Setup window and experiment with the options. Repackage and rerun the lesson file to observe the changes.
   • Create and use a Library. Package the lesson file and embed the Library in the packaged file.

2. Create a mini-lesson that includes a graphic created with a Graphics tool such as Photoshop. Package the file and place the packaged file into an otherwise empty folder. Run the packaged file. What do you notice about the graphic?

   In the same folder that contains the packaged file, place a copy of the appropriate Xtra file needed to display the graphic into a folder titled Xtras and rerun the packaged lesson (e.g., on the Macintosh, you would use the following Xtras: MIX Services; Mix Viewer; Photoshop 3.0 Import; Viewer Services).

   What happens to the graphic now? Why are the Xtras important?

17

Shockwave for Authorware

CHAPTER OVERVIEW

Although local networks and the Internet can be used to transport packaged Authorware files from one location to another, it was only until recently that Authorware files could not be opened directly over networks. In the past, through a process known as file transfer protocol (better known as FTP), files could be transported from one computer to another over a network. However, this approach didn't allow files to be delivered on demand through a Web browser such as Netscape Navigator. Instead, quite sophisticated computer skills were needed by the end user to be able to access and run packaged files.

Shockwave for Authorware allows Authorware files to be delivered directly over networks and to run through a Web browser. Delivering a file via a network (known as "Shocking a file") involves processing a packaged file through a software application named Afterburner. Afterburner prepares the Authorware file for network delivery, allowing users to connect directly to an Authorware file from a local network or a site on the World Wide Web (WWW).

CHAPTER OBJECTIVES

After completing this chapter, you will be able to:

- Shock a packaged file for delivery via a network.
- Load the necessary plug-in software onto your computer to run Shocked files.
- Test the Shocked file from your computer.
- Configure a World Wide Web server to deliver Shocked files.
- Understand the capabilities of Authorware's networking functions.

KEY TERMS

Internet
Web browser
Shockwave
Intranet
FTP
URL

SUPPORT MATERIALS

On the CD-ROM disk, run the file titled **Videos.a4r** and select the button labeled **Chapter 17**. The video shows how to prepare a packaged file for network delivery.

UNDERSTANDING THE DETAILS

How Do Networks Work?

Before examining the intricacies of Shockwave, we must understand how information is transferred over a network and how a Web browser such as Netscape or Internet Explorer works. A computer network (one of which is the Internet) is a cluster of computers linked electronically by communication lines. Computer files can be transferred very quickly between machines that are networked. We call the host computer a server, and the machine that is receiving information is called a client.

A Web browser is a client application that receives files from a server. These files are usually text, graphic, and audio files that are formatted for the browser. The formatting includes instructions on where to place text and graphics, as well as other similar formatting instructions. The process of creating Web pages involves writing instructions to access a server and transmitting files back to the client machine. The language used to write Web pages is titled Hyper-Text Markup Language (HTML).

In addition to displaying information, Web browsers can run application software that will run in a Web browser. Special files known as plug-ins are installed into the browser to add this functionality. As we will examine below, an Authorware plug-in allows packaged Authorware files to run via a Web browser.

What is Shockwave?

Until recently, Authorware lessons could be distributed only by using various delivery media (i.e., floppy disks, CD-ROMs, downloading from a network, etc.) to place copies of lessons onto users' machines. With the development of Shockwave for Authorware, multiple users can now receive lessons through the Internet or a local network; users can be directed to other network locations, such as sites on the World Wide Web; and data from lessons can be returned for central processing.

Shockwave has the potential to solve many existing educational and training needs. Consider the following scenarios:

Scenario 1: A company's Human Resources department regularly delivers updated training to employees via a CD. Copies of the CD are mailed to the employees, in several locations, who then load the training from the CDs onto their desktop computers. Apart from the development costs, distribution expenses include creating and mailing the CDs. Using Shockwave, the training department no longer distributes training on CDs. Instead, a single Shocked version of the training is uploaded to a server, and employees now run the lessons directly from the Internet.

Scenario 2: Students at a university must take a test. The test is given on paper, and students submit answers on mark-sense forms that can be scanned by a machine. Using Shockwave, students now log onto a computer to take the test, and answers are scored and recorded into a database file.

Scenario 3: Shockwave also presents some futuristic capabilities for curriculum development. A biologist working for a pharmaceutical company comes across a problem in her work that she does not understand, but needs to. Typically, she would go to the library to research the question. Such an approach would probably work well; however, going to the library involves leaving the workplace, finding the necessary information, and processing the information sufficiently to be able to understand the information.

Alternatively, the biologist can use an expert system that quizzes her on what she needs to know, as well as what she does not presently know. Once this information has been collected, Authorware can deliver an instructional module on the topic and ensure that she reaches an acceptable mastery level without ever having to leave her laboratory.

Scenario 4: Another benefit of using Shockwave is that transitory information can easily be updated. Consider the simple example of a phonebook. Typically, phonebooks are updated annually at great expense. In the future, a user working in a Shocked Authorware file will be connected with an online database that quickly returns the requested information from a database stored locally or on the Internet.

Shocking an Authorware File

The process of creating a file that can be delivered over a network involves three phases. First, a packaged file must be prepared for network delivery. This process is known as Shocking a file. Second, the designer must ensure that each machine on which the Shocked file is to run contains the necessary software. That is, the necessary plug-in files must be loaded onto the computer. Finally, the computer that will store the Shocked files must be properly configured to deliver the files, and a home page must be written in HTML to create a link to the Shocked file.

The application Afterburner converts packaged Authorware files into Shocked files that can be delivered over local networks or the Internet. Afterburner compresses and dissects files into smaller chunks that can be quickly and efficiently delivered. Afterburner also creates a management file (called a Map file) that controls which chunks will be delivered, when the files should be sent to the user, and the names of any additional files (such as Director movies) that may be needed.

To Shock an Authorware file:

- Package the file without Runtime. The Runtime software needed to run the packaged file will already exist on the end user's computer. We will deal with this issue later.
- **Run** the Afterburner application. The Macintosh version is titled Afterburner-MacFat-AW.

Afterburner-MacFat-AW

- From the File pulldown menu, select Shock... .

- Choose a packaged Authorware file to Shock. Remember that the files with the suffix .a4p are unpackaged files, but those with the suffix .a4r are packaged. In the illustration below, a packaged file titled **file1.a4r** will be selected.

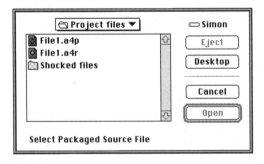

- Next, select a destination folder into which the processed files will be placed. In the example below, the file will be saved in the folder titled Shocked files. This step establishes the location where the Shocked files will be stored and the name of the Map file. Here, the title **file1.aam** for the Map file is given automatically and is taken from the name of the packaged file.

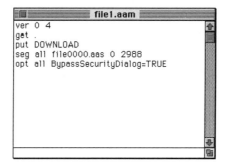

- After selecting the Save button, the Segment Settings dialog box appears. Segmenting a packaged files creates two types of files: segment files and a Map file. Each segment file contains a slice of the packaged lesson. The map file remembers how the slices fit together.

   The Segment Settings dialog box contains two fields. The Segment Prefix field is used to name the segments. The field contains four characters that are used to name each of the file segments that will be produced by Afterburner. You can use the default settings or use your own four-character prefix.

   Each segment is named with the prefix and four digits starting with 0000. Consequently, the second segment of the present example will be named less0001. Each segment also has the suffix .aas. Consequently, the complete title of the second segment will be less0001.aas. The Map file, which is an editable text file, has the suffix .map.

   The Segment Size controls the byte size of each lesson subset. Shocked files are delivered in segments over networks as each segment is needed. Smaller segments are transmitted faster than larger segments, but require more frequent delivery. The default segment size is 16,000 bytes. In general, do not change this setting unless you have compelling reasons to do so.

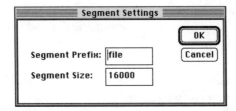

- After you select OK, Afterburner creates the segment files and a Map file that manages each of the segments. The illustration below shows two segments (less0000.aas and less0001.aas) and a Map file (lesson1.aam), although in reality most lessons are made up of many more segments.

Loading Plug-in Software Onto Your Computer

To run a Shocked Authorware file in a Web browser, it is necessary to load special files known as plug-ins into your browser. You must be using a recent version of the browser to be able to load the plug-ins. For example, if you are running Netscape, version 2.0 or a later version is required. When you are developing a Web page, it is a good idea to include a link for users to download plug-ins if they have not been installed previously on their respective computers. The plug-ins necessary to run Shocked Authorware files are presently available from Macromedia at the URL:

http://www.macromedia.com

Plug-ins must be placed into the Plug-ins folder of your Web browser on your hard drive. The illustrations below show a folder containing Netscape Navigator 2.01, together with the Plug-ins folder. The first illustration shows the contents of the Plug-ins folder, including a default plug-in and the two plug-ins needed to run Shocked Authorware files on a Macintosh Power PC.

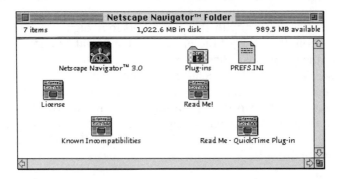

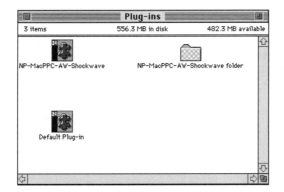

Testing Shocked Files

The folder containing the Shocked files will be placed onto a file server for delivery. Before placing your Shocked file on a server, you should test the file on your own computer. If you have developed Web pages before, you probably know that you can test a page by opening a file that is stored on your computer's hard drive. For example, if you are using Netscape, you can select Open File... from the File pulldown menu in Netscape and open the appropriate file. The file will appear in your browser as if it were running off a file server.

You can follow a similar procedure to test a shocked Authorware file. The file you will open is a Map file with the .aam suffix. In the illustration below, a Map file for the application titled lesson1 is opened. The Map file determines the order in which the segments will be delivered.

When you are sure that the files are working properly, transport the entire folder to the server. However, before you access the Shocked file from the server, the server must be configured.

Configuring the Server

The server you are using to deliver Web pages must be configured to deliver Shocked Authorware files. The method you use to configure a server will vary according to the server type. To configure a Macintosh HTTP server, you must add the following lines to the **MacHTTP.config** file (the file can be found in the same folder as the default Web page for the server):

```
BINARY .AAM TEXT * application/x-authorware-map
BINARY .AAS TEXT * application/x-authorware-seg
BINARY .AAB TEXT * application/x-authorware-bin
```

Information on how to configure other types of servers is available from the Macromedia Web site previously listed.

Writing the Web Page

When the Shocked files have been loaded onto a server for network delivery, you must write a home page that includes a link to the file. Running a Shocked file requires you to use the HTML tag EMBED. The EMBED tag tells the Web browser to place a Shocked file in the specified location.

The instruction is as follows:

```
<EMBED SRC="lessonname.aam" WIDTH=640 HEIGHT=480 WINDOW=onTop>
```

The WIDTH and HEIGHT commands specify the size of the window (measured in pixels) in which the Shocked file will be displayed. The WINDOW command controls the type of window used for the file. Macintosh users may select onTop or onTopMinimize.

The following illustration shows a file and folder as they would appear on the server. The file titled **default.html** contains a link to another page containing the EMBED command. The folder titled Shocked contains the Shocked lesson segments (less0000.aas, less0001.aas, and less0000.aas), the Map file (lesson1.aam), and the file containing the EMBED tag (**shockedfile.html**).

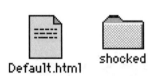

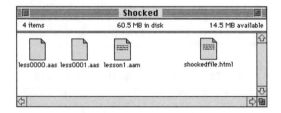

The next set of commands lists the HTML code to specify the link from the home page to the file that includes the EMBED tag. After writing the HTML code, test the commands on your server.

```
File name: default.html
<HTML>
<HEAD>


<TITLE>Link to a Shocked File</TITLE>

</HEAD>
<BODY>


An example of a <A HREF="Shocked/shockedfile.html">Shocked</A> Authorware file.

</BODY>
</HTML>


File name: shockedfile.html
<HTML>
<HEAD>


<TITLE>Shocked File</TITLE>

</HEAD>
<BODY>


<EMBED SRC="lesson1.aam" WIDTH=640 HEIGHT=480 WINDOW=onTop>

</BODY>
</HTML>
```

Networking Functions

Two important networking functions can be used to link to a Web page or to bring information from the Web into an Authorware file. You can use Authorware to connect the user directly to a Web page. The function GoToNetPage sends the user to the given Uniform Resource Locator (URL). URL is the term given to an Internet address where information is stored.

GoToNetPage gives the designer a tool to update lesson content. By connecting to Web pages, you can keep users current with up-to-the-minute information.

Example:
Typing the following command: into a Calculation icon sends the user to the Macromedia home page:

```
GoToNetPage("http://www.macromedia.com/authorware")
```

As well as sending users to Web sites, you can download and use files stored on the Internet. The function NetDownload transfers a file at the specified Web site into a variable.

Example:
Typing the following into a Calculation icon:

```
Latest:= NetDownload("http://www.university.edu/statslesson.txt")
```

transfers the file **statslesson.txt** onto the user's computer. Using the function ReadExtFile, you can now transfer the contents of the data file into a named user variable. The information can be presented in Display icons, placed into dialog boxes, or used in any other way that data can be used in Authorware. As mentioned in Chapter 14, data downloaded from file servers can also be used for data-driven design. Designers can create lesson shells, and lesson content can be accessed from files delivered over the Web.

STUDY EXERCISES

1. Take one of your lesson files that is packaged without Runtime software and prepare it for network delivery. Remember to:

   - Shock the file.

   - Store the Shocked file on a file server.

   - Configure the server.

   - Write a Web page to access the Shocked file.

   - Load the necessary plug-ins into your Web browser's Plug-ins folder.

   Before loading onto a file server, test the files on your computer.
2. Create a Shocked file that directs the user to information stored at various locations on the WWW. You will need to ensure that users have Internet access for this activity to work.

APPENDIX A

What Is Bit Depth?

Before examining bit depth, it is important to know a little bit about how computers store colors. To display realistic pictures, a computer must be capable of reproducing many different colors. Photographs use thousands, or even millions, of colors to make a picture look real. Imagine, for example, how many different colors would be needed to accurately represent all the skin tones of your hand. What would happen if you attempted to paint your hand using only a few colors (assuming that colors could not be mixed)? Obviously, your picture would be less realistic looking than if you had access to a more diverse palette.

The ability to reproduce realistic images on a computer is limited by the sophistication of the computer's color palette. A color palette is a predefined set of colors that can be used to color images. The smaller the color palette, the lower the potential to reproduce realistic images. Computers can usually employ different color palettes. For example, the illustrations below show a 16-color palette and a 256-color palette, and most computers have the potential to display thousands, or even millions, of different colors (i.e., more colors than the human eye can perceive).

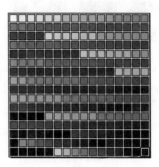

Developers refer to the sophistication of a color palette by the amount of information needed to describe each of the colors in the palette. For example, the 256-color palette is referred to as an 8-bit color palette (see the following section for an explanation). Similarly, a color palette capable of displaying 65,536 colors is referred to as a 16-bit color palette, and one that can display more than 16 million colors is referred to as a 24-bit color palette. In general, the number of bits used to describe a color palette refers to its bit depth.

What Does Bit Depth Really Mean, and What Are the Implications for How Large a Color Graphic Will Be?

Bit depth refers to the amount of computer space needed to specify the color of a pixel. Every color in a color palette is referred to by a unique number, stored in base 2. If a 256-color palette is being used, then only 256 different numbers are needed to describe those colors. When translated into base 2, we can use the following 256 numbers (using 0 through 255):

  0 translates to 00000000
  1 translates to 00000001
  2 translates to 00000010
  3 translates to 00000011
  .

  .

  254 translates to 11111110
  255 translates to 11111111

As you can see, 256 colors can be described in base 2 using exactly 8 digits in base 2. Since each computer digit is called a bit, we refer to this 256-color palette as 8-bit color. If we use 16 digits to describe different colors, we can describe 65,536 different colors, as illustrated below:

0 translates to 0000000000000000
1 translates to 0000000000000001
2 translates to 0000000000000010
3 translates to 0000000000000011

.

.

65,534 translates to 1111111111111110
65,535 translates to 1111111111111111

Since we use 16 digits to describe the colors in this palette, we refer to the palette as a 16-bit color palette. Finally, using 24 digits, we can describe 16,777,216 different colors, so we refer to this palette as a 24-bit color palette.

It takes three times more bits to describe a color from a 24-bit color palette than it does to describe a color from an 8-bit palette, so 24-bit color is more memory intensive than 8-bit color. But just how much memory does it take to store a graphic?

The standard size of a computer monitor is 640×480. In other words, the screen is divided into a grid that is 640 pixels (picture elements) wide and 480 pixels long. Each screen location can be described exactly by a unique number; hence, it takes 640×480 (307,200) different numbers to describe every screen pixel. In addition, each pixel must be described by a number to connect it with the correct color that is to be displayed. The file size is calculated by multiplying the number of pixels in an image by the number of bytes (where a byte is 8 bits) needed to describe the bit depth.

Why Do Computers Use Different File Formats for Graphics?

File sizes can easily become quite large. Large files eat up storage space and are difficult to transport. For example, the chart below shows the approximate file sizes that are required for graphics of three different dimensions and three different bit depths.

FILE DIMENSIONS	8-BIT COLOR	16-BIT COLOR	24-BIT COLOR
640×480 (full screen)	300K	600K	900K
320×240 (quarter screen)	75K	150K	225K
160×120	19K	38K	57K

Most files can be dramatically reduced in size by using compression software. Compression software uses mathematical algorithms to save information rather than remembering everything about every single pixel. Saving a file using an algorithm known as JPEG can reduce a file's size by 90% or more.

APPENDIX B

What Is Data Rate?

Data rate is the speed at which information is transferred from a disk to the computer's CPU. To understand this concept, it may help to use the analogy of water flowing out of a bottle. Obviously, water flow is limited by the size of the bottle's neck. Similarly, information flow from a disk (i.e., a floppy disk, hard drive, or CD-ROM) is limited. Faster, more expensive machines allow information to flow at greater rates than do slower computers. The flow rate is sometimes referred to as throughput rate. Most importantly, if the required data rate for a file exceeds the throughput rate of the computer, the file will "take a hit"—that is, the file will be interrupted while the computer attempts to manage the information overflow. When sound files are interrupted, information is lost and breaks appear in the audio.

It is important that the maximum throughput rate does not exceed the data rate. To find the throughput rate, you need to know some technical information about the computers on which your files will be played. For example, for a single-speed CD-ROM drive, the average throughput rate should not exceed 100 KB per second. Thus, in the illustration below, the date rate (22.050 KB) is considerably less than the maximum throughput rate for a single-speed CD-ROM drive.

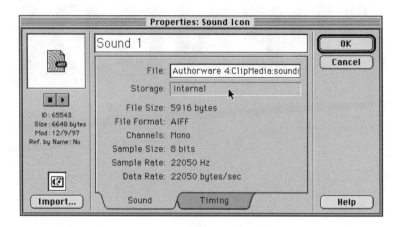

The chart below shows some approximate throughput rates for different CD-ROM drive speeds. Note that the Peak Data Rate (PDR) is the maximum rate at which the speed will operate. The Sustained Data Rate (SDR) is a rate approximately 70% of the PDR. The SDR is a better measure of the true rate at which data is transferred.

CD-ROM DRIVE SPEED

	1X	2X	4X	8X
Peak data rate(PDR)	150 KB/sec	300	600	1.2 MB/sec
Sustained data rates (70% PDR)	100	200	400	800

Index

End User License Agreement

PLEASE READ THIS DOCUMENT CAREFULLY BEFORE BREAKING THE SEAL ON THE DISK ENVELOPE. AMONG OTHER THINGS, THIS AGREEMENT LICENSES THE ENCLOSED SOFTWARE TO YOU AND CONTAINS WARRANTY AND LIABILITY DISCLAIMERS.

BY BREAKING THE SEAL ON THE DISK ENVELOPE, YOU ARE AGREEING TO BECOME BOUND BY THE TERMS OF THIS AGREEMENT. IF YOU DO NOT AGREE TO THE TERMS OF THIS AGREEMENT, DO NOT BREAK THE SEAL. PROMPTLY RETURN THIS PACKAGE, WITH THE UNOPENED ENVELOPE, TO THE PLACE WHERE YOU OBTAINED IT FOR A FULL REFUND.

1. Definitions

(a) "Company" shall refer to Prentice-Hall, Inc.
(b) "Software" means the software program included in the enclosed package, and all related updates supplied by the Company.
(c) "Company Product" means the Software and the related documentation, instructions, user's guides, tutorials, models and multimedia content (such as animation, sound and graphics), and all related updates supplied by the Company.
(d) "End-User Product" means the executable output file generated by you using the Software for use by a third party. Examples of End-User Products include animations, courseware, presentations, demonstration disks, interactive multimedia material, interactive entertainment products, and the like.

2. License

This agreement allows you to:
(a) Use the Software on a single computer of the type identified on the package, and load the Software in that computer's temporary memory and hard drive.
(b) Make one copy of the Software in machine-readable form solely for backup purposes. You must reproduce on any such copy all copyright notices and any other proprietary or confidentiality legends that are on the original copy of the Software.
(c) Transfer the Software and all rights under this Agreement to another party together with a copy of this Agreement, provided the transferee reads and accepts the terms and conditions of this agreement, and provided further you do not retain the original or any other copy of the Software.
(d) Make copies of the End-User Product and distribute those copies: (i) for use by personnel who are employed by you; or (ii) for use by third parties, provided the copies are distributed free of direct or indirect charges to those third parties.

3. Supplementary Licenses

Certain rights are not granted under this Agreement, but may be available under a separate agreement with Prentice-Hall. In each case, if you would like to enter into one of the Supplementary Licenses listed below, please contact the contact person listed below.
(a) Site License: This Agreement does not authorize copying of the Software except onto a single hard drive and for backup. If you wish to make copies of the Software for use with additional CPUs owned by you, you must contact the person identified in paragraph 14 and request permission. The Company may, in its discretion, enter into a Site License with you.
(b) Distribution License: This Agreement does not authorize you to copy and distribute the End-User Product except as set forth in Section 2, above. If you wish to otherwise distribute an End-User Product, you must contact the contact person identified in paragraph 14 and request permission. The Company may, in its discretion, enter into a License Agreement with you.

4. Restrictions

The Software contains trade secrets and in order to protect them you may not decompile, reverse engineer, disassemble or otherwise reduce the Software to a human-perceivable form. YOU MAY NOT MODIFY, ADAPT, TRANSLATE, RENT, LEASE, LOAN, RESELL FOR PROFIT, DISTRIBUTE, OR CREATE DERIVATIVE WORKS BASED UPON THE SOFTWARE OR ANY PART THEREOF.

5. Ownership

The foregoing license grants give you extensive but limited rights to use the Company Product and the Software. Although you own the disk or other medium on which the Company Product and the Software is recorded, you do not become the owner of, and the Company retains title to, the Software and the Company Product, and all copies thereof. All rights not specifically granted in this agreement are reserved by the Company.

6. Limited Warranties

(a) The Company warrants that, for a period of ninety (90) days from the date of delivery (as evidenced by a copy of your receipt)(the "Warranty Period"), (i) the Software will perform in substantial conformance with the documentation supplied as part of the Product; and (ii) that the media on which the Software is furnished will be free from defects in materials and workmanship under normal use. EXCEPT AS SET FORTH IN THE FOREGOING LIMITED WARRANTY, THE PRODUCT IS PROVIDED "AS IS" WITHOUT WARRANTY OF ANY KIND, EITHER EXPRESS OR IMPLIED. THE COMPANY DOES NOT WARRANT THAT THE FUNCTIONS CONTAINED IN THE SOFTWARE AND THE COMPANY PRODUCT WILL MEET YOUR REQUIREMENTS OR THAT THE OPERATIONS OF THE SOFTWARE WILL BE UNINTERRUPTED OR ERROR FREE. THE COMPANY DISCLAIMS ALL OTHER WARRANTIES, EITHER EXPRESS OR IMPLIED, INCLUDING THE WARRANTIES OF MERCHANTABILITY, FITNESS FOR A PARTICULAR PURPOSE, AND NONINFRINGEMENT OF THIRD PARTY RIGHTS IF APPLICABLE LAW IMPLIES ANY WARRANTIES WITH RESPECT TO THE PRODUCT. ALL SUCH WARRANTIES ARE LIMITED IN DURATION TO NINETY (90) DAYS FROM THE DATE OF DELIVERY.
(b) NO ORAL OR WRITTEN INFORMATION OR ADVICE

GIVEN BY THE COMPANY, ITS DEALERS, DISTRIBUTORS, AGENTS, OR EMPLOYEES SHALL CREATE A WARRANTY OR IN ANY WAY INCREASE THE SCOPE OF THIS WARRANTY, AND YOU MAY NOT RELY ON ANY SUCH INFORMATION OR ADVICE UNLESS IN A WRITING SIGNED BY AN AUTHORIZED OFFICER OF THE COMPANY.

(c) SOME STATES DO NOT ALLOW THE EXCLUSION OF IMPLIED WARRANTIES, SO THE ABOVE EXCLUSION MAY NOT APPLY TO YOU. THIS WARRANTY GIVES YOU SPECIFIC LEGAL RIGHTS AND YOU MAY ALSO HAVE OTHER LEGAL RIGHTS WHICH VARY FROM STATE TO STATE.

7. Exclusive Remedies

(a) If the Software does not perform in substantial conformance with its documentation during the Warranty Period, please return the Software to the place from where you acquired this software, with a copy of your receipt and a description of the nature of the nonconformance. The Company will use reasonable commercial efforts to supply you with a replacement copy of the Software or work-around that reasonably conforms to the documentation. The Company shall have no responsibility with respect to Software that has been altered in any way or where the nonconformance arises out of the use of the Software in conjunction with software or hardware not supplied by the Company.

(b) If the media on which the Software is furnished proves defective during the Warranty Period, please return the media to the address in paragraph 14 with a copy of your receipt and a description of the defect. The Company shall have no responsibility with respect to any copy if the media was damaged by accident, abuse or misapplication.

(c) As an alternative to replacement as described above, and as your exclusive remedy in the event of a breach of the limited warranty, the Company may refund to you your purchase price for the Product.

8. Limitations of Damages

(a) THE COMPANY SHALL NOT BE LIABLE FOR ANY INDIRECT, SPECIAL, INCIDENTAL OR CONSEQUENTIAL DAMAGES (INCLUDING DAMAGES FOR LOSS OF BUSINESS, LOSS OF PROFITS, OR THE LIKE) WHETHER BASED ON BREACH OF CONTRACT, TORT (INCLUDING NEGLIGENCE), PRODUCT LIABILITY OR OTHERWISE, EVEN IF THE COMPANY OR ITS REPRESENTATIVES HAVE BEEN ADVISED OF THE POSSIBILITY OF SUCH DAMAGES AND EVEN IF A REMEDY SET FORTH HEREIN IS FOUND TO HAVE FAILED OF ITS ESSENTIAL PURPOSE.

(b) THE COMPANY'S TOTAL LIABILITY TO YOU FOR ACTUAL DAMAGES FOR ANY CAUSE WHATSOEVER WILL BE LIMITED TO THE AMOUNT PAID BY YOU FOR THE SOFTWARE THAT CAUSED SUCH DAMAGES.

(c) SOME STATES DO NOT ALLOW THE LIMITATION OR EXCLUSION OF LIABILITY FOR INCIDENTAL OR CONSEQUENTIAL DAMAGES, SO THE ABOVE LIMITATION OR EXCLUSION MAY NOT APPLY TO YOU.

9. Basis of Bargain

The limited warranty exclusive remedies, and limited liability set forth above, are fundamental elements of the basis of the bargain between the Company and you. The Company would not be able to provide the Software or the Company Product on an economic basis without such limitations.

10. Termination

This agreement is effective until terminated. You may terminate this agreement at any time by destroying the Product together with any permitted copies. This Agreement shall terminate automatically upon your breach of your obligations under this Agreement. Upon termination you must destroy the original Company Product together with any copies in your control.

11. Export Control

The Software is subject to the export control laws of the United States. You agree and certify that neither the software nor any direct product thereof is being or will be shipped, transferred or re-exported directly or indirectly into any country prohibited by the United States Export Administration Act and the regulations thereunder, or will be used for any purposes prohibited by same.

12. Government End-Users

If this product is acquired by or on behalf of a unit or agency of the United States Government, this provision applies. The Software
(a) was developed at private expense, is existing computer software, and no part of it was developed with government funds,
(b) is a trade secret of the Company for all purposes of the Freedom of Information Act,
(c) is "restricted computer software" submitted with restricted rights in accordance with subparagraphs (a) through (d) of the Commercial Computer Software - Restricted Rights clause at 52-227-19 and its successors,
(d) in all respects is proprietary data belonging solely to the Company, and
(e) is unpublished and all rights are reserved under the copyright laws of the United States.

13. General

This Agreement shall be governed by and interpreted in accordance with the internal laws of the State of New York, as applicable to contracts made and fully performed therein. This Agreement contains the final, complete, and exclusive agreement between the parties with respect to the subject matter hereof and supersedes all prior or contemporaneous agreements or understandings, whether oral or written. If any provision of this agreement shall be held by a court of competent jurisdiction to be contrary to law or otherwise unenforceable, that provision will be enforced to the maximum extent permissible and the remaining provisions will remain in full force and effect. Sections 6 and 7 shall survive termination of this Agreement.

14. Inquiries

All questions concerning the Product and this agreement shall be directed to: Prentice-Hall, Inc., One Lake Street, Upper Saddle River, NJ 07458, Attention New Media Department